PARISH MANAGEMENT AND OPERATIONS

PARISH MANAGEMENT AND OPERATIONS

Michael A. Brinda

En Route Books & Media
5705 Rhodes Avenue, St. Louis, MO 63109
Contact us at contactus@enroutebooksandmedia.com

© 2018 by En Route Books & Media

LCCN: 2018930212

There is to be no part of this document that may be reproduced or transmitted in any form or by any means, electronic or mechanical, including photocopying (xeroxing), recording, or by any information storage or retrieval system, without permission in writing from the author.

Cover design by T.J. Burdick

Paperback ISBN: 978-1-950108-85-5
Hardback ISBN: 978-0-9996670-6-4

Printed in the United States of America
1 3 5 7 9 10 8 6 4 2

PRAISE FOR
PARISH MANAGEMENT AND OPERATIONS

In the book of Revelation (3:15-16), Jesus tells the church at Laodicea, "I know your deeds, that you are neither cold nor hot; I wish that you were cold or hot. So because you are lukewarm, and neither hot nor cold, I will spit you out of My mouth." In my travels I have seen many Catholic churches. There are very few that really seem "hot," even fewer that seem "cold," but many that seem "lukewarm." If you are currently ministering in a church that is lukewarm, or perhaps we should say, mediocre, and you are content with that mediocrity, then this book is not for you. However, if you want a church that is hot, or exemplary or superior, then this is the book for you. I would go so far to say that this book could lead to a totally changed Church worldwide. Unfortunately too many people are leaving the faith and many of our parishes are suffering. This book could stop that exodus and actually help to bring people back.

The author, Michael A. Brinda, combines his obvious business management skills with a deep faith that the Church is called to serve God's people. He tells us that we must serve God's people in an exemplary way. There is no room for mediocrity in the Church. This involves all people in all ministries in the Church. We, lay or ordained, are all called to superior service. Thus this book is not just for pastors. It is for anyone in a leadership/ministry role in the parish. There is no doubt that the ways of the pastor most influence the culture of the parish, and it is extremely important for all pastors to read this book. I have worked in parish leadership ministry for over 40 years, 37 plus of them as an ordained deacon. This book changed my thoughts on how a parish should be managed.

At the very heart of the author's message is the idea that each parish needs a good Parish Management person who is trained in how to bring about exemplary, not mediocre, ministry from parish personnel. He believes, rightly so, that we need to look at the culture of the parish (which probably has been formed and perpetuated for many years), and that you cannot try to change this culture, but that you must kill it and then install a new culture. If this seems difficult to you; it is. However, the author gives us many tools to help bring this about. I was very impressed by the tools that he gives us. There is no doubt that this hard work will bring about what God calls us to be and do. Using the words of the author, "And why do we bother with this process? As always, so that we can serve greatly those we are called to serve. If something were worth doing at all, why wouldn't it be worth doing in a superior way? Are the barriers to superior performance too tough and too high for you overcome? No. Never."

I received my degree in Business Administration—Management and worked my entire career in management, and I can tell you that the tools and wisdom given by the author in this book are exemplary. I am also an ordained deacon for 38 years now and have worked even more than that in parish ministry. This book is not just a book written by a businessman to apply to the Church. It is written by a businessman who has a deep faith and knows that the Church is called to use all of its resources in an exemplary way to spread the Good News and to serve the People of God. The Church is in dire need of this book.

The good news is that this book is well written and easily read. Putting what it says in to practice will be difficult, but all of us know that you can't accomplish anything great without hard work. Throughout the book, the author gives us numerous quotes from a wide variety of individuals, from spiritual writers to business writers to pop culture individuals. He makes the book an interesting read. I was really disappointed when it ended. I wanted more. If you are in any type of parish ministry, especially leadership roles, this book is for you. Do yourself a favor and read the book. It will benefit you, the Church and the building of the Kingdom of God.

—Deacon Marty McIndoe

Michael A. Brinda's book on Parish Management Operations deals with the foundational principles of effective pastoral work in a given Parish. It aims at getting better results by avoiding the persistence of a broken culture.

He proposes that using successful business principles without becoming business-like is the way to an effective and successful parish management. This, of course, is worth the try. Identifying the presence of different gifts, needs and sharing responsibilities (delegating) in the parish is the starting point for such successful Parish Management Operations. He writes,

> Culture is the force that animates and motivates people, thereby creating a correct working environment and now bringing us to this important additional insight: it is a derivative of the correct culture that provides the PMO administrator with the foundational framework for accurately measuring all results.

When this does not take place, in the long run culture becomes weighty bureaucracy; hence, instead of helping PMO it becomes a hindrance if not a deviation to it. It becomes a "broken culture," resistant to any novelty.

Mike Brinda's effort to bring new and creative initiative is therefore most welcome. I would like to congratulate him for his commitment to the improvement of pastoral methodology. It is sure that many people of our time will make the best use of such a proposal and benefit from its practical suggestions.

—Archeparch of Asmara and Metropolitan of Eritrea
East Africa, Abune Menghesteab Tesfamariam, MCCJ

There is a very important dictum in orthodox Catholic theology that maintains that "the higher never negates the lower." We see this dictum, for example, governing our understanding of the soul's relationship to the body, correcting our thought on the relationship between the two natures of Christ, and helping us grasp how an act of mercy is related to, and perfective of, justice. Unfortunately, today, this principle—whether found in lofty speculative thought or in its practical application—is often violated. In fact, it may be argued that the eclipsing of this principle is at the root of many of the ailments plaguing our culture and the Church.

As such, Professor Brinda's book is a welcomed correction and proper application of this dictum in the area of parish management and operation. Brinda rightly argues that the best practices and truths found in effective business management models are not at odds with the truths found in the Gospel. Rather he maintains that it is only when these two come together, in a mutually enriching way, that the current malaise and ineffectiveness in parish culture and management will be overcome.

Brinda's text thus provides an accurate assessment of the current crises in parish management and operations and a practical, no-nonsense guide of overcoming the problem by creatively conjoining the wisdom of the Catholic intellectual and spiritual tradition with the art of a highly effective, holistic system of parish management. Brinda's book is a must read for all who are interested in revitalizing parish life.

—Richard S. Meloche, Ph.D.
Associate Professor of Theology

To my loving wife, Kathy.

She worked the window while I worked the grill.

<u>*And she never doubted*</u>*.*

CONTENTS

Preface	1
Introduction	3
Chapter 1: Delegation	13
Chapter 2: The Tyranny of How Over Why	21
Chapter 3: PMO is a Superior Results Paradigm	31
Chapter 4: Applying Business Principles in a PMO Environment	35
Chapter 5: The Church Is Not a Business but…	39
Chapter 6: On Those We Serve Through PMO	45
Chapter 7: The Essence of PMO Service to Parishioners	49
Chapter 8: On Mediocrity in PMO Service	53
Chapter 9: Critical Distinctions Between Administration & Leadership	57
Chapter 10: PMO and the Parish Mission Statement	65
Chapter 11: We Need a New PMO Results-Measuring Yardstick	83
Chapter 12: The Identification and Repair of What Is Broken	91
Chapter 13: Volume of Actual PMO Usage In Relation to Potential Usage	97
Chapter 14: The Creation of Want	103
Chapter 15: Defining the Target Audience	107
Chapter 16: Indicators of PMO Engagement	113
Chapter 17: Removing the Suppression	115
Chapter 18: On the Revelation of Want	119
Chapter 19: The Buck Stops in PMO	125
Chapter 20: Culture?	135
Chapter 21: The Relationship of Performance to Culture	137
Chapter 22: Fundamentals on Culture	145
Chapter 23: Change a Broken Culture?	149

Chapter 24: On the Culture Killing and Replacement Hurricane	151
Chapter 25: Exposing The Grand Illusion	155
Chapter 26: The Attitude of the Receiver	159
Chapter 27: Breaking the Chain of Broken Culture	163
Chapter 28: The PMO Organizational Chart in Relation to Culture	167
Chapter 29: Providing Full Disclosure and Advanced Warning	171
Chapter 30: Statement of PMO Culture	181
Chapter 31: Experience a Broken Culture	189
Chapter 32: What Hats Are on Your Hat Rack?	193
Chapter 33: Either You Choose the Culture or the Culture Chooses You	197
Chapter 34: The Consequences of Wearing the Wrong Hat	199
Chapter 35: On the Primacy of Hat Switching	201
Chapter 36: On the Optics of PMO	207
Chapter 37: Leave the Culture DNA Alone	211
Chapter 38: Facing the Job Performance Mirror	215
Chapter 39: Communicating the Culture	217
Chapter 40: On Turnover	221
Chapter 41: To Share or Not to Share	223
Chapter 42: Why Plan?	227
Chapter 43: PMO Strategic Plan Science	233
Chapter 44: Observe, Question, Listen Through the Culture Lens	239
Chapter 45: The Good, The Bad, The Ugly: Organize and Prioritize	247
Chapter 46: How The Ugly Drives Strategic Planning Work Prioritization	255
Chapter 47: Will You Take the Road Less Traveled?	263
Chapter 48: Execution Overview	269
Chapter 49: The Nature of Execution	273

Chapter 50: But I'm Trying My Best!	277
Chapter 51: The Art of Achieving Superior Execution	281
Chapter 52: The Bottom Line on Execution	291
Chapter 53: Purpose of Planning Tools	295
Chapter 54: Tactical Discrimination and Delegation	303
Chapter 55: Internal and External Strategic Plan Terminology	315
Chapter 56: On the Art and Science of Strategic Plan Creation	319
Chapter 57: Strategic Plan Starts with Communications	321
Chapter 58: The PMO Communications Challenge	333
Chapter 59: On Rejection and Failure	351
Chapter 60: People Make for Superior PMO	359
Chapter 61: Hiring—You Just Never Know	363
Chapter 62: The Primary Hiring Foundational Principle	369
Chapter 63: The A-Player Conundrum	371
Chapter 64: B-Player Reality and the Road to Ruin	375
Chapter 65: C's Lead to D's and D's Lead to F's	377
Chapter 66: On Hiring the Best of the Worst	379
Chapter 67: The Art and Science of Hiring	381
Chapter 68: On Applicant Claims of Prior Experience	391
Chapter 69: Ask for Interviewing Help When You Need Help	395
Chapter 70: The Prior Work Experience Trap	399
Chapter 71: Who Am I Really Seeking to Hire?	403
Chapter 72: Let Me Tell You What You Want to Hear	409
Chapter 73: The Hidden Benefit: Loyalty	413
Chapter 74: On Firing	417
Chapter 75: Methodology	425

PREFACE

Up-front disclosure: *this book asks hard questions, and no-nonsense answers are always given.*

We are past due for an update in our thinking toward all things related to parish management and operations (PMO). This book presents a holistic system of concepts and principles (many of which may be new to you) on the application of available tools that will challenge your basic assumptions about the *definition and scope* of all things PMO.

When you think of a paradigm shift within a Church context perhaps Vatican II comes to mind. Fine. Think of this book as a paradigm shift in the field of PMO. Why do we need a paradigm shift in PMO? Because PMO as it is generally understood and practiced today *fails to serve all those we are called to serve in a most superior way.* And why is that? Easy answer:

You cannot put into practice what you do not yet know.

But what if you believe PMO where you are is just fine right now? If you think PMO isn't broke, why would it need fixing? Or an even more challenging question: what if what you think is so about the methods and purpose of PMO, *is not really so?*

As you read each chapter, challenging your current beliefs one by one, perhaps you may be moved toward a new understanding not only of PMO best practices, *but the very reason PMO exists in the first place.* I can assure you

PMO exists to provide a scope of services far more comprehensive than people think. Further note this mental movement toward acceptance of a new PMO paradigm will more than likely create within you some interior tension, some mental battles—and I am forecasting both as you turn the pages of this book. Be ready for it and fight through it. Our mortal enemy does not want this book read.

You will also note explanations of "Why?" something is so, something must be done in a particular manner, etc., presented (some might say hammered) before "How" throughout this book. Why? The adult mind desires—indeed usually *demands*—to understand "Why?" before being presented with explanations on "How to do…" almost anything. This is especially true with concepts and principles that are not necessarily new, just new to the person or new as applied within a PMO context.

Further note the science of PMO is just not that complicated, but the art animating the science of practicing superior PMO? Oh my, that's a much different story. Therefore, this book does not just present a litany of mechanical "How to" steps to follow in each area of PMO (a read of the table of contents will reveal this fact). Why? Because "knowing the why behind the what" facilitates a more willing acceptance for learning the "How to do" in the adult mind. The answer to "Why?" before "How" also helps us remove a chronic elephant in the adult mind: *resistance to change*.

I pray you gain more than a little from this book. Please keep an open mind as you read. Pray your way through each mental obstacle and you will learn what you need to learn. And if you think you don't have time to read this book—*make the time.*

In Christ,
Prof. Michael A. Brinda
March, 2018

INTRODUCTION

Let's make some sausage now. Why? Because somebody had to actually make the sausage on display in the market. Somebody had to know how to kill and slaughter the hog, grind the pork, add the seasonings, stuff the sausage casing, package the sausage, and sell it to the market. You may not be the sausage maker, but if you want sausage—and since you are reading this book I know you do—you must have recognized that somebody, somewhere, all the time, has to be the sausage maker. This is a book for sausage makers. Let's start here:

Who should care about parish management and operations (PMO), and why?

The topics covered in this book concern core aspects of PMO. Although the principles presented here work on a local level, the truth is we need a movement in PMO toward widespread worldwide adoption of the principles that follow—and this book provides the unifying catalyst for such a movement. Happily, some readers will accept the information contained herein. Yet sadly many readers, perhaps most, will initially reject the content. Why this is so is rooted fundamentally in a lack of patience with accepting new-to-you ideas and principles applied to PMO, before dismissing them as generally inappropriate within a Church setting and/or not a perfect fit for your personality. This challenge will become apparent as you continue reading.

Either you will find yourself nodding your head in agreement, or shaking your head in disagreement and even refuse to finish reading, as in your personal opinion I am teaching concepts, methods, and principles that you feel do not belong in a parish, seminary, or Church environment. In this regard:

> I urge you to resist this temptation and maintain an open mind, because most likely the contents of this book will represent a much-needed <u>paradigm shift</u> in your attitudes and thinking toward most if not all things PMO. I expect much in this book will be new to you, and much of it not intuitively connected to PMO as you currently understand it.

The initial reason for the above attitude of disagreement and rejection of what is presented herein will be that I have failed to persuade you there are certain business principles that can and should be adopted in a parish setting, that certain business principles are not mutually exclusive to what Jesus Christ taught us about how we treat one another, always in love and charity—but that producing superior results also matters to those we are called to serve. To those of you who choose to dismiss what is taught herein and/or take unwarranted potshots, I wish you the best but your diocese or parish or seminary status quo will continue. If you like the way things are operating currently regarding all things PMO, no need to read any further. But if you suspect there is room for improvements—indeed vast improvements—please read on. Perhaps applying this insight in our present context will help:

> Enter through the narrow gate; for the gate is wide and the road broad that leads to destruction, and those who enter through it are many. How narrow the gate and constricted the road that leads to life. And those who find it are few.
> *—Matthew 7:13-14*

The professional and educational backgrounds of readers of this book can vary widely. Likewise, the motivations to read this book can also vary, which

INTRODUCTION

raises the question: *who is this book written for, and why?* Let's breakdown the answer by position because each position carries with it different interactions, motivations, responsibilities, and perspectives on PMO:

Bishop or Abbot: to know *what is possible*, to know *what should be*, to know *what to expect* from every parish Pastor, priest, and deacon regarding all things PMO. To be on the same page concerning approach, attitude, and vocabulary. <u>*PMO is a holistic system*</u>, absolutely not a "this is how we do things here..." variable methodology that should be reinvented by every Pastor in every parish in every diocese all over the world. Parish employees, volunteers, and parishioners should not be treated as experimental guinea pigs under the "management" of a Pastor who is going to leave someday, and who while no doubt well meaning and doing his best does not know what he is doing as he has *never been trained in PMO*. Certainly some Pastors do a superior job with PMO, but do all Pastors do a superior job? If not, why not? What *holistic system* is offered to those who need help in this area?

When the Bishop and the Pastor are on the same PMO page it is a beautiful thing to see, this certainty of a well-managed parish that is in full accord with what Jesus Christ had to say about how we should treat each other with love and charity, *while at the same time delivering superior performance to all parishioners and the community at-large.*

If there is one thing a Bishop wants and needs at all times, it is well-managed parishes that are in accord with the Gospel values of Christ. Homogenous and system-oriented PMO, albeit possibly with some minor adaptations based on local customs and international cultural differences, is how you achieve superior PMO. Leaving PMO to the best _____ (insert descriptor of choice here, i.e. guess, hunch, efforts, etc.) of an untrained Pastor will always result in underperformance, and possibly disaster.

Rector: to know *what is possible*, to know *what should be*, and ultimately to know more precisely and with a finer granularity *what additional course content should be permanently institutionalized* within the seminarian's curriculum in regard to all things PMO. To realize that a few days or a week in the curriculum allocated to classroom teaching on the topic of PMO *is not close to sufficient* time to learn PMO, nor is attending a short post-ordination seminar on PMO a sufficient substitute for a designed course on PMO. To realize that teaching PMO as presented herein *requires an experienced professor* who cannot only teach in a seminary environment and relate to seminarians, but has mastered both the *art and science* of all aspects of a holistic system approach to practicing PMO. To come away with enough conviction in the need for teaching a course in PMO that *time will be allocated* within the existing curriculum to teaching a course in PMO, even if other topics must be shortened, even if there are objections from faculty to such a change, because one now realizes all the reasons why knowledge of PMO prior to ordination and parish assignment is *critical*. Finally but most critically, to realize that the old understudy model of having the newly ordained priest work under the tutelage of a Pastor for a decade or more, this model was broken long ago and indeed no longer exists. At the present time and for the foreseeable future priests are moved into Pastor positions long before any such understudy tutelage sufficiently prepares the priest for the PMO aspect of a Pastor's duties.

Pastor: to know *what is possible*, to know *what should be*, to know *what to expect*, and to know *how to manage* all those working in PMO who by Canon Law ultimately report to them. It is not so much that the Pastor has to do everything in PMO—but the PMO administrator and all employees and volunteers will always *report directly or indirectly to* the Pastor. If anyone reports to you, you may not know step-by-step how to do his or her jobs *but you better know how to manage that person as he or she goes about doing that job*. Indeed, for a Pastor to attempt to do everything is not only a recipe for failure, it is impossible

INTRODUCTION

to accomplish; the Pastor must learn to *delegate*. But the Pastor must also be trained in PMO so he can delegate wisely, converse, and manage all employees and volunteers who work in PMO. The Pastor must recognize PMO not as an endless series of suggestions ("Hey, lets try this idea!") but as a diocese-wide <u>documented and transferable holistic system</u> of parish operations applied to manage those who are actually doing the work.

What administrator can do an effective job of managing anything without knowing how to guide and manage those who actually do the work? Who thinks it is effective "management" to essentially, out of ignorance, turn a blind eye to how the parish operates concerning PMO, allowing untrained and perhaps incompetent employees and volunteers to do as they well wish, to invent their own disparate policies and procedures, by their own prerogative and on their own initiative? This is often the way PMO is practiced, but does this sound wise? And most importantly, who thinks that today it remains necessary to *reinvent the wheel of PMO methodology every time* a new Pastor arrives at a parish? Why can't newly appointed Pastors *expect* to arrive and find superior PMO left to them by their predecessors, operating fundamentally in the same mode, manner, methodology, and vocabulary as the parish they just came from, using the same system-based principles of PMO? There is no reason why this cannot happen, except for lack of widespread knowledge.

Parochial Vicar (PV) or Deacon: to know *what is possible*, to know *what should be*, to know *what to expect* from those who report to you in PMO, and to know *how to perform* as the PMO administrator if called upon to hold this position (which is likely.) All those working in PMO, both employees and volunteers, report directly to the PMO administrator. The PMO administrator reports to the Pastor. If the parish does not have the financial means and/or size to hire a full-time PMO administrator separate from the PV or deacon, after training the PV or deacon should be delegated the job of PMO administrator by the Pastor.

Consequently, *the PV or deacon must master everything in this book—both the art and science of PMO, to the level <u>required for executing in a superior manner</u>*, not simply being "aware of" or merely conversational on any topic. They are the doers, not the watchers. This book teaches PMO as a system, and the person charged with serving as the PMO administrator must master everything in this system.

PMO Administrator: to know *what is possible*, to know *what should be*, to know *what to expect* from those who report to you in PMO, and to know *how to perform* as the PMO administrator. All those working in PMO, both employees and volunteers, report directly to the PMO administrator. The PMO administrator reports to the Pastor. The PMO administrator *must master everything in this book—both the art and science of PMO, to the level <u>required for executing in a superior manner</u>*, not simply being "aware of" or merely conversational on any topic. This book teaches PMO as a system, and the person charged with serving as the PMO administrator must master every concept and principle of this system. If not you, who?

PMO Employee or Volunteer: to know *what is possible*, to know *what should be*, and to know *what is expected* of you by the PMO administrator, and to know the *correct culture* that animates performing your job.

Parishioner or any member of the community: to gain further insight into PMO so as to *discern any interest in working or volunteering* in any aspect of PMO. To better understand how PMO exists to serve you.

Any lay person: note that many of the concepts and principles presented in this book are *ubiquitous, portable, and transferable* in their nature, and can be applied to administrative positions within business, education, government, military, or religious environments. That this may be news to you, that a book written ostensibly on parish management has anything substantial to offer anyone on the topic of administration and management outside of a religious con-

INTRODUCTION

text or setting, well, what can I say? When reading this book simply "find and replace"—mentally replace occurrences of "PMO" or "Church" etc., with the name of the organization where you work, and you will find the concepts and principles presented herein are often transferrable.

Historically speaking crises have a way of changing the status quo. This is good because historically speaking there has been a bias or prejudicial attitude toward much of what is presented in this book. How so? Specifically, the Church has been slow to embrace transferable core principles concerning all things "administrative" *whenever such principles originate from the business world.* Such principles are often summarily dismissed, along with their messenger, without due consideration as to their usefulness and validity within the *temporal*—not spiritual—PMO environment. In other words, proven and standard practices in other fields have not been embraced within a PMO environment based on the faulty assumption that there are essentially no means, methods, or practices applied in the business world that could, or should, be assimilated into the Church; think oil and water. This thinking is deeply flawed and incorrect, as we shall explore and expose.

Note some who are currently working directly in PMO want to learn more. Others are not working exclusively in PMO, but they are or will be managing those who do. Still others may wish to borrow PMO principles for use outside of the context of parish management. This is wise, as with little to no effort you will discover many portable attitudes and principles presented herein. Some will have prior PMO and/or business experience, while others will have little to none. But fundamentally, *these background variables will not matter to anyone when reading this book.* Why?

This book takes the position that whether or not you are working in PMO or will be managing those who do, and no matter what your exact personal motive for reading, or whether or not you have any prior experience in PMO, business, etc., the material presented in this book, if not completely then at least to a very high degree, *will present many new attitudes, new context, and new methods of approaching your job, whatever it may be.* Viewed in this manner, perceived "prior experience" can actually become an impediment to learning if what you think you already "know" inhibits you from learning new ways, new methods, and new approaches that are not really new at all—*just new to you. Believe in the process presented here, especially when introduced to new ways of looking at PMO. There is no concept presented in this book I have not tried and tested not only in PMO, but also in business all over the world.*

The above is a way of politely inviting everyone to leave behind any potential mental baggage, any interference, any background barking noise of preconceived ideas or notions along the lines of, "But, but, but…this is how things work where I am…this is how I do/did things…this is how I was trained…this way works just fine…this is our way…etc." *You are going to be exposed to new ways of viewing, new ways of operating, and new ways of thinking about PMO.*

The book's title, "Parish Management and Operations," is simultaneously innocuous and ubiquitous in the sense that, "Management and Operations" books and classes are available everywhere. So isn't this just another one to add to the pile? A person could reasonably assume this book offers content that can more or less be found anywhere else such "Management and Operations" books and/or course titles are offered, with the caveat that the object of our attention in this book is a parish, and not, for example, a steel mill. Such an assumption is mostly wrong. Why?

Many of the principles that will be presented in this book would in fact work well in a parish, steel mill, or dozens of other enterprises. So, what is the mental challenge herein? Although the principles presented here are taught under the banner of "Management and Operations," that doesn't at all mean you will find what is taught here in any other "Management and Operations" book.

INTRODUCTION

The fact is, for the most part, you won't.

Just because a book shares the same words in the book title *doesn't mean it offers the same content or message.* Look at it this way: what other words can be used in the book title to clearly state the subject to be taught, but not concurrently infer a commonality in content and methods to other books sharing some or all of the same words "Management and Operations" in the title? If there are any other ways, I didn't find them. But I can't tell you how many times I have heard people tell me when I introduced this book to their _____ (insert name of affiliated organization here), "Oh, I already read a book about that."

No. You didn't.

But there are some things you must experience to realize they are true or false. So, maintain an open mind at all times because here you will discover through each chapter you will be exposed to new approaches and ways of thinking about "Management and Operations" in general, but also specifically as it relates to PMO. Collectively, these "new approaches and ways of thinking" form a *holistic system* of management and operations. Key word: *system*. Why is the notion of a system that important?

Because the content of this book teaches a holistic system or view of PMO that is linear and not presented as a buffet line where you should take whatever items agree with your tastes, and leave the rest behind. No proven system works like that, *as to pick and choose is the very antithesis of the meaning of "system."* Indeed, to pick and choose what, when, and how to do something is not a system, but actually an anti-system approach. This book presents a system, brick by brink, concept by concept, chapter by chapter. Embrace the system or not, *but do not pick and choose from what you will learn and expect superior results in PMO.* I can tell you from experience it doesn't work that way, but many people still embrace the buffet line approach to learning, especially learning new and foreign concepts. Such folks produce no better results than before they started.

Why?

Imagine you are shopping for a computer. Ask ten people what computer to buy and you know what you will get? *Ten different answers*, when you are seeking only the one, best answer for you. This book shows you the way to superior PMO—not average, *but superior*.

CHAPTER 1

DELEGATION

All things being equal (i.e. no crisis, no emergency to attend to), this is your general order of work in creating and installing superior PMO:

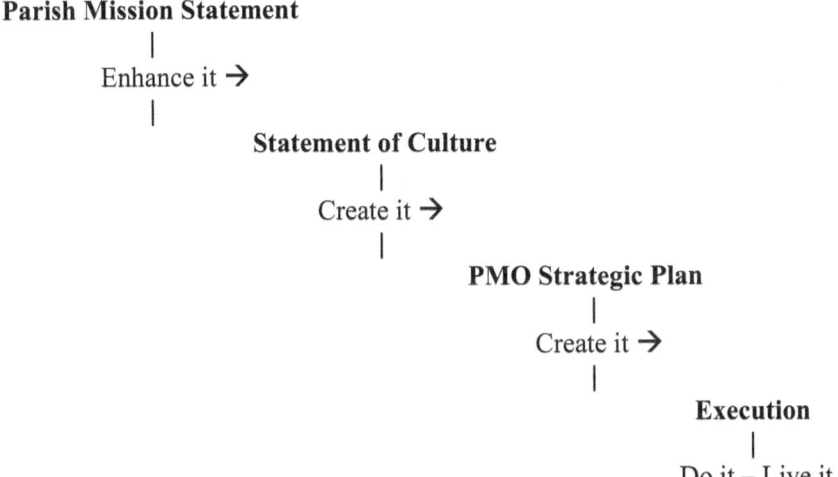

From the above workflow one can gather that certain foundational concepts and principles must be installed prior to discussing the final stage: execution, how to execute "all things PMO" on the job. To use the analogy of new pilot training, notwithstanding a cursory introduction to flight with a flight instructor whereby the pilot-in-training can nominally perform a few non-critical functions in flight, *the new pilot-in-training must start in the classroom and learn*

core aeronautical principles and theory of flight. They must learn how their input to the flight controls directly translates into maneuvering the aircraft, what parts of the plane are responding to their different input, as well as the principles of ground control, airspace nomenclature, navigation, radio usage, emergency procedures, teamwork in a two-person cockpit, etc. In a similar manner, *you must master the prerequisite concepts and core principles of PMO, which is what you will find in this book.*

> **The enterprise we're about is one of the toughest jobs on Earth. It's also one of the best.**
> —*Fr. Robert Stagg*

In the same manner a new pilot perhaps might find some of their classroom coursework less thrilling than actually flying and controlling the aircraft they came to learn to fly, all pilots eventually come to accept and appreciate that their pre-flight education is paramount to not only doing their job well, but also *surviving and thriving in a sometimes difficult and hostile environment.* The degree to which you master the prerequisite concepts and principles presented herein *will directly correlate to your effectiveness in accomplishing your PMO duties in a superior manner.*

> Excellence is an art won by training and habituation. We do not act rightly because we have virtue or excellence, but we rather have those because we have acted rightly. We are what we repeatedly do. Excellence, then, is not an act but a habit.
> —*Aristotle*

Note the goal of the book is to help you become superior in PMO, but help you in exactly what way? Perhaps the answer to this question is best revealed through a sobering fact: the #1 reason given by men who quit the priesthood during their first five years...*was a feeling of being overwhelmed by their administrative demands and duties.*

We all know the feeling of being overwhelmed in life. But you should also know the feeling of being overwhelmed can be mitigated via choosing between two general options:

1. Through enhanced knowledge and increased preparedness, and that is precisely the goal herein—to enhance your existing knowledge in the art and science of practicing superior PMO, either as a direct practitioner or via your delegation and oversight of someone who is, so that you will be better prepared for what is ahead in this dimension of your chosen vocation, or;

2. Administrative demands can simply be ignored. Shrugged off. Dismissed. Forgotten. Or, done poorly. Any administrator can always, and usually quite easily, rationalize that something else, anything else, is more important than what truly is most important. Every day one can find (rationalize, really) more preferable, more enjoyable tasks that can always be substituted for your PMO administrative tasks—especially the tougher ones.

Clearly, you will not feel overwhelmed by administrative tasks if you pretend such tasks don't exist, or are not your job. So let's be crystal clear up front here: this book is meant for people who choose Option 1 above. If you intend to choose Option 2 where you are assigned, if you intend to dodge even a single administrative task on the back of more preferable tasks, reading this book is just a waste of your time.

Like it or not, max busy or not, superior parish administration must become a daily habit. It is part of your kingly role, it is part of your governance role, and it is definitely a part of parish ministry. Therefore, to succeed the PMO administrator must as a habit proactively embrace his or her role—do or do not, there is no try. This point resonated with Aristotle in the *Nicomachean Ethics*:

> States of character arise out of like activities. This is why the activities we exhibit must be of a certain kind; it is because the states of character correspond to the differences between these. It makes no small difference, then, whether we form habits of one kind or of another from our very youth; it makes a very great difference, or rather all the difference (Book 2, Ch. 1).

Indeed, I hope you enjoy the subject and material presented in this book, but on the other hand…this book may solidify in your mind that the very last job on Earth you would ever want is any job that incorporates the principles taught in this book into your day. Fine, to each his own, but let's clear one elephant from the room right now:

If you find yourself in the mandatory, no-way-out position of having to perform tasks you really, really do not want to perform, save souls—offer it up, because it is what it is. Specifically, you don't have to like parish administration, and perhaps you would prefer to spend your time doing something else; duly noted. Let the record show—like millions of other folks, there is a part of your job you do not like to do. Now, let's move forward. We must all do our duty and do it in a superior manner. However, what's the bad news for ordained clergy?

Lack of time to actually perform the PMO job. Do the math in your head: total the weekly time you must spend on your sacramental duties, factor in the additional discretionary time you freely choose to spend on sacramental duties, and what number of hours per week did you come up with? At least forty hours, perhaps fifty or more—and you have not even touched PMO. So let's get real here: on the surface it appears there is no time left in your week to serve the temporal needs of parishioners. If that is the bad news, what is the good news for everyone? Let us consult what St. Luke has to say:

DELEGATION

> About this time, when the number of disciples was increasing, the Hellenists made a complaint against the Hebrews: in the daily distribution their own widows were being overlooked.
>
> So the Twelve called a full meeting of the disciples and addressed them, "It would not be right for us to neglect the word of God so as to give out food; you, brothers, must select from among yourselves seven men of good reputation, filled with the Spirit and with wisdom, *to whom we can hand over this duty* (emphasis added). We ourselves will continue to devote ourselves to prayer and to the service of the word."
>
> —*Acts 6:1-4*

In a word, what did St. Luke just explicitly teach? *Delegation.* Delegation is God-ordained, actually, as the apostles explained in Acts 6:3-4 when they resolved to solve their administrative problems by establishing the permanent diaconate. They continued to do what only they could do, and they *effectively supervised* those who could do that which someone else could do. How do we know they were effective? It's been 2,000 years and counting; that'll do. Through proper delegation, you enlist the time of other qualified personnel.

And what did St. Luke also just *implicitly* teach? Every human being has both *spiritual and temporal* needs and it is not simply "okay" to recognize this truth—it is mandatory you recognize this truth through delegation *so those through their ordination who have the necessary faculties to serve the spiritual needs of parishioners <u>have more time in their day to do so</u>*. Ah, the holy-grail desire of every person has just been revealed: *more time in the day gained through delegation.* Further note:

The very first person named as a deacon is Stephen, who by Acts 7:58 is stoned to death for answering his call to ministry. His reward? A direct vision of

God. An instant saint, not the first since that honor goes to the good thief on the cross, but an important one for us to consider given that his martyrdom arose out of the faith that called him to be the Church's *first administrative assistant*, serving the *temporal* needs of parishioners.

Imagine a railroad yard and visualize a maze of crisscrossed tracks. This image is your PMO administrator life without delegation—complete and overwhelming daily chaos. Now imagine a burning building. This is your PMO life with delegation, but delegating without superior personnel to delegate to. Note the importance of delegation to trained and competent personnel, but part of the challenge in delegating is the wild diversity of educational and experience backgrounds in people choosing to work in PMO. The Pastor must also not only understand the means and nature of spiritual work associated with his ordination, *but also the means and nature of his temporal work so that he can properly delegate and oversee all things PMO.*

As the PMO administrator you can and should *delegate* many or even all PMO temporally oriented tasks to trained lay PMO professionals—*but it is precisely because you will delegate that you must also understand the basic concepts, principles and operating criteria of anything so delegated.* You cannot afford to delegate and then ignore your PMO oversight duty as an area of ongoing administration, much less be unable and/or unwilling to converse at a high level of competence germane to the subject matter. Thus, even if you desire to perform your administrative duty, delegation or not, how can you feel anything but overwhelmed if you are not fundamentally competent and conversational about any PMO topic? You are responsible for the results. Who wants to be responsible for producing superior results in some area, *but yet have little to no idea what to do, or how to do it?*

Only do what only you can do.
—Paul Sloane

DELEGATION

Ultimately, you need to know and meet certain PMO administrator criterion that enables your parish administrative mission and ensures this aspect of your mission is in alignment with the mission of your Superior and the Church. However, it is one thing to define your mission and ensure it is aligned with the mission of the Church—a relatively easy task—but it is quite another thing *to actually know the art and science of what you are doing when you get to working on this task*. In other words, knowing your administrative mission and completing your mission are two different things.

A primary purpose of this book is to help you complete your mission, and to eliminate or mitigate any anxiety, any feelings of being "overwhelmed" that may be derived from a lack of knowledge and/or prior experience in parish management and operations. Let's learn the art and science of parish management and operations—*with emphasis herein on developing the art because the science of PMO is relatively easy*. No matter the size of the task, I have never felt overwhelmed when I was prepared.

Lastly, you will note throughout this book the frequent use of the word "superior" in relation to describing the quality of PMO we must deliver to our parishioners. This notion of delivering "superior PMO service" is not a throwaway thought or symbolic statement—*it is literal fact*. Do not read past what is embedded in these words. Delivering superior PMO is not mere wishful thinking to describe a dream, some idealistic, utopian PMO world that cannot actually exist. We are here to build and subsequently deliver *superior* PMO service and services to parishioners. It not only can, but *has to be* done on a daily basis, and as the Pastor or PMO administrator it is your *duty* to ensure "superior" is the standard of service to be provided by all those who report to you, at all times.

Furthermore, we also desire to *institutionalize* superior PMO wherever we go, such that long after we are gone superior PMO remains permanently enshrined within the parish, and therefore, within the Church. If any lesser standard of parishioner service than superior service were to be embraced as our objective, either consciously or unconsciously, there would be no point for this book to exist. As such, know the content herein is not designed to teach you how to just "get by" in PMO, *but to teach the entire process and a holistic system of how to build and deliver superior PMO*. This point is resonant with Aristotle's point in the second part of the first book of his *Metaphysics* where he writes:

> The superior science is more of the nature of Wisdom than the ancillary; for the wise man must not be ordered but must order, and he must not obey another, but the less wise must obey him....[for] the science which knows to what end each thing must be done is the most authoritative of the sciences, and more authoritative than any ancillary science; and this end is the good of that thing, and in general the supreme good in the whole of nature.

In short, then, here we stress the foundational metaphysical question of "Why?" rather than the mechanical question of "How do I do that?"—though answering those types of "How do I that?" questions remains necessary. But in all likelihood, for all intents and purposes, if you choose to you will be the founder of superior PMO in your parish, if not your entire diocese. Why you? Why now? Because you cannot ever give what you do not have, *and not many people in the Church currently have what you are about to learn.*

CHAPTER 2

THE TYRANNY OF HOW OVER WHY

Stop. Pause here before reading further. Write below or take out a separate piece of paper and list at least three or more points you want to learn from this book:

1.

2.

3.

4.

5.

6.

7.

8.

9.

10.

Obviously I do not know what you wrote on your list, but I am going to make this statement concerning whatever you wrote:

You don't need this book to learn what is on your list.

And why would this be? Let's answer that question with another question:

What is the value of this book, what role would it have, what purpose would it serve, if you could learn all that you need to know about the points on your list by reading the existing articles or books concerning those points?

None. Zero. Stated another way: why can't you just buy any existing books on the specific parish management topics that interest you, read them, perhaps supplement them with a short seminar, and learn the same things you would learn from this book? Because such books and seminars only teach the well-known science animating PMO, *but we must go much further, far beyond the relatively simple science to meet the goal of providing superior PMO*. We must address the reasons why passing the dysfunctional PMO buck must stop. Why? The answer resides in the wisdom of this statement:

Those who know <u>how</u> will always work for those who know <u>why</u>.

Have you considered all the ramifications of this insight? More specifically, how does the above statement apply to anyone reading this book? Precisely this way—*and the following point being of paramount importance*, will be emphasized in this chapter:

Generally, people have been taught to believe the person who knows *how* will always have a job and this is the person to emulate on the job; learn the "how" and you are set for life. Not so fast. While partially true, this is not the whole story. How so? *It is not a complete thought for delivering, much less building, superior PMO—or anything, really.* Why? Because:

People are hyper-focused on learning the, "How do I ___?...How do I ___? ..." and still more "How do I ___?" But they habitually overlook the part about learning the, "*Why* do I ___?...*Why* do I ___?" and still more "*Why* do I ___?" in their rush to learn how, how, how. That's not how this book works, and you should resist the urge to skip the why and simply jump to the how. Why? Because:

A "Why" is a hope, a goal, a meaning and purpose to your life.
—Peter Kreeft

For example, decades ago an entrepreneur created a book title, *DOS for Dummies*, that at first glance appears to alienate and insult the very buyers he was seeking to attract. But a funny thing happened in the book-buying marketplace: turns out when you tell people the truth about their situation, *mature people react positively to the truth when it is presented to them fairly and plainly*. And so an entire ____ *for Dummies* media franchise and publishing empire was born with book titles ranging from, *Catholicism for Dummies* to *Piano for Dummies*.

But there's just one catch to the "Dummies" teaching formula: they teach you how, *without teaching much or any why*, and the Achilles' heel of their decision to skip teaching the why is to create a human robot, a savant, a scripted learner who has mastered how to follow a series of proscribed proven steps that work beautifully right up to the point…BOOM! Real life meets them and they are forced to deviate from their limited, scripted bubble world and solve problems that not only require them to know "How to ____," but also *why* things work, *why* things don't work, *why* things sometimes work, *why* things deviate from the proscribed and scripted solution set, and more why, why, why. This is also the unscripted daily world of PMO.

Reread the above statement and realize this truth: the only reason anyone who knows "How" ever had a job in the first place *is because of the man or woman who knew "Why" that job should exist in the first place, and created that job at all*. As such, this pesky "Why?" inquisitor, this is the person whose thinking we are also here to learn and emulate—the master of asking why, the "'Why?' Master." Those who know how will not only always work for those who know why, *those who only know how are severely handicapped, static, robotic situational thinkers of limited bandwidth and usefulness.* You might as well wear cement shoes to work. Such folks are not going to excel at PMO. Why? Because:

There are too many daily variables in PMO to be scripted into a series of, "How to _____" formulaic responses. Everyone working in PMO will be pushed off-script by some random event practically every day, and those who know the root "Why?" behind every "How" are always in a much more agile, stronger position than the robotically inclined "How to" personnel.

> **Man can endure almost any how if only he has a why.**
> —*Viktor Frankl (from Auschwitz)*

In light of the above, this is the superior PMO administrator:

> The superior PMO administrator is concerned with first learning the "Why" in order to best enable learning the "How" for themselves, and to teach the how and why to each person who reports to them.

As such, herein we teach the PMO practitioner the *art* derived from understanding answers to the more complex "Why?" questions standing behind every "How?" If you only know the science of PMO—the how—you will be the epitome of *PMO for Dummies, a robotic "how" practitioner in whatever you do,*

THE TYRANNY OF HOW OVER WHY

but you will never become a superior administrator in the perpetually changing, dynamic world of PMO. Therefore, in sequence:

First you must face the, "What do I do?" Next you face the, "How do I do it?" Paramount lesson here: the how and what to do in all phases of PMO *is just not that complicated, so relax*. Most people stop paying attention after hearing the "What do I do?" or in other words the description of the task in front of them, and subsequently learning the "How do I do it?" solution. Too bad most people stop here, because the final challenge is in deeply understanding *why* this or that must be executed in order to produce superior results in our ever-changing and ever-challenging PMO work environment.

Further note here that you must be of high intellect, *but also an extremely agile thinker* to learn the "Why?" animating the "How?" Key word: *thinker*, not a mechanically minded, script-following robotic practitioner. Thus, the only people who fit the "thinker" description are people who first know what, then how, and finally why—*but mostly why*—and they are also holding an attitude that is *willing to take direction* in their never-ending quest to answer "Why?"

Note, "willing to take direction" necessarily also implies, "subjugation of ego." If you are unwilling to ask questions out of some misplaced concern that asking questions will reveal you are not as smart as people think you are or must be, you will miss learning the "Why?" Indeed, learning the "Why?" begins with a willingness to ask "Why?" in most any setting and under most all circumstances. I will trust the employee or volunteer who asks "Why?" far faster than the stoic know-it-all types who pretend through their silence to know more than they actually do. Too many people have sacrificed their sense of curiosity at the altar of conformity in today's hyper concerns over personal sensitivity and tolerance, which leads to the demise of asking "Why?" questions as something that is politically incorrect. We don't ask "Why?"—that's not polite, that's rude, etc. Nonsense. You are conspicuous no matter if you ask

"Why?" or not, so for right-minded thinkers it would usually be wiser to ask why than to remain silent.

> **The true sign of intelligence is not knowledge but imagination.**
> —*Albert Einstein*

PMO mediocrity exists in the first place because people do not properly value knowing the "Why" that animates adult behavior—they just think, fixated really, in terms of knowing "How" to do something, without regard to the larger consequences and impact of their actions in a fluid environment. Using a baseball metaphor, what happens when the catcher (aka: the reality of life) knows you can hit the fastball? The catcher calls for any pitch *except* a fastball—a curveball, slider, change-up, *any pitch except the one the fastball savant hitter can hit*. When you understand why something must be done, you simultaneously and necessarily start down the road of independently thinking about the consequences of, *"What happens when this or that thing is done differently than before, or done poorly..."* And this is precisely the thinking we seek to foster and blossom in every PMO employee and volunteer. *We do not want mechanical, non-thinkers in PMO—and you don't build non-mechanical deep thinkers unless you model this inquisitive "Why?" behavior as the boss.* Anyone reporting to the PMO administrator who is not asking "Why?" must be taught—shazzam!—why they need to ask why! More on this point in the chapter on culture. So:

There is nothing wrong with learning how to do something. Indeed, as a practical matter you must learn how to do the nuts and bolts job of PMO administration. But if all I presented here was just PMO "how…how…and more how…how…how…" I will have failed you. Why? Because learning the mechanical processes of "How" *is the lesser part, the relatively easy part, the rote part, of what you need to know to develop and deliver superior PMO.*

Wherever you find poor PMO service to parishioners, which exists in epidemic proportions, you will find a gathering of people who at best know how to do their respective jobs…*without a clue as to why they do what they do the way they do it.* To such folks the catcher in the real world routinely calls for a curveball instead of their anticipated pitch, and for the mentally cement shoed "I only know how, not why" savant, *a PMO parishioner service strikeout is very often the predictable outcome.* How could it not be?

The much more challenging part to PMO is learning the "Why?" Learning the why *and* effectively *learning to teach all others* who report to you the why—*this is where we find the art of PMO.* Therefore, the critical *art of PMO administration* is also taught here, presented in a chapter-by-chapter content layering process. Note the real world can be simulated in any classroom, but never duplicated—which only highlights why savant students can excel in any classroom, but often fail miserably outside the classroom—it's that "Dummies" prepared batter vs. the curveball of life thing. Learning to hit the curveball is simply learning to be fully prepared by asking "Why?" before you see the pitch. Because as sure as you are reading this, PMO curveballs are coming for you every day—you just don't know precisely when or which PMO topic they will address. Therefore:

Each chapter herein adds another layer that you must know and why you must know it, and each layer added is designed to logically build upon the prior chapter's content. Like an artist painting a portrait, the learning process is gradual and builds. You will not see the complete picture of the merger between the *art and science* of PMO until the final chapter—*but you will see the critical art of building superior PMO emerge further with each chapter.*

> People in any organization are always attached to the obsolete—the things that should have worked but did not, the things that once were productive and no longer are.
>
> —*Peter Drucker*

It is the lack of understanding the "Why?" dimension of duties, tasks, and responsibilities that animates a broken, careless, and dysfunctional workplace—be it in a business, government, military, or religious setting. When any employee or volunteer, *and this very much includes you as the PMO administrator*, does not know the "Why?" of what they are doing, by definition they lack the larger picture of why what they are doing really matters: "Why this way?... Why not that way?... We have always done _____ this way, why change now?... Why do we do this?... etc." Furthermore, how can you possibly teach those who report to you the fundamentals of why something is done in a particular way, or done at all, if you don't know why yourself—just the rote how?

Ask most employees how to do something, and they will immediately demonstrate. But first ask them why they do something, drill down searching for an explanation and understanding of the larger ramifications of why something is done before getting into the how, and you will often be disappointed. You will receive a blank stare, or an incoherent ramble: "Well, that's just the way we do things here…that's the way we have always done it…that's the way I was taught…." As the PMO administrator you cannot build and deliver superior PMO derived from such a workplace culture, one that exults knowing how without knowing why (much more about culture later). How so?

The degree to which someone cares about the *quality* of their service to parishioners is directly proportional to their understanding of *why* the task not only has to be done, but must also be done in a superior manner. And *why* is that? Because PMO, in any capacity or form, <u>is a results oriented endeavor whereby mediocrity is not our goal, and "good enough" is never to be accepted</u>—a sentiment far easier read or talked about, than executed upon.

Absent knowing "Why?"—and the art of PMO is in knowing and teaching the how *and* why—many employees and volunteers tend to be content with less than superior results—not necessarily abjectly poor results, just less than superior. In other words, there is an unspoken but ever-present tacit understanding of, "Hey, man, it's just a job. I'm doing my job. Relax." Therefore, in addition to teaching the "How" of what you want to learn regarding PMO administration, a relatively easy task, *we also invest time teaching the why (the art) that animates the how* (the science: a rationally organized body of knowledge).

The above "Why" over "How" has been very much emphasized above *because it is foundational to delivering superior PMO*, which is the primary objective of this book.

CHAPTER 3

PMO IS A SUPERIOR RESULTS PARADIGM

However beautiful the strategy, you should occasionally look at the results.

—*Sir Winston Churchill*

This book makes the assumption that every reader, either now or in the future, will at some level be directly involved in PMO. But what does "directly involved" mean in this context, exactly? *Directly involved means you will have your hands directly on the levers of some consequential decision-making, one or more paid staff and/or volunteers will report to you, and you will be <u>responsible</u> for the results produced by your decision-making—or lack thereof—for yourself and all those who report to you. You may not have to directly perform the work, but you are <u>responsible</u> for those who will do the work.*

You will in some capacity and at some organizational level work as the PMO "administrator" as we will come to define the "administrator" title, whether you are laity or professed religious. You are always directly responsible for the results of your efforts, or the lack thereof—good or bad. You will be held accountable for your PMO performance by some superior—because everybody has a superior in one form or another; even those with their names in the top box of the Organizational Chart (Org Chart) report to somebody higher.

Note any PMO results not deemed "superior" *are bad by definition in the correct culture—there are no acceptable in-between permanent states when the discussion topic is "results."* Anything less than "superior" in terms of results had better be in the transitional phase—and never accepted as the terminal end state of our work. *Further understand and acknowledge that "good enough" is always the enemy of "superior performance."*

Acceptance of "good enough" as a terminal end state of our PMO efforts is to institutionalize mediocrity (more on this point later in following chapters), and mediocrity is the bane of those we are charged to serve. Mediocrity invites and opens the door to unwarranted and unnecessary misery in those we are meant to serve. This is immoral. *To knowingly and willingly accept less than superior as a terminal end state of your PMO efforts is actually sin hiding behind a veil of excuses:*

> I'm too busy, I'm too tired, I didn't know, I wasn't trained, I'm not good with details, I'm not a leader, I need more support, I'll get to it later, I deserve a break, nobody told me, it's too hard, too many obstacles, it doesn't feel right, people doubt me, people misunderstand me, I'm afraid of failing, other things are more important, I'm a thinker not a doer, I'm a doer not a thinker, I'm being reassigned soon, I'm not certified, I'm too old, I'm too young, I'm no good with technology, and my personal favorite: *that's not how we do things here.*

If you find the above teaching difficult to accept, know that things are going to get more difficult as this book unfolds because the above demand for superior performance that produces superior results is a bedrock, fountainhead principle. You do not have to like all aspects of the work you are called to perform; *you just have to do it in a superior manner, and this is a non-negotiable principle—the buck just stopped.*

Poor performance will not be overlooked, nor will it be acceptable in PMO personnel. But this has just as much to do with simply *looking in the mirror and facing yourself*, as it does with any formal oversight or extra motivation initiated by your superior. Since you would not accept poor performance from someone who reports to you, *why would you as the leader of the band accept poor performance within yourself?* Mediocrity in PMO is just another name for "failure." Sure, everyone makes mistakes. Everyone has a bad day. Everyone makes mistakes on a bad day. Problems come with any job. *But institutionalized mediocrity is inexcusable and must end.*

Nobody has to take my word for that as Jesus has some very clear, and profoundly harsh, teachings on failure to develop and use the talents God has blessed each of us with. Superior is the standard for our results. There is no other. Accept no other.

CHAPTER 4

APPLYING BUSINESS PRINCIPLES IN A PMO ENVIRONMENT

To correctly explain this point we must from the outset be crystal clear in admitting to a different purpose, a different goal, than others who might study many of the same principles presented here. Notice I did not say we must admit to serving a different Master, as no matter if your destination is to journey to priest or CEO or lay volunteer or paid staff, the Master of all remains the same: God. However:

One cannot assume, indeed one *must not* assume, that the principles taught in this book are principles that in some way are sullied by the fact others serving different goals—but not a different Master—use these same principles to earn a profit and make money, govern, or defend their nation. Do not make the mistake of thinking that earning a profit in a manner consistent with what Christ had to say about such matters is a corrupt end, and do not compound that error by dismissing *dual-use management principles* simply because some people apply those principles to create a business empire—especially those who blend sound business principles with criminal intent, to deceive and defraud people to build a criminally-driven empire. It is not the core and universal principles that are at fault when crooked people do crooked things, so don't cast blame on them and think the principles are in some way corrupt or tainted. *There are always a few practitioners who are corrupt and tainted in all fields and endeavors.* Increase the granularity and nuance of your thinking; be sure to make these distinctions yourself, *and also correct any others you may meet who hold to these erroneous beliefs. Business principles can and must coexist in a PMO environment side by side with the foundational tenets of our faith.*

> **Yes, the church is not a business, but there's the credibility of it that has been terribly damaged by poor management. The mission has to trump the management, yet the mission is constantly enhanced by good management and diminished by poor management.**
> —*Thomas Groome, Chair of Boston College's Institute for Religious Education and Pastoral Ministry*

The entire notion that a principle—any principle that is legal, ethical, moral, and virtuous—should be restrictively applied, such as only applied within the so-called "business world" or "government sector" or "military industrial complex" is absurd, overly restrictive, and naïve. Such thinking is too narrow in scope and counter productive to using many *dual-use* principles in every situation where such principles should be deployed and employed. In the same manner that the Church has much to teach those working in the business, government, or military sectors, *people in those sectors have significant useful experience, best practices, and general wisdom to share with the Church.* Do not dismiss otherwise brilliant ideas and strategies simply because they were not invented and did not originate within your chosen field or profession. Only the naïve, ignorant, or intractably biased would dismiss receiving such rich experience and wisdom *simply because the source is not from a fellow in their same profession or sector*. However:

There are differences to our *primary mission*. What are those differences? The application of business principles in a parish environment by priests and/

or lay personnel *must directly or indirectly further the goals of saving souls and leading souls to Christ, which is in full accord with Canon 1752 which states in part, "[The] salvation of souls is the supreme law in the Church, is to be kept before one's eyes."* Peter Drucker labeled the outcome of such an effort as a "changed human being." But whatever the precise language used, Drucker is making the same basic point using secular language as the Church does using more theologically friendly wording. Fr. Paul Holmes calls this same understanding, "the theology of management." However, we must continue to drill down on this "I'm anti-business principles… I'm against all things business" elephant in the room that might hold some back—*especially those you might report to*—as illustrated by this superior observation made by Drucker:

> **Forty years ago, "management" was a very bad word in nonprofit organizations. It meant "business" to them, and the one thing they were not was a business. Indeed, most of them believed that they did not need anything that might be called "management." After all, they did not have a "bottom line."**
>
> *—Peter Drucker*

Although we admit to using many of the same principles as are used in business, *we do not admit to the same goal. The why we do what we do in PMO is different than business, government, or military sectors.* The goal of business is to make money, to earn a profit. Let's be very clear about that, and also be equally clear that this goal is a noble goal when done in accordance with Christian principles and scriptural values. *So do not make the mistake of blaming the principle itself for its historical misapplication in the world.*

Making money is not our goal in the Church, and never will be our goal in applying business principles within the Church and PMO environment. The goal of the universal Church *is to save souls and lead souls to Christ*. However, *we must accept and execute in a superior manner principles that help us serve this goal—even if the principles originated in the business realm.*

CHAPTER 5

THE CHURCH IS NOT A BUSINESS BUT...

Who and what are responsible for core change in a person? Is it money? Is it environmental improvement? Better housing? More food? Toxin-free water? Job promotion? Improved health? In our exact context, not really. At the core we believe it is cooperation with God, the grace of God through the Holy Spirit working within, entering the people who give themselves over to Christ; this is what changes the heart of a person. But clearly note that the fact our goal is to save souls rather than to turn a profit, *does not admit to any acceptance of mediocrity in our PMO efforts* just because we are not driven by the profit motive. Certainly, the Church does not answer to shareholders but rather will answer to a much *higher authority*. However, this point is paramount: when you remove the profit motive from the work environment, yet simultaneously still require superior job performance, *this workplace reality confuses many people*—including job applicants, current employees, and often your superiors. How so?

If it's important you'll find a way. If it's not you'll find an excuse.

—Anonymous

Each person must do his or her part. We cannot, as it were, buy a ticket and become a spectator, watching the game of PMO. We are not spectators to the work of the Holy Spirit. *The key to effective PMO is to incorporate the mission of the Church with the methods of how we administrate and lead people—and some of these methods will be imported from the business world.* Granted, we will be learning some of the same concepts used in other fields such as business, and we are clearly in the service of different ends. But does this mean we should accept mediocrity and stubbornly reject proven methods simply because they were invented elsewhere, or are sometimes subject to abuse in another field, just because we are not chasing a monetary profit?

Or just because someone is labeled as a "volunteer," does that translate to, "Hands off! Do not proactively manage them, they are volunteers!" Should we not terminate the employment of someone for repeated failures, simply because such an action is misunderstood and incorrectly labeled—by anyone or everyone, as "uncharitable behavior"? For example, it is precisely because some people are volunteers, and largely or totally untrained in what we are seeking from them, *that you must recognize your PMO volunteers need the highest level of management, oversight, and training.*

Indeed, one could argue that between the two distinct goals of making money and bringing souls closer to Christ, if anyone were to enshrine mediocre service as their norm we should pray it would always be the business earning its profits, *and never the Church in its mission to serve others and bring souls to Christ.* There is no place for mediocrity in PMO, yet it is so common as to be the norm. Why is that? This is why:

In understanding those called to serve in PMO as paid staff or volunteers, we commonly observe the prototypical applicant or current employee is animated primarily by their desire to *serve the Lord*. Work in the business sector? Make money? Get rich? No, no, and more no—they are not interested in those pursuits at all. Fine. *But what often follows from this attitude?* For such people it is easy to consciously or subconsciously dismiss job performance concerns when you are animated primarily, if not exclusively, by a simple desire to serve God. Further note all things being equal, *we know they know their career or volunteer choice to work in PMO does not lead to climbing the proverbial ladder of success or material treasure, but spiritual treasure.* PMO employees and volunteers willingly—if not joyfully, accept this fact. Fine. But why do these insights matter? Because the purity of their intentions tends to *set aside or mute* the requirement that *standards of superior job performance must still exist where they work*, and delivering superior results still matters to the parishioners we all promised to serve.

Oh.

People working in Church environments like to think their daily job performance is going to be held as a secondary concern, or even in full abeyance, to their good and noble intentions of working for God and the Church. This is a false paradigm. *You do not relax job performance expectations and standards just because you are working in and for a nonprofit organization.* It is in this regard the label of "nonprofit" can negatively influence and mislead people into believing in the false formula of: "Nonprofit entity = any level of job performance will be accepted; and that's the place where I want to work! No requirements to actually perform! Woo-hoo, do I love working here!" Recognize it is more than likely you will inherit PMO personnel and volunteers who silently hold to one or more such beliefs, as if there is some unwritten rule or understanding to this effect—not to mention perhaps years of non profit prior work experience explicitly reinforcing such notions. Therefore:

We acknowledge the desire and/or pressure of having to, "strike it rich" so to speak, to secure high-paying, high-flying career paths with top-tier firms, etc., *do not apply to those attracted to work or volunteer in PMO*. Fine. Given our free will this is exactly as it should be. However, those working or volunteering within the Church sometimes mistakenly believe that working under the umbrella of PMO services *is somehow a refuge from being held accountable for producing superior output in a results-oriented environment.* Furthermore, sometimes those willingly working or volunteering within the Church mistakenly create an invalid correlation: *they mistakenly believe that working for less than market wages excuses them from superior performance standards.* This point of view is wrong on two fronts:

1. The wage you choose to accept of your own free will is never to be connected to the quality of your job performance. The standard that describes employee and volunteer job performance is always and simply "superior."

2. *The PMO administrator should not as a matter of budget design and default wage policy offer less than market wages in the first place simply because, "We are a Church and not a business."* (More on this topic in the chapters on hiring and firing.) We do not ask applicants and employees to take a paycheck haircut just because we are a non profit religious organization. We offer market wages in order to ensure we have talented job applicants ("talented job applicants" will be defined in the chapters on hiring and firing).

What is the truth? While working in PMO must be a safe refuge from uniquely profit-based and profit-driven workplace pressures and demands such as posting quarterly profits or achieving production quotas, *there is a distinction to be made here between profit-driven and performance-driven work environments. We are performance driven and results oriented in PMO—this is our culture* (more on culture in another chapter). There is no exemption from superior performance expectations for the non profit employee or volunteer simply because they declare themselves to not be motivated by profit, or willingly out of love and devotion freely choose to work for below-market wages. You do not have to earn a profit or be paid high wages to be driven to provide superior service to those you are committed to serving. *And it is the duty of the PMO administrator to personally model this truth in his or her own job performance to all employees and volunteers.* However:

You will note sometimes it is as if the employee is saying, "Hey! If I wanted to work in that type of results-oriented atmosphere, I would have taken a job in the secular world! I work in PMO specifically to avoid all that accountability and job performance stuff!" This attitude is misguided and mistaken, *as it fundamentally and implicitly demeans the importance of who we have been called to serve.* Just because you chose to work for the Church in some capacity, does not mean we eschew performance-based metrics or lack a performance-based results-oriented culture toward those we have been called to serve. *How insulting that attitude is to those we serve.* Further note, office commotion and observed all-around employee or volunteer busyness *does not necessarily equal delivering superior PMO results.* More on this point follows.

CHAPTER 6

ON THOSE WE SERVE THROUGH PMO

And what of the parishioners PMO employees and volunteers are called to serve every day? What can be said about them? Predictably, such people are by their fundamental nature not as apt to speak up when they receive mediocre or below-average service. Why is that? *It is because the entire paradigm of the parishioner-PMO interaction/transaction lends itself to a servant-master mentality.* In other words, "Parishioner, be happy with whatever you receive—if you receive anything from us at all—and do not complain because complaining would be considered as uncharitable behavior." In such an environment, a veritable performance feedback desert, "nothing" is the expected level of service. Furthermore, how in the world is an administrator holed up in an office going to accurately know what level of service his or her parishioner base is actually receiving from the PMO personnel? In the land of the blind parishioner, the one-eyed PMO administrator becomes king.

Of course, we are speaking here in generalizations and there are always individual exceptions, but *generally speaking*, the typical parishioner-PMO relationship paradigm contributes to a lack of loud, clear, timely, and accurate performance feedback about any mediocre parishioner-PMO experiences. In this sort of passive daily, "see no evil, hear no evil, speak no evil," PMO administrator's utopian world, the uninvolved PMO administrator naïvely if not gladly remains behind the curtain holding to the illusion that all is well in PMO Land—when all is not close to well. While existing in their truth-starved bubble, naturally there is no apparent need for the administrator to prioritize their daily to-do task list to include any time, or at least enough time, *to monitor the functionality and quality of PMO services*. What happens next? *Mediocrity quickly becomes the accepted cultural norm and performance standard.* But anyone who has spent any time watching cooking competitions knows that in all cooking competitions the judges keenly watch for one thing: *do the contestants taste the food before they serve it to the judges?* Do the contestants have any idea how their food actually tastes and what quality they are serving, or do they just go by best visual guess and fall for the illusion that their professed busyness while cooking—through some mysterious default alchemy—produced superior results? For example:

Some years ago David Copperfield appeared to make me disappear from the stage of a packed auditorium, and mere seconds later, appear to reappear standing at the back of the auditorium (my wife was disappointed I reappeared, but that's another story). What really happened is an entirely different story. But this example illustrates that even when you are paying close attention you can be fooled—*so just imagine how bad PMO can be if you are not watching at all, or do not fully understand what you are seeing and misinterpret employee and volunteer busyness for effectiveness.*

To assist in the saving of souls is why we must learn to become superior PMO administrators, but we can and should embrace business principles to further this end. We should not naïvely and in some knee-jerk fashion refuse, rebuff, reject, or otherwise defeat the application of sound business principles in a parish setting simply because someone dismissively and naïvely pushes back your efforts with, "You know, the Church is not a business!" *We already know that. We admit to that.* Now, can we discriminate between the goals of business and serving God, *but share certain dual-use attitudes, practices, principles, techniques and culture that produce superior results?* Will you accept this premise? Will you put it into practice in PMO? *Will you teach it to others who might struggle accepting "dual-use" principles?* Can we move forward, or do we refuse to change and remain trapped where we are? The main reason people resist change is that they focus on what they think they have to give up, *instead of what they have to gain.*

As the leader of the PMO band, it is your job to help anyone overcome his or her mental barriers to accepting qualified business principles within PMO.

CHAPTER 7

THE ESSENCE OF PMO SERVICE TO PARISHIONERS

What does it mean to "administer" a parish, specifically in a PMO context?

To "administer" the parish in a superior manner is to mean performing any task, whereby it can be said that in the performance of that task we are directly or indirectly furthering the goal of saving souls.

Remember, *"saving souls" is a multi-faceted, multi-dimensional activity*. It does not require a huge leap of faith to make the connection, for example, that an efficient and competent parish office staff furthers the saving of souls by serving the many and diverse non-sacramental needs of parishioners—clearly not in the same spiritually profound sense as participating in the Sacraments, *but in the sense that a parishioner who is apathetic or frustrated by a lack of superior services provided by the parish is certainly in a less than optimal mental state to receive the Sacraments and the Word, than one who is well served by robust PMO.*

For example, a parishioner who is given the wrong start date for the parish's RCIA course—or no date at all because the person who answered the phone not only has no idea, but lacks the "why" training necessary to capture the caller's information in order to call them back—in her frustration over now starting the course late chooses to *not join the course at all*.

Oh. That's not good.

And precisely who benefited from that blown PMO information exchange and predictable outcome? Nobody. What about the long-time parishioner who is dying; his family calls for their priest to administer the Anointing of the Sick sacrament, but the message is lost, the parishioner dies, *and no priest ever shows up?* How is that acceptable PMO service to parishioners? What about when payday rolls around, but your new-hire employee does not receive her first paycheck—but everybody else does? Did you ever have two funerals or weddings scheduled on the same day, at the same time? That's just a lovely scene, said the comedy movie screenwriter, especially when the people arriving are not yet aware they are present for different events and begin to gather and mingle together. Here you should feel free to insert your own personal PMO-based horror stories. However:

What is paramount is that you do not insert yourself and your personal reaction to any such situations and in so many words declare, "But those mistakes would not bother me… I would understand being poorly served… It was just an accident… Mistakes happen… I would forgive…." Why must you avoid this line of thinking in this context? *Because this is not about how you would react, that's why.* Here is the cardinal rule to follow in PMO:

We must meet people where they are, **not where we wish them to be.**

It makes no difference whatsoever that you would not be angry at the person who gave you the wrong RCIA start date, or who failed to inform the priest your mother was dying, or submit an accurate payroll, etc., etc. It makes no difference that you personally would not shake your fist at God for missing administering the Anointing of the Sick sacrament due to someone else's failure to perform and/or to be adequately trained and supervised. What matters here is that you understand that these are potentially the very real reactions of community members meant to be served by the parish, and in the failure to serve them—and serve them in a superior manner, *we are actually working against our goal of saving souls.*

Oh. That's not good.

It is not for any of us to demand a holy and saintly reaction to poor service, or anything less than superior service, from people who are fundamentally at a different point in their faith walk with Christ. *We meet people where they are, not where we wish them to be.* People will walk away from their Church—if not their faith as well—and not come back *over what you might consider a trivial matter.* It is imperative a PMO administrator possesses the so-called "view from the pew," which is the ability to mentally walk in the same shoes as *all* those they have promised to serve. If you cannot relate to those you serve—regardless of where they are on the faith spectrum—you will more often than not do a poor job in serving them. *Your personal opinion and point of view is not the yardstick by which others measure PMO results or react to being poorly served.*

So we return now to revealing the more nuanced meaning of, "Those who know how will always work for those who know why" in our specific PMO context to be precisely this: we have now come to accept and understand *why* tested, tried, and true principles of business management and operations such as those presented here will fit and lead to the saving of souls, either directly or indirectly, within a PMO environment. We will joyfully commit ourselves to learning these principles, both the art and the science, and not eschew or avoid them simply because the realm of "business" is not our personal vocational calling. We embrace this belief with a charitable heart so that we might be of greater service to Christ and His Church. No obstacle will become an excuse crutch for us to do little or nothing about less than superior service. Indeed, we will sometimes leave the riverbanks of our typical comfort zone in the pursuit of service of others, because one glance at Christ on the cross certainly tells us… He left His comfort zone for us, don't you think?

The reality is that by embracing and subsequently teaching others who report to you business principles categorically can and will apply in a PMO environment—perhaps even though you may have no desire to ever touch such principles in your vocation—by accepting your duty to do so you are demonstrating the historical character of self-sacrifice that has been demonstrated to date by all the saints for His sake and the building of His Kingdom.

That is not a bad group to be a member of.

CHAPTER 8

ON MEDIOCRITY IN PMO SERVICE

We are fortunate today that the issues summarized so far have been recognized in the Church at-large. We now have great (not merely good) educational resources to read and learn core principles germane to practicing sound PMO science. However, the Catholic Church family, as we well know, has been in existence for hundreds and hundreds of years—which is to say it has operated without such insights and understanding for a whole lot longer than this information has been readily available. As such, you would be wise to expect much, if not all, of what is presented here to be mentally deposited by those who receive it from you—incorrectly, into the category of "new information," and ultimately come to represent in their mind the dreaded C word: *Change*.

> **All happy families are alike; each unhappy family is unhappy in its own way.**
>
> *—Tolstoy*

There are as many ways to fail in PMO as there are different services to be rendered. Suffice it to say that most people in or out of authority are prone to resist all things perceived as "new," and to resist "change." People most often resist change under the misapplied banner or rubric of, "If it ain't broke, don't fix it." What is the problem with this attitude in our PMO context? What if it is broke, *but you don't want to do what it takes to fix it because you like things just as they are?* What if you fear change?

Many daily PMO related issues are terribly broken—at least in relation to measuring against what could and should be—and yet administrators, staff, and volunteers don't realize this fact. Why is this? *It is because the boss has quietly accepted mediocrity as the unspoken, de facto performance standard in PMO.* Mediocrity is sometimes even mislabeled as superior, usually via an overabundance of misguided praise cast about as if uttering words of false praise has no consequences. The PMO administrator has accepted "good enough" instead of the "superior" level of service that parishioners deserve. Indeed, *many do not even know what superior PMO looks like because they have never seen consistently truly superior performance in any organization they have ever been a part of.*

Why do people accept such mediocrity at all? The most likely reason is not that they are infatuated with mediocrity and strive just to be average—although such folks do exist. No, it is because they do not know how to perform any better, at a higher level, *thus all anyone can deliver is defined and derived from the upper limits of what they currently know and have experienced in their life to date.* It is therefore most often a simple lack of knowledge via training that creates a less than ideal PMO environment. This is why employees and volunteers deliver mediocrity, or worse—*they don't know any other standard of job performance.* Ask budget motel customers how they define superior service—*after they have stayed at a five-star resort.*

Further note that since volunteers do not receive a paycheck, on the job achievement is their sole reward—*but what can/do they achieve if they are poorly trained and/or unsupervised?* To dream of superior PMO service to all parishioners does not make it so, and certainly does not begin to define what that ideal even means to the parishioner. Your mission as the PMO administrator is to prayerfully and respectfully *change the PMO cultural paradigm,* first through your own servant leadership example, your actions being animated by a written Statement of Culture (fully explained in a later chapter) and supplemented by patiently training those who report to you until they demonstrate an inability and/or unwillingness to learn what you are teaching, or in business parlance, "they refuse to buy what you are selling." Precisely what you do in such cases is covered later in this book. But I will tell you this much now: you do not accept mediocrity or worse as the status quo from any current personnel. *You also do not accept mediocrity and brokenness in PMO just because it is challenging to change your status quo.*

Make no mistake about this: if you do not make the time to train people (and yourself) in precisely why and how you want something to be done, you are failing in a PMO context. You will enshrine mediocrity, guaranteed. Further note people are more than willing to do things your way...*if you train them in your way.* Did you catch that? Given bright personnel in PMO who are willing to take direction, *overcoming institutionalized mediocrity is simply a training challenge for the administrator—provided you start with bright people in PMO who do not resist change and are willing to take direction.* Uh-oh? What happens if the people you inherit or hire in PMO are not bright, and/or willing to take direction? What do you think happens? It's not rocket science: *they go, or you fail.* More on this point later.

If you fail to proactively train *you will end up with a mish-mash of daily disparate and non-integrated PMO ways and means that at best produce mediocrity, and at worst deliver poor service creating an untenable and miserable working environment for everyone.* Do you want that? Obviously not, but that is what you will get. Perhaps you are already familiar with such dysfunctional working environments? Have you ever worked in such an environment? Did you enjoy the experience? Are you enjoying the experience now? Would you like to repeat the experience, forever? More importantly, would you like those who follow in your footsteps to inherit such a dysfunctional working environment? Do you not have a duty to solve this problem of institutionalized mediocrity, or at least try? You know there is no joy anywhere such working conditions exist, not for the worker or those they are meant to serve. The cycle of broken PMO must end, everywhere, and if you will not end it, who will? Will you look the other way at PMO mediocrity, or fix what is under your control? Will you pass the buck, or does the buck stop with you? However:

Note the above does not infer you must do everything for yourself in a PMO context. Quite the contrary, *as that would be a recipe for personal burnout and PMO disaster*. You must master two skills:

1. The art and science of *delegation* of work and;
2. Training of personnel (both paid staff and volunteers), and you may choose to delegate the training of PMO personnel once you have installed a functional Org Chart.

CHAPTER 9

CRITICAL DISTINCTIONS BETWEEN ADMINISTRATION AND LEADERSHIP

> There are **different kinds** of spiritual **gifts** but the same Spirit; there are different forms of service but the same Lord; there are **different workings** but the same God who produces all of them in everyone. **To each individual the manifestation of the Spirit is given for some benefit**. To one is given through the Spirit the expression of wisdom; to another the expression of knowledge according to the same Spirit; to another faith by the same Spirit; to another gifts of healing by the one Spirit; to another mighty deeds; to another prophecy; to another discernment of spirits; to another varieties of tongues; to another interpretation of tongues. But one and the same Spirit produces all of these, **distributing them individually to each person as he wishes**.
> —*St. Paul, 1 Corinthians 12:4-11*

Any discussion on management and operations in any realm must include an explanation on the nature of leadership and the distinctions between administration and leadership. Technically, when we think of management and operations we think namely of the science of operating, but the reality is that the operating science without the animating art behind it simply devolves into a series of mechanical processes, without an artistic mind serving as the overall organizing principle. *Mechanical processes without an artistic mind behind them are bleak, robotic, static, and soulless acts ultimately unsuited to the fluidity of human-to-human interactions.*

To be effective in PMO we must understand what "effectiveness" means in terms of the *art* of administration or leadership—or lack thereof, that animates both. For instance, the parish can increase in its wealth or decrease in its wealth depending upon the skill of the parish business manager. But *what to do* with the wealth that is generated to better support the parish mission—*that requires a mind that understands the art of PMO and not just the mechanical science of fundraising.*

This next point may read counterintuitive to what you think is the central objective, or at least a primary objective of this book, and that is: *no book or course will ever create a leader.* We are not, per se, teaching here how to be a "leader." Why? *Because that is not possible.* Leadership is a God-given gift—repeat leadership is a *God-given* gift. The goal here is not to make leaders out of those who do not have the *gift of leadership*—because you can't. God chooses who will receive the gift of leadership—not any teacher or book author.

A quick internet search will confirm how confused the world is on the above distinction, with an equal number of articles claiming that "Leaders are born, not made" and "Leaders are made, not born." To be clear: you can teach a leader how to be a better leader, *but you cannot teach someone who has not received the gift of leadership how to be a leader.*

> Some people **God has designated** in the church to be, first, apostles; second, prophets; third, teachers; then, mighty deeds; then, gifts of healing, assistance, **administration**, and varieties of tongues.
>
> —*St. Paul, 1 Corinthians 12:4-11*

CRITICAL DISTINCTIONS BETWEEN ADMINISTRATION AND LEADERSHIP

So, what can be taught to anyone? *Administration can be taught to anyone designated to serve as an administrator*, but leadership is a God-given gift. You were either given this gift, or you weren't. The notion that learning some number of steps, "How to be a leader in 12 steps!"—*or any number of steps*—will make a leader out of someone who fundamentally does not have the God-given gift of leadership, is false. People come to believe that reading such articles and/or books will backfill what they are missing to become effective leaders. *Nothing a person reads, views, hears, will backfill for the lack of God's gift of leadership*, and unless and until God gives someone the gift, he or she will not gain it. *But such people can become very effective administrators.*

Perhaps you can now detect the spiritual gift of leadership is *closely related* to the gift of administration, *but administrative skill is not the same as the gift of leadership* (more on this point below). If you already have the gift of leadership—and perhaps you don't even know it but may realize it as it is *revealed*—wonderful. If you don't, *please relax now*, because turning you into a leader without the gift is not possible *and therefore is not our objective here*. In this book we are here to:

1. Reveal—not create, simply *reveal* the gift of leadership that God may have given to you according to what gifts God has given you. And;
2. Although no course and/or book, video, etc., can create a leader out of whole cloth, a course and/or book can create a better leader if someone is so gifted, *and;*
3. *We can create an administrator from whole cloth if someone has been designated to an administrative position*, and this is what we are specifically here to do through this book: *reveal the gift of leadership in those who have the gift,* and in anyone *create a supremely competent administrator.*

Derived from the above, it then becomes a fair question to ask: *what is the difference between an administrator and a leader?* Or more precisely for our purposes, what is the difference between a *parish administrator* and a *parish leader?*

Administrators are responsible for running an organization. In plain English, they must at a minimum keep the wheels on the figurative parish bus going 'round 'n 'round in the same direction, every day. Administrators keep the operations they inherit running smoothly if they are already running smoothly, and they also must detect and repair what is genuinely broken or in need of improvement in order to deliver the superior service God expects—not man expects—*God expects*, from their PMO. This will also involve the ability to teach not just the "How" but also the "Why" to those who report to you.

We must also note that "leader" does not have a relatively simple, or one-size-fits-all definition as stated above for an administrator. To be a leader is to include all of the above that defined an administrator in basic terms, *but also includes* integration of the art of personnel management, multiple disciplines, sciences, and skills related to (not listed in order of blending percentage or priority): organizational culture creation, delegation, empathy, founding, financial matters, creativity, humility, listening, motivation, inspiration, consistency, flexibility, objectivity, risk assessment, risk-taking, fearlessness, self-sacrifice, subjugation of ego, team building, extreme focus, failure management, forecasting, intuition, passion, sense of humor, conviction, diverse skills acumen, results driven, superior persuasive abilities, self-aware, and long-term strategic vision. Are you starting to see why there are so few authentic leaders?

Here is the distinction between the administrator and leader succinctly stated: *an administrator <u>does not have to posses all</u> of the aforementioned skills to be an excellent administrator—a few key ones will suffice—but a person without a high degree of mastery of all these skills can never be an excellent leader, or really, a leader at all.* Although we all know of people who *masquerade as leaders*

CRITICAL DISTINCTIONS BETWEEN ADMINISTRATION AND LEADERSHIP

and hold positions where a leader is optimally required—at least temporarily, over an administrator.

In regard to claiming to be something that you are not, perhaps Abraham Lincoln described this disorder best:

> **If you call the tail of a dog a leg, how many legs does a dog have? Four. Saying that a tail is a leg doesn't make it a leg.**
> —*Abraham Lincoln*

Thus, if you call yourself a leader or have a title that infers "leader," this does not make you a leader any more than mislabeling the tail of a dog affords the dog five legs. Leaders have an intuitive sense to the aforementioned daunting list of characteristics of leadership—*this is the God-gifted dimension of leadership in action that man must acknowledge—and often fails to acknowledge in a futile attempt to become a man-made leader, not God-created leader, and lead.* The leader's mind can capably process the overall situation, however complex, in a holistic manner that *an administrator's mind and inventory of talents—try as they might—cannot possibly replicate.* Throughout history and to this day in business, government, military, and religious circles, so much misery is inflicted upon the world when people without true leadership skills somehow end up holding an office that intrinsically requires leadership skills.

Clearly note we are not labeling or implying in any way "smarter" or "better," but simply pointing out the characteristics that define the key/core distinctions between a leader and an administrator. *Why is this point so important to understand?* Answer for yourself. Pause and reflect here: how many people do you know who can articulate the difference between an administrator and a leader, and in order to do their current job most effectively should absolutely know these distinctions *but do not know them and cannot explain them?* When you cannot identify the differences between an administrator and a leader, what are the usual consequences?

You will inevitably place an administrator—who are far more in abundance—in a position that demands a leader—with predictably disastrous results.

What have been the consequences of placing an administrator in a position that demands a leader? Look at it this way: notice how the only person who suffers when a leader is incorrectly placed in an administrator's chair *is the leader*, because the only problem is that the leader owns a skill set that is being underutilized. *But what about the administrator who is incorrectly placed in the leader's chair?* Oh my, how everybody can suffer when the task at hand requires the skill set of leadership as mentioned above—and it is not provided. Note this lesson well for the good of the Church. It is not for me to tell you at this time if you are an administrator or a leader—but you better figure it out if you don't know, *because the last thing you want to do is be an administrator assigned to a role that requires a leader, or be a leader stuck in a position that is wasting your gift of leadership.*

The gift of leadership is part art, part science. The science of leadership can be taught, the art of leadership cannot, *and therein lies the God-given origination of the gift.* How so? Among other things, a leader needs to be ready for what is *going to happen,* and not simply dither or dwell on or plan to remedy what has *already happened.* Shouting "Iceberg ahead!" usually doesn't turn out so well for the ship—or the captain. As such: a good leader sees tomorrow, a better leader sees the day after tomorrow, *and the greatest leaders see the day after the day after tomorrow. This is an art, not a science.*

Do you understand? This is strategic vision, a paramount ingredient to leadership, but an ingredient—all things being equal—*that an administrator does not need to have to excel at day-to-day PMO administration.* Does there need to be a leader somewhere on parish Org Chart? Yes, *but it does not have to be the PMO administrator.* This is one reason God did not create an overabundance of authentic gifted leaders—as that would give us a tribe of chiefs that clearly

CRITICAL DISTINCTIONS BETWEEN ADMINISTRATION AND LEADERSHIP

could not function. We don't need a plethora of leaders to daily administrate—*we just need the leaders God gifted as such to be placed in the correct organizational positions*, and it is often the ego of others—which is to say the sin of pride—that blocks what should be happening in personnel promotions, transfers and advancements, from actually happening. As such:

As stated it is not our goal here to create leaders out of those who do not posses the gift of leadership. It is our goal here to teach the principles of effective administration, *and reveal*—not teach—the gift of leadership in those who may have been gifted it by God. In short, you are either capable of becoming an administrator by learning this craft, or you already have the God-given gift of leadership, but perhaps need more education on the *science side of administration or leadership*. Fine. You will find both the science and the art of PMO presented here. However, notice that by pure definition a leader has the skill set to perform the duties of an administrator, *but an administrator does not have the skill set to perform the duties of a leader*, nor can an administrator acquire the skill set of a leader without the gift of leadership coming from God. This point is one of the most misunderstood points in any realm, be it business, government, military, or religious operations. Far too many people strive for positions that demand leadership skills and gain them, but they only possess the skills of an administrator—and sometimes not even those skills—to the severe detriment of their organization.

The Church requires both administrators and leaders, and there is positively no inference here, expressed or implied, that the nature of one skill set is better or more important to building the Kingdom of God than the other. However, it is vital to you that you understand your own self, to understand what you are, *and it is paramount that we do not place administrators in positions that require leaders*. Simply re-read the characteristics that define a leader as listed above, and then imagine the problems within any organization that gets this wrong and installs an administrator where there should be a leader. That this mistake is an everyday and common occurrence speaks to the depth and lack of understanding people have in regard to the nature of leadership, and the distinction between leadership and administration. Many an administrator will clamor for a leadership position, but should they be given such a position? No.

I would be surprised if you have not already been on the wrong end of these truths about the distinctions between leaders, leadership, administration, and administrators at this point in your life. Note such positional and talent mismatches are not easily forgotten, *especially by those on the receiving end of the mismatch*. Apply the above teaching whenever you are now, or are in the future, given the authority to do so. *I covered this point to this detail because to get these points wrong is to cause much trouble for many people and waste an enormous amount of time and energy.* Note these lessons well for the good of the Church.

CHAPTER 10

PMO AND THE PARISH MISSION STATEMENT: A CODEPENDENT RELATIONSHIP

I guarantee what follows will be new to most readers, so please read it closely. Let's start here: what guidance and/or direction does the 1983 Code of Canon Law provide us concerning the creation of the parish mission statement?

None.

Okay, let's try this: what guidance and/or direction does the United States Conference of Catholic Bishops (USCCB) provide us concerning the creation of the parish mission statement?

None.

You mean there have been a whole lot of well-intentioned people for a whole lot of years writing the ever ubiquitous "parish mission statements" *without knowing all they needed to know about the entire mission of the mission statement?*

Exactly. Let that sink in.

The USCCB includes and invokes various mission and vision statements throughout their website, but nowhere in their website do they provide any guidance and/or direction *concerning the creation of a parish mission statement and the <u>entire</u> mission of the mission statement.*

For many millennia the world, including the Church, operated without any formal written mission statement whatsoever. Why? Because the very notion of a "mission statement" had not yet been invented. There is no absolute historical proof of the first use of a "mission statement," but the oldest citation found in a newspaper archive dates from Nov 29, 1973, where there is a phrase in the proposed "mission statement" for the University of Wisconsin's freshman-sophomore campuses, which implies that the two-year campuses exist only or primarily for those who cannot afford to go to school elsewhere. *The Oxford English Dictionary* references "mission statement" in military usage in 1967. The earliest business management educational application seems to be 1971 from *The Journal of Higher Education*. Logically speaking, perhaps the "mission statement" was military in origin, subsequently picked up by academia, followed by business adoption, and ultimately adopted from the business realm by the Church. In other words:

The use of a "mission statement" has organically evolved and spread relatively recently via what we could best characterize as a committee building process of, "Hey, that looks like a good idea… That sounds good… Yeah, I like that" adoption and propagation. At first glance, such committee-written mission statements seem to quite nicely and tidily communicate the purpose of an organization, be it business, education, government, military, or religious in nature.

But first glances can be deceptive.

Who drilled down on this "mission statement" spread and adoption in the world? Who kicked its proverbial tires? Anybody? Who looked at the complete mission of a *parish* mission statement—indeed, who in the room understood it? Does your parish even have a mission statement? When was the last time you looked at it? Most importantly for our purposes, what happens if the mission statement you craft quite nicely and tidily *appears* to fully communicate the mission of the parish *but unintentionally omits a critical point*? Oh my, that's not good. Why? Because language that is integral and paramount for you to complete your PMO mission in a superior manner— *Oops!* <u>Has not been iden-</u>

PMO AND THE PARISH MISSION STATEMENT:
A CODEPENDENT RELATIONSHIP

tified as being an integral part of your mission. The critical additional language needed by the PMO administrator never makes it into your parish mission statement, thus handicapping the ability of the PMO administrator to do his or her job in a superior manner.

And what happens now—and forever more until the mission statement is enhanced—if this integral enhanced language is not specified in such a foundational statement as your "mission statement," a statement universally accepted and understood today to be publically and proudly proclaiming to the world the summarized total essence of the reasons your organization purports to exist? It's not what does happen, *it's what doesn't happen that we must identify*.

By definition, the missing point(s) cannot be a focus of anyone's attention—*because missing language does not exist to be focused upon, and that's not good from the PMO administrator's perspective*. Why? Because from the PMO administrator's perspective you must be able to make the following statement to any PMO applicant, current employee, or volunteer:

> Do you see this piece of our mission statement language? This particular language is also a key point animating your daily job performance, and my review of your job performance. It is also integral to the foundation of our culture. This language both literally and figuratively is a public promise to everyone in our community that we will serve them in a superior manner in both temporal and spiritual matters.

The problem? You can't make the above statement unless the requisite language enabling the above sentiment is part of your parish mission statement.

Oh.

And what happens if such language is *not* present in the mission statement? That's a simple formula:

Missing mission statement language = no PMO administrator leverage, and that can't be good. Why?

> **If you don't know where you are going, any road will lead you there.**
> —*Lewis Carroll, author of (appropriately) Alice in Wonderland*

Since we don't live in a fantasy world, we are stuck with the reality of things as they are, not as we wish them to be. So, if we apply the sentiments animating Carroll's "any road will lead you there" statement, but apply them to the realm of missing critical language in the mission statement, what we stand to generate is a mental image whereby parish paid staff and volunteers are never fully clear—or perhaps never clear at all—*that to reach their destination they must deliver the superior results that their mission statement publically promised.*

And why do PMO employees and volunteers often fail to deliver superior results? First, because this commitment to provide superior results was never publically promised to anyone in the first place, and secondly because their training was poor to non-existent concerning their exact duties, responsibilities, how to perform them, how their work aligns with the larger mission of the parish, and most importantly a simple but profound point—*why we even bother to do what we do to the standard of superior has not been publically articulated.*

Therefore, it becomes a fair question to ask: how in the world can one serve the parish in a superior manner (not merely "good enough") without an <u>underlying written foundation</u> of some sort that universally and publicly establishes the direction and core purpose of the organization? Answer: you can't. *You will never be able to relate the fruit of your efforts to the mission of the parish without a parish mission statement that <u>also</u> reasonably expresses the purpose and performance standard of what you do in your paid staff or volunteer roles.* In other words: can employees and volunteers connect the dots from their role in

PMO AND THE PARISH MISSION STATEMENT: A CODEPENDENT RELATIONSHIP

PMO, *to some explicit and clear language in the parish mission statement that fundamentally supports what they do, and why they do it that way?*

What exists to provide the aforementioned "direction and core purpose of the organization"? How is this accomplished? Where do we start? The *parish mission statement* is the place we start building our PMO foundation. *The parish mission statement is the stem cell from which we derive all PMO guidance, direction, and culture—and it has deep and sobering Biblical roots.* Thus, before we do anything we must ask: does what we intend or plan to do in PMO jibe with our current parish (or any enterprise for that matter) mission statement? However, notice the potential crack in our PMO foundation? *Missing mission statement language does not help us do our job as PMO administrators.*

> **Knowing the specific mission of an institution and being dedicated to its fulfillment are crucial for the well-being and effectiveness of any institution—certainly for a religious one.**
> —*Fr. Donald Senior*

Let's turn the issue around: if the parish mission statement is ignored and/or poorly crafted, *it cannot be used for the purpose just expressed—it cannot be used as a foundational statement to support our efforts in PMO.* What happens then? We are building a castle in the sky, that's what. *We have no foundation upon which we can build a correct organizational culture.* As such:

Your PMO is potentially untethered from this core source of guidance—a properly constructed parish mission statement, something that you so desperately need in order for anyone to know—especially you as the PMO administrator—if the work performed and service provided is in accord with...*anything, any objective performance targets whatsoever*. Without a parish mission statement that includes some language—and it is brief language—that endorses and supports delivering superior PMO, *you have no authority as the PMO ad-*

ministrator to do what you must to build superior PMO. You are broken before you even start, and you will remain broken unless and until your parish mission statement contains the enhanced language necessary to provide the community with superior PMO. Why? Because:

If you cannot map the culture animating everyday PMO to the parish mission statement, *you will have no way of measuring whether or not parish paid staff and volunteers, who no doubt "look busy," are actually busy according to meeting the needs of those they exist to serve and promised to serve in a superior way.* Why? *Because you didn't publically commit your PMO to serve anyone or anything to any standard, much less a superior standard, in your parish mission statement.*

Note we are not proposing that a properly constructed parish mission statement will in and of itself ever be an awe-inspiring motivational force for most people. Let's be real here: the parish mission statement is something that is printed in the weekly bulletin or posted on the parish website and largely ignored—*except when it is not ignored, except when it is needed by the PMO administrator to lean on*. And when might the parish mission statement not be ignored, but leaned on instead? *Whenever the PMO administrator needs to reference and invoke the specifically crafted language it contains that supports the goal of providing parishioners with superior service.*

Oh.

Applying the above, we are not asking the parish mission statement to do more than it can, *but we are asking it to do all that it should to assist the PMO administrator*, that is to say become the publicly proclaimed foundational language that promises superior PMO service to parishioners. This very brief but critical enhanced language that supports delivering superior PMO is placed in the mission statement to inform the parishioner of our intentions, *but primarily this language exists for the internal benefit of the PMO administrator, who*

PMO AND THE PARISH MISSION STATEMENT: A CODEPENDENT RELATIONSHIP

needs this language to exist in order to properly hire, manage, motivate, and train PMO employees and volunteers.

Oh.

What PMO under your administration promises to the parish in content and level of service, when *untethered* to some language in the parish mission statement, *is whatever it chooses to be about at any given moment—and that is no way to run anything, much less PMO.* Isn't that just a lovely image of how things operate wherever there is no publicly professed PMO standard of performance, much less a superior standard as your only standard? As Carroll so wisely stated above, you are certainly on some road, going somewhere, but where? When? Why? What? How? Who? The benefit of a public declaration is that it *implicitly demands fidelity to the declaration,* and this fidelity to a quest for superior will subsequently compel the PMO administrator to now embrace a *holistic PMO system* to achieve and institutionalize superior PMO—there is no other path to superior. *Note that holistic system of PMO operations starts by adding missing language to the parish mission statement.*

It is precisely here where the distinction between business and Church is most pronounced. In the business realm, it is common knowledge based upon common sense that the boss expects superior performance to achieve the highest possible monetary profit, not to mention crush the competition. But as previously acknowledged, *the Church is not animated or motivated by earning monetary profits or crushing competitors.* As such, we must make it expressly clear to PMO personnel that although we are not motivated by these factors, we nevertheless remain highly motivated, and as we have publically promised in our parish mission statement, we have committed ourselves to delivering superior PMO service to our community *for the sake of serving Christ and saving souls.* I believe we can agree this is a worthy calling?

The key point here is that we want this commitment *declared in writing* in the parish mission statement. *We do not expect that any, much less all, the ramifications of this promise are assumed to be understood by anyone, much less everyone.* As such, whenever the PMO administrator needs to cite it, lean on it, teach it, etc., for whatever reasons—*the language you need to exist must actually exist to be leaned on*. This is why we consider such language in the parish mission statement to be *foundational in nature, because without it, you have no foundation to support taking the culture-building actions in personnel management that you must follow.*

Here we begin to see creating superior PMO is a holistic challenge, and a properly crafted mission statement is but the first step in a series of steps to creating superior PMO. Merely "being busy" is not only an insufficient indicator, it is a misleading indicator to the untrained observer. How do you know the "busyness" you no doubt see in some PMO paid staff and volunteers maps to greatly serving those in need, if your parish mission statement doesn't at least give a nod, have a few words to say about serving your parishioners' temporal needs? Note this well: busyness, in and of itself, *tells you nothing as a leader and/or administrator about delivering superior results.* Busyness simply allows every person to self-declare they are highly effective in their PMO service, when nothing may be further from the truth. Busyness and delivering superior results are two different things, but the busy but ineffective person *usually overlooks this point until it is pointed out—and when you point out such things while wearing your PMO administrator hat, you will at that precise moment be very glad certain language exists in the parish mission statement to enable you to say and do what you need to say and do.*

> **It's not enough to be busy, so are the ants. The question is, what are we busy about?**
>
> —*Henry David Thoreau*

PMO AND THE PARISH MISSION STATEMENT: A CODEPENDENT RELATIONSHIP

The parish mission statement when used as a foundation for all PMO is the clear line of demarcation between stating the distinct mission and purpose of the parish, vs. the mission of any business enterprise. From the outset you should be able to charitably explain to anyone who questions the veracity and/or wisdom of the application of business principles within a PMO setting, that although we may apply some of the same core principles and techniques, *we do so in the service of distinctly different ends as evidenced by comparing the mission statement of any business with the parish's mission statement.*

This distinction makes all the difference. Thus, it is acceptable to use time-tested and proven means, methods, and terminology shared by other disciplines, *provided their application is also in accord and alignment with all Christian objectives, values, and virtues.* We test this accord by crafting a parish mission statement that lends itself to addressing both the *spiritual and temporal* needs of those we serve. Not one or the other; *serving both the spiritual and temporal needs of those we serve must be reflected in the fully inclusive parish mission statement language, otherwise the poor PMO administrator—who might be the Pastor—has no solid foundation from which to manage and achieve superior PMO.* Who thinks serving the temporal needs of parishioners through superior PMO is already also included in the parish mission statement of their own parish? It is highly doubtful, and therein lays not only a major problem—*but also an institutionalized problem within the Church.*

Ignoring the temporal needs that are met through PMO services offered to parishioners and the community at-large is made so much easier by a parish mission statement that omits any acknowledgement whatsoever, any comment, any testimony, any witness to serving parish or parishioner *temporal* needs. But for the parish mission statement to ignore acknowledging the service of temporal needs through superior PMO, is to ignore an integral need. This is not necessarily an equal need, *but still an integral need of the parishioner that can* add, or detract, from their spiritual development—and anything that detracts from spiritual development is by definition a bad thing.

When we fail to acknowledge our total mission is defined by servicing the *dual needs*—both the spiritual *and* temporal composite needs of any person—when we unilaterally dismiss the temporal by omission, by ignoring acknowledging in the mission statement such needs exist and must be served by PMO, we are making it much easier for PMO to exist in mediocrity, or worse. Why? Because we have not made any promise, any public commitment or profession to our parishioners or the community that we are also fully committed to serving their needs *as a whole person, temporal and spiritual*. By omitting necessary and critical language we are in fact loudly declaring to our parishioners:

> Oh my, yes, we are here to serve your spiritual needs! But those potholes in the parking lot, that leaky roof, perpetually deferred equipment maintenance, poor landscaping, poor janitorial service of the parish office, rectory, hall and Church, unanswered phone calls, unreturned messages and emails, lost paperwork, outdated website information, low event participation relative to potential participation, abandoned or ineffective ministry leadership positions, broken music ministry organ, inoperable parking lot lights, cracked sidewalks and other safety hazards, out of date fire extinguishers, use of our parking lot by the nearby public school, double-booked or forgotten wedding and funeral services, double-booked or forgotten parish hall usage, poor promotion of parish retreats and events, lost schedules of all sorts, dropped parish bulletin entries, missed bulletin submission deadlines, missed announcements, failure to order required ministry course materials, missed bank deposits, parish debt

PMO AND THE PARISH MISSION STATEMENT: A CODEPENDENT RELATIONSHIP

mismanagement, parish accounting statement errors, lack of accounting statements, our chronic shortage of _____ (and we are not even addressing potential parish school issues), lack of outreach programs to lapsed and lost souls, well...*that's not addressed in our parish mission statement because we don't think you really need any of that.* Those things are just icing on your spiritual journey development cake. We know what your needs are better than you do. You see, *at this parish we demand you meet us where we are, we don't promise in any way to meet you where you are.* Step up! Become a more mature Christian! None of these temporal things really matter! Be strong, my friends!

Like the ring of the above? Like the message? Like the mental imagery? Think it is a valid message? Check your mission statement, because if your mission statement is one-sided, one dimensional, and tone-deaf in regard to also serving human temporal needs, *this is precisely the message you are sending, shouting really, to your parishioners by your silence.* Ignoring making a public declaration to serve the temporal needs of a parishioner is as unwise as it is unnecessary, as the parishioner has a composite of needs, and all needs must be greatly met—not just spiritual needs—by the PMO administrator and his or her team of paid staff and volunteers.

Thus, the parish mission statement with fidelity to the *composite needs* of parishioners must be crafted to meet both *spiritual and temporal* realities so the PMO administrator—who may also be a priest and clearly serves the parish's sacramental life and spiritual needs—also has a foundation, *and best/closest friend*, in the parish mission statement from which they can legally, publically, and/or privately support their PMO actions and decisions. Such a well-crafted parish mission statement no longer constitutes Carroll's, "any road will get you there" travel rubric. By no longer neglecting to address temporal needs in the parish mission statement—as if in some fog of denial such needs did not exist or need to be expressed—we lay down a specific starting point and road to follow from which we *publically* acknowledge at a very core level the parish's commitment to serving the temporal needs of everyone we meet. However:

Upon further reflection, we can surely realize the mere existence of a parish mission statement *does not necessarily mean we have exactly what we need within the mission statement text, to properly support and teach the PMO mission within the parish, or set the correct PMO internal culture.* This brings us to the next observation:

> **One of our most common mistakes is to make the mission statement into a kind of hero sandwich of good intentions.**
> —*Peter Drucker*

The parish mission statement need not, and likely will not, contain a balanced, 50/50 word count with language equally split between serving the spiritual and temporal needs. *Would you believe a mere well-crafted single sentence on serving the temporal needs of parishioners can suffice?* Clearly, we are not looking for a hero sandwich, a kitchen sink of good intentions thrown into the parish mission statement. Drucker provides us with some excellent general guidance on the proper formation of the mission statement. Drucker's goal is to ensure that the mission statement—no matter what type of organization it is meant to serve—is actually crafted and achieves what it was meant to do. Fine.

But what happens when the parish mission statement is poorly crafted? Oh, that's not a pretty picture. Drucker states, "For the ultimate test is not the beauty of the mission statement. *The ultimate test is right action.*" That pesky notion of "right action" in PMO is clearly derived from somewhere—*and now we know where.* The parish mission statement should be the fountainhead, the foremost

PMO AND THE PARISH MISSION STATEMENT: A CODEPENDENT RELATIONSHIP

touchstone, for developing "right action" in all PMO personnel. Fine. *But what if it is not?* What if the mission statement, usually through omission, is poorly crafted? Precisely this:

What is the name of your parish? You know that. What is the city of your parish? You know that. What is the phone number of your parish? You know that. What is your parish's mission statement? I bet you can't recite that. Why is that? Why is it that you don't know something that is, in theory, so foundational and vital to PMO? How about because...*nobody cares.* Why? Because since few understand the purpose and value of a properly-crafted mission statement to PMO and temporal needs—*the mission statement is ignored by everyone and used as a foundational tool at work by no one.*

Oh. That can't be good.

A "mission statement" is neither a "mission" nor a "statement" when it is poorly crafted. What it is, *is habitually and universally ignored.* A poorly-crafted mission statement is not helpful, much less vital to creating and animating the correct *culture* of any organization. It is simply a pro-forma but futile exercise, a hand-me-down historical tradition perpetuated by popular demand and now rendered as necessary window dressing demanded to exist by someone in authority, and then promptly forgotten. Equally, as Fr. Senior wisely notes: to neglect to adapt and update an existing mission statement to the changing circumstances of the world in which we live, is also a serious error, *as our PMO tools must adapt to the times.* The parish mission statement is a tool, but when your parish mission statement language fits just as well today as it would during the lifetime of St. Peter and St. Paul, as the famous saying goes, "Houston, we have a problem." Why?

Just look at the tools available to the enemy today: countless drugs, internet enabled pornography and immorality, nuclear war, the scourge of relativism, the "her body, her choice" abortion movement, IVF, societal legitimization of homosexuality, and the list goes on. You must understand that PMO informs little to nothing as to its contribution to bringing souls to Christ, *solely from the typical lofty and soaring language in the parish "Mission Statement" forming some generic, perpetual call to "right action."* Only the people who have a hand in creating the parish mission statement are passionate about such statements, and even then, only during the discussion of its formation. After formation, such statements become invisible and fade into the background. Such mission statements miss the mark by the *commission of omission*—what they leave out, not what they include—and do nothing to create and sustain the correct culture of the organization. The mission statement in essence is a tool at our disposal in PMO that is unnecessarily wasted.

As you will read, *building the correct culture is vital to any organization—and it is the centerpiece of the art of PMO*. This culture-building process *begins with, but does not end with,* promulgating a well-crafted mission statement in which *the purpose of parish PMO paid staff and volunteers is presented to the community as integral to the mission of the Church universal, your diocese, and your Parish*. You empower delivering superior PMO through a properly-crafted parish mission statement. You make a *public promise* to deliver superior PMO. You weave delivering superior PMO into the fabric of your parish DNA. Delivering superior PMO service becomes as transparent as breathing. Most importantly—absent the monetary profit motivation—the PMO administrator now has a statement that contains your public pledge to provide superior PMO services to parishioners—*and all PMO staff know this truth as a condition of their continuing employment*.

In the above comments we have established in a general sense that for the parish mission statement to be used as an effective foundation for PMO, *it must be crafted and presented from the outset in recognition of serving both the spiritual and temporal needs of every person*. To promise to serve spiritual

PMO AND THE PARISH MISSION STATEMENT:
A CODEPENDENT RELATIONSHIP

needs through the mission statement while ignoring temporal needs *would not be in the best interest of serving the parish as an entity, nor the person as a whole being.*

We are not here to minimize serving the spiritual needs of the parishioner, nor are we attempting to overemphasize the temporal needs of the parishioner. *We are seeking a reasonable balance expressed in the parish mission statement that gives the proper recognition that is due to both needs, so that a PMO culture of excellence can be created that will serve both the spiritual and temporal needs of the person.* So long as the personnel who report to us know the above, we are doing our jobs in this regard.

In light of the above, there is no need to dismantle your current parish mission statement. The question posed here is: what language should be added to *enhance* your existing parish mission statement—assuming there is one—in support of publically promising the community you will serve their temporal needs as well as their spiritual needs? The first thing to note here is the avoidance of the word "change" in this process as in, "We need to change our mission statement." You are only proposing to *add* language to *enhance* the existing mission statement. None of the current mission statement language has to be changed. Indeed, there is no quicker, surer way to make this language enhancement task more difficult, if not impossible, than to propose to "change the parish mission statement." Why? Because every stakeholder—real or imagined—that ever had anything to do with the creation of the current mission statement language will immediately go on high alert: "Who dares to change our parish mission statement…our parish mission statement has been around for years and is fine just the way it is…there's nothing wrong with the statement we already have…etc." This parochial, almost "turf protection" attitude is perfectly understandable given the fact that expressing support for serving the temporal needs of the community *within the parish mission statement* has historically been overlooked.

Let us look at three sample before and after enhancement parish mission statements (added enhanced language in **bold**).

Before enhancement:

We, the members of _____ (insert parish name) baptized into the body of Christ and filled with the Holy Spirit, are called:

To form ourselves in the Gospel and the teachings of the Church.

To celebrate the sacramental life, especially the Eucharist, until the Lord comes in glory.

After enhancement:

We, the members of _____ (insert parish name) baptized into the body of Christ and filled with the Holy Spirit, are called:

To form ourselves in the Gospel and the teachings of the Church.

To continue the corporal and spiritual work of Jesus as we minister with excellence to those in our home, in our community, in the Church, and in the world.

To celebrate the sacramental life, especially the Eucharist, until the Lord comes in glory.

We acknowledge and accept Jesus' call to make disciples through excellent corporal and spiritual service to the community.

Before enhancement:

The mission of _____ (insert parish name here) is to proclaim the good news of Jesus Christ confidently and completely. We do so in order to build a joyful and welcoming community of faith that reaches out enthusiastically to all throughout ministries of word, worship and service.

After enhancement:

The mission of _____ (insert parish name here) is to proclaim the good news of Jesus Christ confidently and completely. We do so in order to build a joyful and welcoming community of faith that reaches out enthusiastically to all throughout ministries of word, worship and service. **Our corporal and spiritual service to the community will be excellent.**

Before enhancement:

We are a reconciling, healing family of Christians celebrating life through worship, service and Catholic Formation.

We are committed to creating an atmosphere within our parish family to come together in body and spirit as a living faith community to help each other become better servants, mature in faith formation, feed the spiritually and physically hungry, create a stronger faith formation and bring people to the light of God.

We invite you to come and worship with us.

After enhancement:

We are a reconciling, healing family of Christians celebrating life through worship, service and Catholic Formation. **Our corporal and spiritual service to the community will be excellent.**

We are committed to creating an atmosphere within our parish family to come together in body and spirit as a living faith community to help each other become better servants, mature in faith formation, feed the spiritually and physically hungry, create a stronger faith formation and bring people to the light of God.

We invite you to come and worship with us.

From the above examples you can see the language of virtually every parish mission statement can be kept intact—no incendiary "change" imagery need be invoked. Why wave a red cape in front of a bull? Your objective is the simple addition of *enhancement language* to the parish mission statement, done to extend support for serving the temporal needs of the person. Through implication this is also to say you publically promise to deliver an entire gamut of superior PMO services to the community.

Why this enhanced language becomes paramount will be further explained, but suffice it to say here that *a properly worded mission statement is foundational to the implementation and delivery of superior PMO*. If you do not have this enhanced language in your mission statement it is not impossible to deliver superior PMO, *it is just that the job of doing so just got a whole lot harder,* and unnecessarily so, for the PMO administrator.

It is most likely you are not a practicing business major if you are reading this book, nor did you choose the field of business as your final career path. The most likely reason for this mindset is the simplest: you did not feel business was your highest calling to serve God. Fine. But that said, *do not be fooled into thinking that your chosen vocation is a refuge from all things business*—it is not.

The fact is that the Church desperately needs more men and women with at least a basic understanding of the art and science—especially the art—of sound business practices. Why? There are several reasons, but they all terminate here: at best superior PMO will bring your constituencies closer to Christ, which is our goal, but at worst poor PMO will drive people away from God in every imaginable way—and perhaps for some, petty and unimaginable ways. Nevertheless, this is the world we live in. Rather than retrofit this critical knowledge to you in some Band-Aid fashion—especially when there is no time to do so for some after their ordination and placement in a parish—I applaud your wisdom, insight, and commitment to perhaps leave your topical and vocational comfort zones and read this book before you take on duties and responsibilities for which you are not so well equipped or prepared to handle.

CHAPTER 11

WE NEED A NEW PMO RESULTS-MEASURING YARDSTICK

We don't like their sound, and guitar music is on the way out.

—Decca Recording Co. rejecting the Beatles in 1962

Nuclear-powered vacuum cleaners will probably be a reality in ten years.

—Alex Lewyt, President, Lewyt Vacuum Cleaner Co.

And one of my personal favorites...

One day Apple was a major technology company with assets to make any self respecting techno-conglomerate salivate. The next day Apple was a chaotic mess without a strategic vision and certainly no future.

—Time Magazine, February 5, 1996

Who says such things as above? Wrong question. *Why are such things said?* That is the better question to answer.

The number one market capitalization company in the world today as of this writing? Apple, on its way to a $1 trillion valuation. If whoever wrote the comment above about Apple would have invested 10% of his or her paycheck in Apple stock at that time, this person surely would not have to work today. It appears some folks need a new results-measuring yardstick.

So, who makes such comments as above? Doesn't really matter—*why matters*. People who have no idea what they are doing, lack vision, mistakenly exclusively focus on the how and not at all the why, and critically…*somehow have managed to find their way into a seat with authority and influence—this is who says such things to this day.* And what is the fruit of their efforts? That would be choking new ideas and killing so-called "mavericks" in society. Here's a tip: don't kill your mavericks; they might save your life one day.

Now, ponder working at Decca under the Decca "management," etc. Sound like fun? Sound like a bright future? Visionary enterprise? Or in our paradigm: do you want to do work in PMO solely to provide routine services to the currently active parishioners? I pray you do not, but how do you think superior PMO services to active <u>and lapsed</u> parishioners come into being? Oh? Wait. We are here to also address lapsed Catholics via PMO? Yes, we most certainly are. But can we do so by redoubling the same efforts that produced mediocre results and hemorrhaging parishioner attrition in the first place? No. When you redouble the same principles that produced mediocrity and attrition in the first place, guess what you get? *More entrenched mediocrity and more attrition.* Why? To start with, bum results-measuring yardsticks. How so?

In the previous chapters the point was made rather strongly that in PMO our performance standard is not merely "good enough," but superior. We achieve superior results by understanding a new why/what/how paradigm in PMO. We were also clear that we are responsible for producing results (aka: outcomes) and mere busyness is not only not enough, *observed busyness is a terrible yardstick upon which to measure actual performance.* We further learned that we must have a defined direction and roadmap, otherwise we might travel any road.

WE NEED A NEW PMO RESULTS-MEASURING YARDSTICK

As sure as you are reading this, while not impossible, there is only a one in 360° chance we will end up where we desire to be without a predefined direction and roadmap to take us there. It's that, "Even a broken clock is right twice a day" thing, yet people often interpret circumstantial luck for brilliant strategic planning. It's time we wake up and embrace a holistic system of PMO. While I will gladly accept luck, I will not rely on luck.

Most importantly, we established that no matter how you may feel personally about being poorly served by any aspect of PMO, *there are people who may react very negatively*—possibly to the detriment of their soul, by being poorly served by PMO employees or volunteers. This raises the question: we know superior PMO is the objective, *but what constitutes "superior results" in PMO?* Will you—can you, even recognize superior PMO when and if you see it? More specifically, *what is your performance-measurement yardstick?* Clearly, if you cannot answer these questions, how will you know if you have achieved your objective? Do you simply and unilaterally declare managerial and operational victory, go to bed, and sleep well under the illusion that your mental and physical exhaustion is tantamount to having achieved superior results in your area of PMO responsibility? If so, there is no need to read any further. Indeed, there is no need for this book to even exist if certain people do not want to build and operate superior PMO wherever they are. *Superior PMO starts with the foundational desire to create superior PMO.*

Recall that the purpose of business is to produce a profit, in other words, to make money. We acknowledge the Church does not share that purpose or mission, and in one sense, that is too bad. Why? Because it is far easier in a business for the boss to measure whether or not "superior results" were achieved, when the most prominent results-measuring yardsticks are the proverbial, simplistic, and universally understood "bottom-line" results expressed in black and white numbers. In this reporting column we have one simple number representing profit, in another column a number representing profit margin expressed as a simple ratio, here is our share value, etc., etc. *But the fact the parish does not sell its services means that PMO results are not measured using the traditional business indicators of personal or departmental success.* The upshot? There is no direct link between PMO performance and the rise or fall of profits—because we do not operate in the realm of such profits. *We deal in the realm of spiritual gains or losses, not monetary gains or losses.* Clearly, we require a different performance-measurement yardstick—*but we still need yardstick metrics, and we will apply those metrics to determine such things as who remains employed and who doesn't.*

For those who must measure and manage their personnel towards a financial results-based performance standard, there are no grey areas when mentally mapping profit numbers, P/L ratios, etc., etc. to performance, because such numbers speak directly and plainly to performance, or the lack thereof. This observation raises an important question: *how the heck can a PMO administrator know how they are doing in their job, without access and reference to such numbers?* Without the profit/profit ratio et al yardsticks, *is there a way to measure, recalibrate, view, and review PMO results in relation to the primary mission of the Church,* which as we know is saving souls and bringing souls to Christ?

Yes and no.

> **I shall not today attempt further to define the kinds of material I understand to be embraced within that shorthand description ["hard-core pornography"], and perhaps I could never succeed in intelligibly doing so. But I know it when I see it.**
>
> —*Supreme Court Justice Potter Stewart*

No, there is no number or ratio to reference in PMO that is akin to the bottom line numerical yardsticks of profit, loss, profit margin, etc., that are universally

WE NEED A NEW PMO RESULTS-MEASURING YARDSTICK

accepted in the business world. Also, note that the government and the military also have their own unique performance-measurement rubrics, yardsticks, and vocabulary. Although we do acknowledge there is a link between bringing a soul to Christ and PMO, and we do desire to do our best, *mere desire does not constitute a strategy, nor does hope, and observed busyness is not a valid performance yardstick as to how well PMO is fully serving the needs of parishioners.* However:

Since we admit the mission of the Church is radically different than the mission of business, it follows that the metrics of business—*not necessarily the core principles, but the metrics*—must be different in a PMO environment. So although different, *we still need* a yardstick and vocabulary unique to nonprofits in general and PMO in particular, in order to evaluate, measure, adjust, and constantly monitor PMO performance and results. Why?

1. So that everyone in PMO knows how to recognize superior performance when they see it, and conversely, everyone in PMO can recognize when they see mediocrity, or worse.
1. To ensure the proper PMO culture has become institutionalized and always exists (much more on culture later).

Note that the above use of "1." for both line items is not a typo—it is deliberate. This nomenclature is used whenever we are discussing two or more points of equal and vital importance. There is no difference in importance, priority, or value between the above two points. Achieve both, or you will fail.

So, if we do not have access to the same profit and loss performance-measurement yardsticks as used in business, *what do we have available in PMO?* The answer to this question is found in the processes used to form the sum of the answers to the following four questions:

1. As administrators, against what *written standards* do we grade the level of PMO employee and volunteer performance—both our own and those

who report to us—in order to continually evolve and improve the service we provide to the parishioner we have a duty to serve? Most parishes have none.

2. Since we do not sell anything per se and we do not record profits/losses in the traditional sense, are we stuck without any PMO performance-measurement tools? No, but the metrics we do have are not often embraced, much less understood, by most PMO administrators. In essence, this means most PMO administrators have no performance-measurement tools except the seat of their pants.

3. Without easy to measure and report numerical indicators, what do we look for to know the difference between abysmal, poor, average, above average, and superior PMO performance?

4. *And very critically*, what is the triangular level of activity, engagement and utilization between your PMO services, PMO personnel, and parishioners, *in relation to the size of your parishioner base?* Viewed as an illustration:

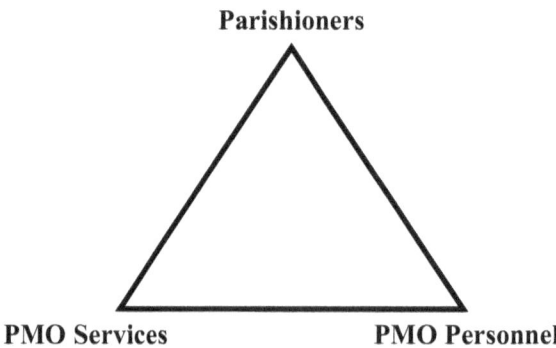

In the above illustration the critical point is not made simply in affirming there exists a relationship between parishioners, PMO services, and PMO personnel. Most people already intuit this relationship. The critical point in order to understand the results yardstick we invoke in PMO is to *measure our results*

WE NEED A NEW PMO RESULTS-MEASURING YARDSTICK

from the above relationships *within the context of the size of your parishioner base*. In other words:

How much activity do you see in this triangular relationship, vs. *how much activity should you see?*

Oh.

You mean we can't get by, we can't measure results, we can't rest in PMO by measuring how busy we actually are, *we have to also know and consider how busy we are in relation to how busy we should be, and the results we see must correlate to the size of our registered parishioner base and community population at-large?*

Correct. Useful performance measurement is always relative to your circumstances, to the facts of the ground. Take that point in for a moment. Again, busyness alone as our performance-measuring yardstick is a very poor yardstick for measuring results *in relation to our demographic potential.*

The answers to the above four questions collectively represent a blending of PMO art and science in order to deliver to PMO administrators *defensible, effective, sustainable, and enduring* performance-measurement tools and data. In other words, if you truly want to know how effective your busyness in PMO is in terms of producing superior results, you can know. But if you simply want to be busy and conclude without actual data-based justification that you are producing superior results for everyone in your geographic area, well, it's a free world—you can choose that road, too. But that road has a name: the road of denial. You would be living in denial, in a dream world of phantom performance.

CHAPTER 12

THE IDENTIFICATION AND REPAIR OF WHAT IS BROKEN

Perhaps you have read or heard the phrase, "Must be present to win" associated with various contests, ticket drawings, lotteries, etc. We borrow from that statement here, as the same principle applies to being a superior administrator or leader—*you must be both physically and mentally present to observe what those who report to you are doing, or not doing, on the* job in order to ever repair what is broken. You must initially, *but not perpetually*, perform this observation aspect of your job personally, not delegated through any staff you may have available to you. You can't remain static in your office, nor can you be focused on performing any other task so much you avoid responsibility to all your duties. Why? Because how in the world can you know if your many and diverse parish constituency's needs are being greatly served by PMO paid staff and/or volunteers, guest speakers, ministry leaders, etc., *if you do not bother to occasionally observe everyone in action, actually in the process of serving their parishioner constituency?* Not in some heavy-handed manner of grimace-jawed green eyeshade and tightly gripped clipboard oversight, but in the background you must observe all those who report to you until such time you are 100% certain, in a variety of scenarios and situations, these people are doing their tasks not just "good enough," but superior as you have defined it to them through their training and via the correct culture. Note: *superior* is as *you* define it.

Everybody has an opinion. Wonderful. Collect them all. Listen well. Consider all input. Adapt. Adjust. Be collegial when collegiality is called for. But at the end of the day after all the input has been collected, heard, and sifted: *you make a decision and people do what you want, the way you want it done*. In this regard, beware: *do not make the mistake of treating PMO employees as family and close friends—do not cross that line* (more on this point later). An employee is an employee no matter where they work—*maintain a professional working relationship and make your friends elsewhere*. And further note the clear distinction between "asking" and "requiring."

Whether you realize it or not, people naturally desire clarity and direction in their work. Providing such clarity and direction while holding people accountable, *these are simple precursor points crucial to setting and sustaining the cultural expectations of the correct workplace environment*. As the PMO administrator, you are responsible for setting this expectation within anyone whose work product you are ultimately responsible for. And if any mediocrity is allowed to exist, *mediocrity will expand over time to become the cultural expectation throughout all PMO*. As such, if systemic mediocrity exists within an organization it is never the employees or volunteers who are at fault—*it is always the fault of at least their direct management, if not higher*. But mediocrity will not long survive educated scrutiny—so get out of your office and observe those who report to you doing their respective jobs. *Your system-educated and proactive informed scrutiny is cultural Kryptonite to PMO mediocrity.*

Further note this "get out of your office and observe" aspect of PMO administration is not as time intensive as it might first appear—*it is mind intensive far more than time intensive*. What is required is that the wise PMO administrator must skillfully recognize what they are looking for in terms of employee/volunteer production and results—right, wrong, good, bad, poor, average, superior, etc. They must also know what they are looking for in per-

THE IDENTIFICATION AND REPAIR OF WHAT IS BROKEN

formance, in relation to what they actually see occurring—*or not occurring that should*. Again, this is not time intensive, but mind and know-how intensive. Specifically: *does what you see being done reconcile with what you want done? Should you see something being done, which is not actually being done? Should there be people in your community being served by robust PMO who are not even present?* (Now, there is a question that is so often overlooked.) This point brings us here:

> **Non nobis solum nati sumus. (***Not for ourselves alone are we born.***)**
>
> —*Marcus Tullius Cicero*

Do you fully appreciate how many diverse parish and diocesan constituencies PMO exists to serve, each constituency with their own parochial interests and unique demands—some daily, some weekly, some monthly, some annually, and some are at odds with the PMO resources allocation of other constituencies? All of these diverse constituencies that need to be served contact someone in PMO, who reports to someone, and eventually...*that someone they report to is you as the PMO administrator.*

It is in this manner we arrive at this observation: as explained above, personal observation of those who report to you is paramount, and there is no substitute for personal observation, *but one must also know what he or she is observing in relation to what should be observed*. Repeat: one must also know what he or she is observing *in relation to what should be observed*. In other words, this is knowledge of what is <u>in relation to what should be</u>. The blind leading the blind never works, unless being lost is your goal. This is what it means to have knowledge of what is, in relation to what should be: *to know what you are observing in relation to what you should be observing is paramount to delivering superior results*. For example:

Suppose I am observing a student-artist paint a self-portrait. The portrait looks terrible at the start, looks terrible at all points during its creation, and predictably—looks terrible when it is completed. Can you see that if it were my duty to help the artist paint a superior self-portrait, of course I must be present from time to time during the painting process, *but I must also know what I am observing and talking about* in order to be of any service to this artist-in-training? I must have an understanding of what I am seeing, not simply as it presently looks, *but also in relation to where it is heading and what it should look like upon successful completion of the assigned task*. I must have vision. Moral support is wonderful, *but ultimately moral support without precise training and technical guidance in the art and science of what I am attempting to accomplish is just so much feel-good noise.*

Moral support without the requisite specific guidance leads all parties into an otherwise avoidable train wreck. You can question later how you ended up as the PMO administrator, but for now you have a job to master. Therefore, abject silence and ignoring manifest brokenness—even though you probably did not create the brokenness in front of you—is also not an option for the superior PMO administrator. You must know what you are doing and what you are talking about, and by the way—*you must turn thinking into right actions*.

For whatever aspect(s) of PMO that report to you and for which you are responsible, from a technical point of view do you know what you are doing in that realm? Are you trained in that discipline, at least enough to be conversationally fluent? As the saying goes, "Do you have a clue?" If so, *speak up and take action*. When those who report to you stray from proper methods and techniques and you are looking right at them, do you know enough about the task at hand to tell the difference between a poor self-portrait and a masterpiece? If so, *speak up*. And if you are not willing to take such action for whatever reason:

Why did you accept the position of PMO administrator without the attitude

THE IDENTIFICATION AND REPAIR OF WHAT IS BROKEN

required to do the job in a superior manner? Do you think your good intentions ultimately matter to those who are poorly served by PMO administration? And how can you train those who report to you if you don't know what you are doing? Do you think you are assigned to be a token office caretaker? *Do you know enough about the subject to teach me,* your employee or volunteer, such that I can deliver to you what you want the way you want it? Or are you going to observe me performing poorly, remain silent, take no action, *and thereby certify by your complicity in silence my mediocre performance as normative PMO culture and acceptable as the workplace standard?* Silence—for whatever reason, in the face of less than superior performance is the number one reason PMO mediocrity will become enshrined as your normative workplace standard.

Oh. That's not good.

You must understand and accept that in a results-oriented culture and working environment—and make no mistake "results oriented" is the correct and proper PMO culture and working environment—if your euphemistic "good intentions," if your, "above and beyond the call of duty…yeoman efforts…etc." and commensurate extreme personal exhaustion at the end of the day have not yet *produced superior PMO results,* know this is the predictable outcome when an administrator had the greatest of intentions to do a great job…*but has little to no idea what he or she is doing on that job.*

Does this sound harsh to you? If so, further reflect on the above. Reconcile that requiring superior PMO performance as a prerequisite condition of continued employment *is not at odds with Scripture-based values on the dignity of the human person.* We are called to *actually* serve in a superior manner, not merely look busy or even truly be busy while producing poor fruit. Additionally, we must not actually be busy *and naively fall for the illusion we are greatly serving anyone, much less everyone, in our busyness.* How so? Keep reading.

CHAPTER 13

VOLUME OF ACTUAL PMO USAGE IN RELATION TO POTENTIAL USAGE

We have gathered that as the PMO administrator we must not only observe those who report to us and further train them as necessary, but we must generally know how the job we are observing should be performed so we can distinguish mediocre performance from superior performance in each job. In other words, *to be effective we must know what we are doing.* Fine. But if we frequently observe those who report to us, if we truly know what we are doing in our oversight and training roles, if people actually do their PMO jobs in a superior manner, is our work done? No, our work is not done. *It is not close to being done.* Why?

You claim, "We have superior PMO, we monitor, we train, our operating culture is correct, so what more is there to do?" That question is answered by returning to this revealing question posed earlier:

> Do we have the overall demands for the sum of all our various parish ministries and services <u>that are commensurate with the size of our registered parishioner base</u>?

Oh. You mean there's a catch. You mean that merely being busy in PMO—even extremely busy—is not the tell-all all-informing yardstick for determining PMO effectiveness?

That is correct, 100% correct.

It is when this question is posed in the business world—or to PMO personnel for our purposes—that people start to look down at their shoes, shuffle their feet, and fade into the back of the room. Why? Because the truthful, *no-nonsense answer* to this question shreds the Hollywood movie facades, the huge back-lot PMO mansions revealed to be what they truly are: false fronts. Why? Because the answer to this question more than any other reveals your *actual* level of engagement in relation to what your level of engagement *should be* based upon *the size of your registered parishioner base. This perspective represents a huge paradigm shift in understanding the duty and role of truly vibrant community-wide PMO service*, for so many people only consider what is, *and do not consider what should be* in PMO. How so? As follows:

We operate in a world of potential, and to pretend we have no influence over *cultivating greater activity and engagement from our geographic potential* is an invalid premise. We are not passive order-takers in PMO. Indeed, *such a notion is contrary to Scripture*. Order taking and reacting to a metaphorical ringing phone is not our only role in PMO—*we are also here to proactively do things that make our parish phone ring.* Do you see a drive-thru window attached to the Church or parish office? Neither do I. So why do some folks pretend there is one in PMO? *PMO is the agency within the parish that is responsible for making the phone ring, understand?* If PMO is not ringing this community outreach bell, *this bell doesn't ring.*

Yet, there are some people with overall responsibility for PMO who are far too passive in their attitude and approach to this work. In their world PMO is placed on general autopilot: provided there are no emergencies or complaints, however PMO runs is fine with them. There is no critical analysis or evaluation of whether PMO is delivering all that it should, or rather, if to the proactive and trained eye PMO is actually falling short in many ways. The passive PMO practitioner wants no part of installing a culture that aggressively and proactively serves existing parishioners *while simultaneously implementing strategies seeking those souls who have quit on their faith*. Indeed, passive PMO could care less about those who are not present, not engaging the Sacraments, acting as if reaching lapsed and lost souls is not intrinsic to PMO. How wrong such people are. *Nothing about passive PMO is Christ-like.*

It is disingenuous to rest on what you perceive to be an active and vibrant parish community, while at the same time knowingly or unknowingly refusing to consider the activity you see *in relation to the results you should be generating based upon the size and potential of your geographic base*. It is only when the results you are generating correlate rightly and tightly to the results you should generate based upon the size of your geographic base—*and across the entire suite of potential PMO-offered services*—that one may have any results worth endorsing. Anyone who talks about how busy he or she is in PMO without also making a *corresponding correlation* to fully serving the size of the Parish's geographic base is just making noise. Again:

> Do we have the overall demands for the sum of all our various parish ministries and services *that are commensurate with the size of our geographic base?*

Do you understand the importance of the answer to this telling question? More to the point, can you feel the texture of this question as you map it to your specific PMO utilization level? Assuming you even have well-oiled PMO, *it is not enough for well-oiled PMO to merely exist because mere existence is not the goal. The proper gamut and highest possible utilization of superior PMO services in relation to the size of the geographic base you serve is the goal*.

Thus, we must ask: what do you judge to be your *true level* of *PMO services utilization?* Do not miss answering this tough but revealing question. Do not allow those who report to you to be satisfied with an abysmal level of true utilization of your PMO services in relation to the size of your geographic base. *The answer to the above question tells all about how <u>effective</u> you are in reaching your community.* And why do we bother asking this question? Because we don't exist to serve ourselves—*we exist to serve all others*. As such, are you proactively engaging the number of "others" one would expect to have *in a parish of your size, with your total population?*

Perhaps now do you begin to see PMO as more than parking lot repair and various ministry events management? Mere existence of PMO, even superior PMO, *is simply your starting point*. But to casually accept relative *trivial community engagement* of your PMO ministries and services is to enshrine evangelization mediocrity—*and you are not reading this book to learn how to enshrine any form of mediocrity*. To further develop this point:

In approximate terms: what is the size of your parish, not in terms of geographic boundaries, but in terms of souls? In terms of registered parishioners <u>and lapsed Catholics</u>? How many families? How many adults? How many children? How many sick? How many homeless in your area? How many unemployed? How many cultures? Are all cultures equally served and engaged by various ministries in your parish? Do all the various ministries that should exist, actually exist? Robustly? If not, why not? The real indicator of PMO effectiveness: *the volume of actual engagement and usage of all parish ministries and services <u>in relation to their potential volume of usage</u>*. What is the potential of your geographic area? Have you thought about that? Have you reached your potential? Clearly, if a parish ministry that should exist does not exist or is dormant, the level of community and parishioner engagement is zero. And when the volume of engagement is not where it should be we do not pass the buck in PMO—*this buck stops in PMO*.

The lesson: no matter how well trained, well managed, and how ready we are in PMO, *without the level of utilization of PMO ministries and services that properly correlates to the size of our population base, <u>we are failing in PMO</u>*.

VOLUME OF ACTUAL PMO USAGE IN RELATION TO POTENTIAL USAGE

Note this well:

> We are only superior in PMO to the extent we are fully engaging the number of souls that the population in our geography infers we should be engaging. To willfully and chronically ignore and permit underutilization without a strategic PMO effort to further engage our current and lapsed Catholic base and the population at-large, is not only the epitome of deficient PMO—it is immoral.

CHAPTER 14

THE CREATION OF WANT

In relation to the critical observation made in the previous chapter, one could mistakenly, sadly, adopt the incorrect, diminished, watered-down, apathetic yardstick of mere busyness to measuring PMO effectiveness. In other words, your expressed or implied servant attitude could be:

> It is what it is in our parish. If someone contacts us, we are very ready and willing to serve! But if the phone doesn't ring, if there is minimal walk-in, phone, email, website, or social media communication between registered or lapsed parishioners and the parish relative to our geographic potential, little to no attendance at parish events, missing and/or vacant ministries, etc., which is to say there is little to no interest or demand for what we are providing our community in a PMO context, oh well, that's not our problem. In fact, we probably wouldn't even notice such things. That's not the way we measure things here.

Honestly, have you deeply reflected on the level of utilization of your parish services *in relation to the size of your registered and potentially active parishioner base?* Does the level of usage of your collective PMO services *generally correlate to the number of people, active and lapsed, in your parish geography?*

If it does, wonderful. Your work here is done. However, what if:

1. You cannot truly answer these questions, and;
2. If PMO engagement and utilization could be substantially improved upon in most parishes, *whom do you think is responsible for changing this condition?* In other words: *who is responsible for the creation of want?*

Is this underutilization of services scenario truly "not your problem" to at least partially address via adjustments in PMO? Is "that's not my problem" the Christ-like response to lapsed parishioner and community apathy and an underutilization of parish services? Are we going to embrace the escapist's mentality, a duty-dodging path hiding behind such comments as, "That's the Holy Spirit's job…God will provide…." No, we cannot allow this. As Drucker insightfully stated,

> **The absence of results indicates only that efforts have to be increased.**

In essence, what we are describing in the above paragraphs is a case where you threw the most extravagant party imaginable…and either nobody attended or too few people attended. Either way, you did not receive the results you were seeking—assuming you were even seeking results over falling for the mere illusion of busyness as defining a fully engaged level of service. Now what? How would you personally feel about that? I suppose when the stakes of throwing a party that nobody attends is merely the loss of having fun we can afford to adopt an, "Oh, well, it is what it is" attitude. But when the stake of nobody or too few attending our celebration is the proper spiritual disposition of souls or the strengthening of souls, *there is no place for an attitude of, "Oh, well, it is what it is in our Church."*

We must directly challenge such apathetic trends within PMO, *as defeating parishioner apathy and mindless mechanical roboticism is an integral part of our job as PMO administrators and leaders.* The "creation of want" is part of our job in PMO. And if you are of the opinion, as I am, that we can supremely defeat apathy through the Eucharist, you are most correct, except for the fact *the Eucharist does not benefit those who do not receive Him and are no longer attending Mass.* We must therefore meet those people where they are to be found *and stop whining about where we wish them to be.* The fact they quit on their faith *cannot stop creative, PMO-based, Holy Spirit guided initiatives from proactively seeking them out.*

It is our *duty* as administrators to satisfactorily reconcile *actual usage* of PMO services with *potential usage based upon the potential of our geographic parish size*, and if we cannot satisfactorily reconcile the usage level, *develop a suite of outreach programs via our PMO strategic plan to identify and remedy the discrepancy to the best of our ability.* Yes, man has free will and free will shall not be impinged or overruled—but without concrete feedback or evidence of dismissal, *you must not blame massive scale underutilization or rejection of PMO services on the exercise of parishioner free will until you know that for a fact, per soul.*

Widespread lack of engagement and underutilization of PMO is far more likely than not indicative of *general and systemic religious apathy*, not a conscious and free will hardcore rejection of engaging Jesus Christ through His Church. Over time and with the right strategic plan, apathy and disinterest can be overcome. How? Read on.

CHAPTER 15

DEFINING THE TARGET AUDIENCE

Let's break down the previous critical point: "variance in actual usage in relation to potential usage" of parish services. With an investment of some of your shoe leather and some phone calls, we can question, poll, and/or observe people to learn the level of actual engagement of the various PMO services within our parish. Fine. *But how can we infer what the level of engagement should be*, at least approximately, in our parish? In other words, how do we know when we are not busy, halfway busy, and fully busy in PMO in relation to the geographic size of our parish?

We do this by investigating what I will label as some *conspicuous indicators of humanity* to detect how these indicators inform on the *level of correlation* between our registered parishioner base and overall population in our geographic area in relation to various aspects of PMO service engagement. We observe some informative *human benchmark indicators* that intuitively provide us with a discussion and investigative framework. We apply some very basic math. We logically extrapolate. This information will be used for your mental mapping and reflection in order to fairly answer—not necessarily precisely answer down to the last decimal point—the paramount PMO resource utilization question:

Do we have the overall demand for the sum of all our various parish services *that is commensurate with the size of our registered parishioner base and overall geographic population base?*

What is meant by, "mental mapping and reflection"? It is that state whereby you map in your mind the points that follow—and any other indicators you are aware of that are peculiar to your area—to the overall population of your home parish service geography. *You reflect on and approximate the number of times per day someone in your parish will be touched by one or more of the events named below.*

All things being equal, these events could/would/should necessitate some contact with, some services provided from or coordinated through, your PMO—*but do they in your parish?* Or have you made the mistake of accepting whatever you offer today as good enough? With the volume of good and bad events happening in daily life, with the daily occurrence of good fortune, misfortune, and everything in between that life sends our way, *can you infer, do you intuit, do you perceive, do you know if you actually have the full range of PMO ministries you should and a level of activity that correlates to the number of people registered in your parish or geographic area touched by such events each day?* Or do you have a need for some "creation of want"? *Do you sense that for whatever reason(s) there is far more potential than you are serving?*

Consider the following facts and events:

(Note: since for our purposes we are looking for general framework indicators, fractional numbers have been rounded up or down to nearest whole number.)

_____ Insert total population in your parish geographic area

_____ Insert total number of registered parishioners

DEFINING THE TARGET AUDIENCE

National average: 3 persons per household

Average size of parish: 1,167 households

Average parishioner count per parish: 3,501

Marriage rate: 7 per 1,000 total population

Birth rate: 13 per 1,000 total population

Infant/child baptism rate: 14 per 1,000 Catholics

Death rate: 8 per 1,000 total population

Unemployment rate: 7 per 1,000 working population

Divorce rate: 45%

Alcohol-impaired driving: 479 episodes per 1,000 adult population

Drug overdoses resulting in death: 14 per 100,000 of population

Cancer per 1,000: 44

Diabetes per 1,000: 12

Crime Rate per 1,000 inhabitants: 62

Murder rate per 1,000: 4.5

Televisions per 1,000: 755

Mobile cell phones per 1,000: 980

Percentage of population addicted to pornography: 3–6%

Misery index*: 9.41

The misery index is an economic indicator created by economist Arthur Okun, and found by adding the unemployment rate to the inflation rate. It is assumed that both a higher rate of unemployment and a worsening of inflation create economic and social costs for a country.

Notice the above activities/indicators will necessarily generate data that varies between parishes. Rural parishes will naturally have lower numbers than major metropolitan areas. The nature and type of ministry work will vary between inner, suburban, and rural areas. No matter. This truth simply puts a spotlight on the fact that each parish and PMO administrator *must do his or her own data collection*—clearly, an excellent raw data survey task for *delegation* to a competent parish volunteer. However, what would be most helpful is if parishes could share with other parishes, both neighboring and distant, their data survey collection methodology and collected raw data mapped to their proactive outreach ideas, and coordinate offering some of their PMO strategic event-services together.

But in order for there to be any such sharing there must first be established a *common understanding*, not only of the general role of PMO, *but a common holistic system of PMO thinking, and a common vocabulary must be shared between parishes—and that doesn't exist right now*. But do not let that stop you. For now, you go it alone, and your success will be adopted by others in due time. You go it alone while you work to bring this methodology to others—but it does not take a great deal of imagination to visualize what would happen if every parish around you carried out this PMO survey and data collection initiative. Indeed, no need to reinvent the wheel, either. An internet key-word search will reveal to you survey forms already in parish use to collect some of the necessary information, and all you have to do is modify the forms to fit your specific needs.

> **I'm gonna reveal something to you that's going to come as a shock: If you're a stupid young man, you're usually a stupid old man. Most people, including myself, keep repeating the same mistakes.**
>
> —William Shatner

DEFINING THE TARGET AUDIENCE

There is absolutely no reason whatsoever for each parish PMO to operate in its own orbit, independently and redundantly creating its own core policies, procedures, methods, information surveys, and data collection mechanisms as if they are alone and on their own island. Indeed, the Church acknowledges this truth in publishing, "In Fulfillment of Their Mission." This document first establishes that there are nine essential duties of a Roman Catholic priest, and then divides each of those duties into a set of tasks. It then runs down each task and shows how to assess a Pastor's level of proficiency for each one, categorized as: novice, approaching proficiency, proficiency and above proficiency. Notice point number 4 in this document is, "Leads Parish Administration" and includes nine tasks, one of which is "Employs and Manages Parish Staff."

The metrics for basic proficiency are these:
1. Maintains a healthy work environment.
2. Nurtures a spirit of discipleship among staff.
3. Makes personnel decisions following principles of good stewardship and Gospel values.
4. Hires qualified individuals who support the needs/mission of the parish.
5. Reviews contracts and evaluates employees on a regular basis following diocesan policy (e.g., annually).
6. Mediates conflict among parish staff in keeping with diocesan policy, the parish mission and the good of the Church.
7. Provides for the supervision of staff.
8. Provides opportunities for continuing education of staff.

But here's the key point—to work above basic proficiency there is but a single metric:

9. **Empowers staff to develop their full potential.**

Now, one wonders why a group of seminary formators came together to develop this document if not because of a single realization: that if there really are nine essential duties to being a priest and one of them has to do with parish administration, *then it would make total sense to invest time training seminarians in how to be proficient in this critical duty.* Yet, without a common and holistic system of study to define and unify PMO culture, procedures, terminology, etc., each seminary—and therefore by logical extension each parish—works in isolation and at best loosely shares successful and unsuccessful ideas.

Unfortunately, in their own unique way, each parish or seminary must necessarily and by design write their PMO managerial script in isolation. This is not only inefficient, it is as Shatner pointed out: young man stupid will inevitably grow into old man stupid, or if you prefer, "Born a piglet, die a pig." Why do we do this to ourselves? Here the Church must simply borrow a proven operational blueprint from the business world—franchising: when one man or woman invents a superior system others copy it, *and rather than perpetually reinvent the wheel, all succeed by using the same basic core model and principles.*

When you consider what would be reflected in the daily life of people through all of the life activities and indicators listed above, can you now correlate the level of parishioner contact and interaction with your PMO services, to the registered size of your parishioner count and your geographic area of service? *Think it out.* Collect this information and spreadsheet it where you are, because without the information you not only will not be able to know if you are as busy in PMO as you should be, you will not have the necessary foundation you will need to address a broken culture (more on culture later), or build a strategic plan to address the issues.

CHAPTER 16

INDICATORS OF PMO ENGAGEMENT

Are you as busy as reasonable math would lead you to think you should be in your PMO, given the size of your registered parishioner base and geographic area mapped to life in the world as reflected by births, deaths, disease, crime rate, marriages, divorces, etc., happening within your parish geography? Or perhaps you may have now instinctively detected <u>severe underutilization of PMO services in relation to the size of your parishioner base and geographic area</u>?

To assist in this analysis we must answer: what are the upper and lower framework indicators of an engaged, or poorly engaged, PMO? What yardsticks do we use in PMO? For instance:

Indicators of low PMO engagement and utilization: parish staff phones rarely ringing, low traffic volume and low correlation of registered parishioners to incoming emails transiting the parish email server, zero/low parish website visits, low time spent engaging parish webpages, parish website uninteresting, not updated, and presenting out of date information, zero/low Catholic social media adoption, implementation, and utilization footprint in the parish, zero/low understanding of social media, low foot traffic through parish office, low enrollment for parish events and retreats, not enough meaningful and substantive work for paid staff, little to no impactful or substantive work for parish volunteers, too few new volunteers, too few new registering parishioners for the geographic footprint of the parish, too few active and robust ministries, lack of diverse ministry types, lack of parish ministry proactive leaders/leadership, physical premises in poor condition, youth ministry chronically under-enrolled.

Indicators of high PMO engagement and utilization: high level of inbound and outbound phone calls, high correlation of incoming emails to parish email domain and number of registered parishioners, robust implementation of Catholic social media, high website traffic, high foot traffic through parish office, high enrollment for parish events and retreats, more than enough truly substantive work for paid staff, more work to do than volunteers to do it, high volume of new registering parishioners, numerous active, diverse, and well-led parish ministries, physical premises in excellent condition, parish website interesting and always displays current information, large and vibrant youth ministry.

Do you see how proactively, systematically, engaging all indicators of low PMO engagement and utilization can be used as an insightful roadmap for the clear identification of what is broken or deficient that must be addressed? Do you see how such indicators can be used as data collection points and drivers to ultimately weave a PMO strategic plan for yourself, and perhaps be further shared across multiple cooperating parishes? Certainly you can, as it is obvious to the most casual observer who bothers to investigate, to look under the hood of PMO as it were. And provided you bother to look it is fairly easy to observe when nothing is happening, or not enough is happening in relation to the size and scope of your registered parishioner base and geographic area. However:

The straightforward, "identification of what needs to be addressed" *is the easy part*. Anybody can make a list of broken stuff, but not just anybody can remedy what is on the list of broken stuff. Read on.

CHAPTER 17

REMOVING THE SUPPRESSION

It is easier to suppress the first desire than to satisfy all that follow it.

—Benjamin Franklin

Every enterprise has its so-called low-hanging fruit. We have low-hanging fruit in PMO. Fine. We should always pick such fruit. Why? Because it's there and it's easy, so we pick it. Now what? We want the rest of the fruit—*we want all the fruit on our tree, especially the fruit that is very high up on the tree.* How do we pick the high fruit? *We must create want.* In other words:

> *Sometimes we have to persuade the high fruit to want to meet us where we are in the same manner we are always willing to meet them where they are.* However:

The first point to make is that, "the creation of want" is not a euphemism for traditional "marketing." How so?

> Traditional marketing takes an *external* and attempts to push it upon you until it becomes an *internal*.

For example, I market the _____ product or service image to you (insert image of choice here), and if I am effective in my marketing, you will then choose to buy my product or service in order to embrace that image. Hence, *the external becomes the internal.*

But the "creation of want" does precisely the opposite as traditional marketing: the creation of want spearheaded by PMO proposes to take something that is *already internal* to man—specifically man's innate desire to seek and know God—that for now in a person (the high fruit) is not desired. Why? Because the desire to know/want God is being *willfully suppressed.* Thus:

Traditional marketing pushes something external upon a person, *but the creation of want is a vastly different principle.* The creation of want is an attempt to *reveal* that which is *already internal* within the person—indeed, imbued by God in every soul at birth, *by addressing and removing whatever issue is suppressing the want.* Understanding this point is paramount to accepting that the *true duty of PMO extends beyond simply fixing parking lot potholes, scheduling events, etc.*

The second point to make is another revelation based upon the first: if the "want" we are seeking to create already exists within every person who is apathetic or has quit on his or her faith and the Church—technically speaking we're not creating anything, *we're revealing what already exists, and revealing what already exists is so much easier than building desire from scratch.*

Traditional product marketing is stuck trying to develop desire from scratch, but we are not at this disadvantaged position in PMO—God imbued the desire to want to know Him in every soul. This is a paramount revelation. If we remove what is suppressing the want imbued by natural law, *the soul will return to its natural state and resume desiring to seek God in faith* (faith seeks understanding) where it once left off—no matter how long ago that was. The suspension of desire in each person might have occurred a year ago, or fifty years ago, it really doesn't matter. The "want" to seek and know God is indelibly and permanently imbued on every soul. The problem, our challenge to overcome, is that "want"

REMOVING THE SUPPRESSION

is being suppressed, *and our job as PMO administrators is to remove the suppression of want.*

Oh. That's interesting. *It turns out PMO is ultimately responsible for a lot more than most people think.*

As human beings, our souls are designed to incline unto God. But as people living in the world…*shiny things easily distract us*. And attention spans seem to be shorter. ("Just because I have a short attention span doesn't mean I.") We turn away from our Creator toward that created shiny thing or noisemaker, but unless we can see through the worldly creation to our Creator—and assume our proper role as stewards of creation (Genesis 1:28)—we will fall into idolatry, forsaking the Creator for the creation, or rather, exalting creation (e.g. that shiny thing) to the level of our Creator. Some thing and/or event is ultimately what is habitually suppressing our want, and it's made up in part of all those obstacles we will hear when we try to engage people in our awakening call to action. But notice once we remove what is suppressing that want in a soul, we are free to market the spiritual and temporal benefits to which any member of our faith community is entitled. Therefore:

While it can be said we are "creating want," it is actually more accurate to say/understand/frame our issue as: we are *removing the suppression* of an inherent, imbued, God-given desire to know and seek God that is within every person. The challenge for us in PMO is now more refined, more clear, more precise:

How do we reveal the want that already exists within a person but is being willfully suppressed, through proactive PMO?

CHAPTER 18

ON THE REVELATION OF WANT

We have the choice of two identities: the external mask which seems to be real...and the hidden, inner person who seems to us to be nothing, but who can give himself eternally to the truth in whom he subsists.

—Thomas Merton

What superior PMO is also about, far beyond fixing the potholes in the parking lot, etc., is the implementation of ideas crafted to reveal the expression of the natural desire to know and seek God in those who suppress it. *The "revelation of want" is the cultivation of desire within parishioners strong enough to overcome the suppression of want and to further and deeply engage them with their parish.* Is this easy? No. Is this the essence of our job in PMO ministry? Yes, and since people respond to the marketing of material things, how much more might they respond to the spiritual realm when attracted in a manner that reveals the spiritual hunger and desire God imbued within them? When a person is drawn to the spiritual, he or she will act in the same way as the temporal—engaging in such a manner as to fulfill the desire that is no longer suppressed. This is a transparent migration back to God that the soul cooperates with, but does not necessarily have to fully realize is happening until after it is happening. Further, note this movement of the soul back toward God begets more movement, even astounding exponential movement in accord with the degree of cooperation facilitated by each soul. Now, where to start?

To help serve as a framework for your PMO marketing practices is a document from the Pontifical Council for Social Communications entitled "Ethics in Advertising." The document distinguishes between "advertising" and "marketing" in this way:

> Advertising is not the same as marketing (the complex of commercial functions involved in transferring goods from producers and consumers) or public relations (the systematic effort to create a favorable public impression or "image" of some person, group, or entity). In many cases, though, *it is a technique or instrument employed by one or both of these.*

So, *the marketer uses advertising to achieve his or her goals*. The document also explains the benefits and harms of advertising, continues with some ethical and moral principles (namely, what is advertised must be true, and foremost, it must respect human dignity and be socially responsible), and concludes with some practical steps. Overall, note that within our Catholic faith tradition there is already a good deal of important guidance for us in how to apply such methods, but most importantly in our context note marketing and advertising, per se, *are proposed by proper Church authority as fundamentally defensible principles that are not antithetical or hostile to Church teaching.* Never mind you may have known that—*how many people who in some manner interact or report to you in PMO know that?* You will want to remember this source of authoritative and valid endorsement when facing those who do not choose to understand this proactive dimension of PMO, and shun all things business.

For the lapsed person(s) we must help them view their parish community and Church as a helpful spiritual and temporal resource in living their daily life as a Catholic Christian—not just a place where they must by threat of some eternal damnation and punishment make a mechanical guest appearance at least once a week. Of course we desire the parish to become the *organic center* of personal and family life—but as you must know, mere "desire" is not a strategic plan. *Mere desire will not overcome years, perhaps decades, of the suppression of want.* We must therefore with some sadness reflect and note…

There is a good reason you may observe the parish phone is not ringing often enough, the email volume is too low in relation to the size of the registered parishioner base and geographic area, social media campaigns do not develop any traction, there is little to no foot and website traffic, enrollment in parish retreats is undersubscribed to nonexistent, and there is overall and on balance, not nearly enough substantive or substantial across-the-board PMO ministry engagement taking place. And what is the reason: too many people reject what the parish is offering, or not offering, by suppressing the desire God imbued in every person—*and PMO is not doing their part to help souls overcome this obstacle of suppression.*

> **Insanity: doing the same thing over and over again and expecting different results.**
> —*Albert Einstein*

Before we proceed further let's ask this elephant in the room question: if not PMO, then who will seek these apathetic or disconnected souls? To answer we must first understand these three critical points:

1. Those who serve the temporal needs of the parish must always ultimately *defer to the authority of the ordained who serve the spiritual needs*. In other words, what you want to do in PMO outreach and what you are permitted to do by the powers that be may be two different things. However:

> And if a house is divided against itself, that house will not be able to stand.
>
> —*Mark 3:25*

2. A house divided against itself cannot stand. There must exist a *positive and symbiotic relationship* between those who serve the spiritual, and those who serve the temporal needs of active or lapsed parishioners. If such a positive and symbiotic relationship does not exist between the respective personnel, *it must first be created in order for a high level of innovation and quality of PMO engagement to exist*. In plain English, if parish paid staff and volunteer personnel are either at odds with the ordained in the parish over what to do and how to further engage active or lapsed/lost souls, or if PMO personnel and the ordained are either not rowing or rowing in different directions, or if the PMO administrator adopts a too narrow and restrictive view of the role and purpose of PMO, until this situation is addressed and remedied *you are wasting your time trying to improve PMO in the manner proscribed herein*. In others words, *first and foremost everybody in authority must get on and stay on the same vision page, or developing PMO "want" that is commensurate with your geographic size will never be achieved*.

3. Although those who serve the temporal needs of parishioners must defer to the final authority of the ordained parish leadership—not only because they serve the sacramental needs of parishioners but because as a matter of fact they ultimately report to the ordained at the top of the parish Org Chart—that does not negate the fact that when highly effective ideas are implemented for serving the temporal needs of souls, *this fact ultimately and inevitably has the additional benefit of leading souls to a higher level of spiritual and sacramental engagement with*

ordained clergy. There is a symbiotic relationship between the ordained and PMO personnel. As such, there are mutually shared motivations for the ordained leadership and PMO administrator to resolve any differences in creating more robust, effective, and results-oriented evangelical outreach PMO.

To consciously and willfully neglect serving well the spiritual and temporal dimensions of the parishioner/person through superior PMO is tantamount to one limb of the body declaring another limb to be less valuable—if not utterly useless. The body will not die, *but it is certainly not what it could and should be when it is denying a critical piece of its very self.* Hence, the symbiotic relationship cited above is only achieved when PMO administrators and the ordained in the parish *work in harmony together* such that the "whole" parishioner or lost soul—both the temporal and spiritual—is mutually served. This necessity must be recognized and acknowledged. The key point: do not adopt the ridiculously narrow position that PMO exists, "for doing parish administrative stuff, etc." Expand your PMO horizons. *Do not bifurcate serving the needs of any soul along rigid lines of spiritual and temporal parochial interests and turf protection. Work together.*

This lesson has largely been lost in many parishes today, with invisible walls, but nonetheless present, isolating and locking people into their respective artificial fiefdoms. Mutual inter-parish and intra-parish PMO cooperation—not to mention mutual professional courtesy between those who serve the spiritual and temporal needs of parishioners—is often poor to non-existent. Why? *Because this foundational principle of a symbiotic and reciprocal relationship between serving the spiritual and temporal needs of all souls is not acknowledged or recognized by those holding final authority over PMO.* And who suffers in this broken scenario? *The entire Body of Christ suffers.* We all suffer, but most directly the lost souls who are not served…needlessly remain lost.

It is in part your job to identify this broken condition within your parish and become part of the solution—*if not the fountainhead solution provider*. Notice this entire problem is initially addressed strictly through the recognition that comes from the art of asking the PMO "Why" rather than clobbering the science aspects of practicing PMO: "How, how, how!" We must first ask why the Church is trending toward empty—the answer being the *free will suppression of the want imbued by natural law*—before we can discuss what to do about it.

So, if we observe that the volume, type, and/or nature of PMO utilization is not what it should be and could be, we must proactively create demand through the "*revelation of want*," which necessarily implies, "*removal of suppression*." To do so we start where? Read on.

CHAPTER 19

THE BUCK STOPS IN PMO

What is "revelation of want"? Before answering, first be advised some people only want to shop at the market, buy their sausage, and go on about their business of preparing the meal. Fine. *But somebody first has to actually make the sausage.* Somebody has to discuss and know how to *kill and slaughter* the hog, *grind* the pork, *add* the seasonings, *stuff* the sausage casing, *package* the sausage, and *sell* it to the market. You may not be the sausage maker, but if you want sausage, and I know some people do, *you better acknowledge and respect that somebody, somewhere, all the time, has to be the sausage maker—and right now, that person is you.* Therefore:

Let's review the aforementioned sausage-making process, but place it within a PMO working context:

1. Kill = precisely target the removal of the suppression of want
2. Slaughter = sectionalize all marketing ideas into actionable pieces
3. Grind = begin to grind out solutions to each challenge
4. Season = adjust your work efforts according to feedback and results
5. Stuff = ensure everyone is working and rowing in the same direction
6. Package = create processes and procedures to publically promote efforts
7. Sell = present the fruit of your work to current or lapsed parishioners

Start by doing what's necessary; then do what's possible; and suddenly you are doing the impossible.
—*St. Francis of Assisi*

It is in this sense one must gain an appreciation for the PMO aspects of parish life. Whether or not you are reading this and wishing with all your might to avoid the PMO aspects of parish life, whether you wish to devote 100% of your time strictly to serving the spiritual dimension language of the parish mission statement, this is not an option for you. Why? *Because somebody has to oversee PMO temporal works and implement robust outreach ideas, in the same manner somebody has to make the sausage.* If nobody is willing to do this—shazzam! No sausage for anybody! Translation: *the buck stops with you.* Therefore:

We are now about to go deeper into a discussion akin to the graphic business of how the sausage is made. Why? *Because somebody has to do it, and that somebody is you.* Most people—including many ordained, PMO lay employees, or volunteers—would prefer not to know about, much less participate in, this aspect of PMO. People would prefer to live in their fantasy world of choice, a world where everyone is just like they are—alive in their love for the Lord and active in their faith and on the right road to becoming saints. While this is a wonderful sentiment, *mostly it does not reflect the world in which we live.* Tough PMO decisions must be made, usually every day, and somebody has to make them. Thus proactively, not passively, but *proactively* we must approach certain aspects of PMO that are akin to making the sausage. At times, this is no doubt rough duty, tough duty. You do it anyway. However:

Perhaps you consider PMO administration not your primary calling—or your calling at all. Too bad. You were called. Dislike of an assigned duty, while it may be understandable, is never a valid excuse for ignoring your duty. If dislike of the PMO "creation of want, removal of suppression, etc." dimensions of your job is giving you grief, consider the sentiment expressed by Cardinal John Henry Newman that those who only want to serve the spiritual needs of people...*should be Chaplains not Pastors*, because a Pastor has to absolutely serve both the spiritual care of souls and temporal needs of people—especially those who have lapsed and quit on their faith.

Note well that PMO is a *ministry* for those who work in PMO, and as with any ministry, *the ministry of PMO has to, from time to time, make some sausage.* Yes, we all rely on and trust in the Holy Spirit—but nowhere in Scripture does reliance on the Holy Spirit mean we are exempt from also doing our part, our jobs, our duty. On the contrary, Scripture gives very clear and sober warnings (Matthew 25:14-30) to those who neglect to use their gifts in the service of others and for the glory of God.

Although in PMO we borrow principles from the business world, *we cannot borrow all of their vocabulary.* Some business vocabulary is not applicable (i.e. IPO, stock split, shareholder, etc.) because we do not serve an economic cause; *we serve the whole person in pursuit of a higher spiritual cause.* But what about the business vocabulary that represents concepts and principles that *are* applicable to PMO—but to the misinformed or uninformed may sound crass, vulgar, and/or out of tune with the mission of the Church? This is a nuanced distinction in assimilated thinking that makes a huge difference, not so much in what we actually do in PMO, *but in understanding the frame of mind of those we speak to about PMO*—especially those outside the realm of PMO who do not want to know, much less discuss, how the sausage is actually made. How so?

Imagine talking to the person buying the sausage about how his sausage purchase was made. How many sausage buyers would want to engage you in such a discussion? Do you see the PMO training challenge facing you if you land—and you can bet you will land—in an underperforming and underutilized PMO environment and begin to address the paid staff and volunteers in the

PMO sausage-making vernacular? (More about this scenario will be presented in chapters on culture.)

We have established that if we observe the volume, type, and/or nature of PMO utilization is not what it should and could be, we must proactively create demand through a "revelation of want," or in other words, unleash the innate desire in souls to engage with our various PMO services and ministries, *which is to say unleash the desire to know and seek God*. But in the business realm "creation of want" or creating desire is simply stated as "marketing." Marketing is how you "create want" for your product or service. See where this explanation is going? Sometimes we must be pragmatic and give a nod to the reality of our circumstances, and this is one of those times. While "creation of want" and "marketing" both appear to speak to performing the same general activities—and we already acknowledged they really don't—*there is no way in a Church setting or environment we can use the term "marketing."*

The mental imagery conjured by "marketing" anything associated with faith, religion, God, etc., is simply not appropriate imagery. However, and this is paramount, this point explains to you where our proverbial PMO buck has been passed: *just because we cannot use the term "marketing," <u>does not also mean we are banned from employing marketing and the principles of marketing in PMO</u>*. Indeed, *we must proactively market certain temporaly-oriented aspects of what the parish offers in order to reveal the want being suppressed by some souls*. It is precisely our failure to market—to reveal suppressed want—that causes many aspects of what the parish offers its parishioners and community at-large to be chronically underutilized. In concrete and practical terms, here are some examples of failure:

Do you think apathetically listing a "Christians in Commerce" meeting, a "Crisis Counseling Center Grand Opening" or a "Rediscovering Catholicism" class in the weekly parish bulletin is really the quintessential definition of "revelation of want and removal of suppression," *or is it just going through the motions and looking busy while pretending to do so?* Do you think the equivalent of a weekly bulletin entry represents the be all, end all, best efforts, and practices embodiment of how similar events would be marketed in the business realm? But yet I know you would not be surprised at all to learn that these relatively passive and milquetoast efforts at developing the "revelation of want and removal of suppression" *are typically all PMO offers in support of these great endeavors in most every parish today.*

And we wonder: why are parish events poorly attended, why are participation levels pitifully low *in relation to what they could and should be?* Why people leave the Church for a church where they airily claim to feel, "more connected"? Why do people quit on God? We must here and now stop passing the buck and reject the notion that in PMO we can hide behind abysmal marketing efforts. Especially when the inevitable and predictable poor attendance hits us all in the face, while such pithy bromides as, "Well, it must have been God's will..." or the absurdly narrow, "That's not our job in PMO" are tossed around to explain away such terribly disappointing results—if the results are even properly recognized as such in the first place. Perhaps the worst predicament is to not even recognize the distinctions between the results of your PMO efforts you see, *and the results you should see.*

We routinely refuse to look in the mirror and critique our own PMO methods used in the "revelation of want and removal of suppression," and instead lay the personal failure at the doorstep of such shop-worn bromides as, "It was God's will" and, "Oh well, that's all God sent us." Of course embracing such attitudes is 100% acceptable, *but only after you have 100% done your part.* We are not fast-food restaurant drive-thru window order takers in PMO. *Order taking is not our culture in PMO.*

Do not grow slack in zeal, be fervent in spirit, serve the Lord. Rejoice in hope, endure in affliction, persevere in prayer.
—*Romans 12: 11–12*

In PMO we must analyze our results through the results-oriented lens labeled, "What didn't we do that we should have done? What could we have done better?" and not simply invoke "God's will" or a litany of other excuses to cover our own failures to proactively execute our PMO duties. Such passive positions and views have failed and sadly continue to fail the Church, and must not be accepted—much less perpetuated wherever you work. You are either part of the problem and perpetuate mediocrity by continuing to robotically embrace narrow PMO methods and procedures *that are already known to produce little to no fruit whatsoever in relation to what could and should be produced*, under a broken rubric such as, "It must have been God's will," or alternatively:

You here and now declare you will stop passing the buck. You will embrace proactive efforts and innovative ideas to "reveal want and remove suppression of desire"—expressed in a PMO strategic plan (another chapter) for the many and wonderful events and services offered by the parish *in support of the needs of the whole person, active or lapsed, both spiritual and temporal*. Enough with the insulting invocation of "God's will" as a flimsy cover for rationalizing away ineffective, stale, and autopilot PMO. Do not engage in this tactic. *Face the mirror and own the results your PMO administrative efforts produce, or more to the point, don't produce that they should produce.*

It is time for a better and proactive way to practice PMO, a way that complements a properly constructed parish mission statement and overall mission of the Church. You should now see and acknowledge that the PMO status quo cannot continue. It is a team approach in PMO that is driven off of a holistic system of adoption of step-by-step procedures and operations, *starting with a correctly worded parish mission statement.* You should more clearly see that serving the spiritual needs of parishioners comes part and parcel with effective methods of serving their temporal needs, and we can no longer define "effective methods" as merely inserting critical information in the weekly parish bulletin or website posting, wash our hands, and believe this is in any reasonable manner a proactive definition of "revelation of want and removal of suppression." See this nonsense activity for what it is: *busyness masquerading as effectiveness, and fooling nobody anymore—or at least nobody who reads this book.* Furthermore:

The greatest problem is often not the level of busyness you observe—perhaps much of it *inconsequential and inefficient and superficial activity* when you really drill down and analyze it—*but the busyness in PMO personnel you don't see that you should,* but you won't because you have not embraced any or enough proactive ideas for reaching people who have quit on their faith and are no longer active in the parish. You want to see busy, truly busy? *Mobilize those who have quit on their faith. Bring those souls back to the Church—then you will see busy and effective.*

Oh. You mean it is within the duty of PMO; *in PMO ministry is where we find the obligation* to unceasingly try reaching *all* souls in our geography who have quit on their faith? Yes, that is what is meant. Why? Because when you don't explicitly designate an owner of an obligation and publically place it where it belongs, the duty of achieving that obligation becomes the lovely, amorphous, and utterly ineffective, "Everybody's job"—*which is to more precisely say all those agenda items just became <u>nobody's job</u>.*

The revelation of want has to go somewhere that is not passive by default, *but proactive in its very nature.* Ask anyone in authority, "Who has the job of cleaning the Church?" You will receive an exact answer. Ask anyone in authority, "Who hears confessions?" You will receive an exact answer. Ask anyone in authority, "Who is in charge of Youth Ministry?" You will receive an exact answer. Ask anyone in authority, "Who is in charge of crafting a strategy to reach out to souls who quit on their faith and God?" *You may get an answer but even if you do, you will not receive a complete answer.* How so?

Q. Who is in charge of reaching out to souls who quit on their faith and God?

A. The Holy Spirit!

And in this answer we have exposed the cloaked elephant in the room. Which elephant? The elephant labeled, "I have faith in God. God will provide."

This elephant brings us precisely here, to a story you may have heard before:

> A fellow was stuck on his rooftop in a flood. He was praying to God for help.
>
> Soon a man in a rowboat came by and the fellow shouted to the man on the roof, "Jump in, I can save you!"
>
> The stranded fellow shouted back, "No, it's okay, I'm praying to God and he is going to save me."
>
> So the rowboat went on.
>
> Then a motorboat came by. The fellow in the motorboat shouted, "Jump in, I can save you!"
>
> To this the stranded man said, "No thanks, I'm praying to God and he is going to save me. I have faith."
>
> So the motorboat went on.
>
> Then a helicopter came by and the pilot shouted down, "Grab this rope and I will lift you to safety!"
>
> To this the stranded man again replied, "No thanks, I'm pray-

ing to God and he is going to save me. I have faith!"

So the helicopter reluctantly flew away.

Soon the water rose above the rooftop and the man drowned. He finally got his chance to discuss this whole situation with God, at which point he exclaimed, "I had faith but you didn't save me, you let me drown! I don't understand why!"

To this God replied, "I sent you a rowboat and a motorboat and a helicopter. What more did you expect?"

No doubt, the Holy Spirit will always do His part—but PMO administrators cannot just buy a ticket and watch as a spectator; we are not spectators. *PMO must take the initiative because it is a PMO ministry duty to take the initiative.* Or stated another way, "Man proposes, God disposes." As such:

You mean we can no longer ignore the fact that the number of souls we serve in PMO *might not sufficiently align with the number of souls you projected PMO should serve?* You mean the PMO administrator must not only look at the actual level of busyness and active parishioner engagement level—the low-hanging fruit—but also forecast the level of busyness he or she should see based upon common mitigating factors of daily life, parish size, total population, etc., and devise creative evangelical strategies to reach those souls?

Yes, that is the role of PMO.

CHAPTER 20

CULTURE?

The role of organizational culture is poorly understood. Why? You can literally get your hands on and read an organizational policy handbook or procedure, but how do you "get your hands on and read" a culture? We are not speaking of different national cultures, which are a completely separate concept; we are speaking of organizational culture.

Organizational culture truly exists and has a profound impact, but it is not tangible—it is a force that influences, but what does it do? What is its purpose? Is culture really that important? Why should you care about culture? Where does culture come from? Do you serve culture, or does culture serve you? If culture erodes, can it be restored? How do you create something, yet it cannot be touched? How is culture sustained? And a critical question: do you change a broken culture? No. (Much more on why you do *not* change a broken culture and what you must do instead, below.)

Given the innate and natural transparency of organizational culture, very often little to no attention—much less deeper thought—is given to the role of culture. Employees and volunteers alike are allowed to perpetually operate under the unspoken illusion that "things just operate." As such, when one is finally introduced to "all things culture" it can be a bit of a shock to learn the true role of organizational culture, subsequently take the measure of the culture that exsists where you work, and then face the fact your culture is a perpetual train wreck in progress and you must do what it takes to first create and then maintain a correct culture. Specifically: you must create, install, and maintain the correct culture, *or you are just wasting time in PMO*. For example:

> **Behind the scenes, one of the first things new Microsoft CEO Satya Nadella did was start to upgrade Microsoft's culture.**

And why did Nadella do that? Because culture is akin to the human heartbeat, and if your heartbeat has a problem, *your entire body will necessarily also have problems*. Some samples of people trying to describe a broken culture:

> Something will be off in the energy at work, and little by little you'll see and feel the dysfunction. You'll see it in the way colleagues communicate with one another, face-to-face and via email.
>
> You'll feel the bad energy in the way meetings are conducted and the fact that everybody spends their mental and emotional energy trying to deflect blame rather than solving problems and beating their goals.
>
> A friend will ask you "How do you like the job so far?" You'll say, "Honestly, there's something wrong in that place. Nobody speaks candidly. Nobody wants to speak up, even about obvious things that are broken."

If the study of organizational culture is new to you, keep the above reflections in mind as you read what follows. Please do not jump to conclusions. Read, then reread if you do not understand. When your culture is broken, *you're not going to improve your organization until your culture is 100% correct—no matter how much you know and what else you do*.

That's a sobering reality.

CHAPTER 21

THE RELATIONSHIP OF PERFORMANCE TO CULTURE

We never set our performance-measurement bar in PMO to past results. Never measure performance in anything by looking at where you are in relation to how far you have come. *Nobody cares how far you have come, understand? We are not giving out participation ribbons.* The only valid performance-measurement yardstick is to take a long, hard look at where you are, <u>*in relation to where you should be*</u>. Make sure you understand this point. Therefore:

A. Claiming to *desire* superior PMO, and;
B. Having what it takes to *achieve* superior PMO, and;
C. *Doing* what it takes to actually *be* superior at what you do in PMO are three different points, *yet they must harmoniously learn to dance together in a blending of both art and science.*

Blending the above points is an impossible blend to master when uninformed about culture. This is precisely why there are many who would claim to desire superior PMO, many who present empty claims to realizing superior PMO based on incorrect measurement yardsticks, but there are so very, very, few that actually attain a superior level of PMO. Never mind what people think they have achieved, and absolutely never mind measuring performance through the sadly misinformed thinking of, "Hey, everybody! Look where we were and look how far we've traveled! Isn't it wonderful!" *This is a ridiculously stupid and flawed performance-measurement yardstick*. Only look at reality, objective truth, *and most especially where you are <u>in relation to where you should be</u>*. Further, know most people can't measure by this yardstick because they have no context by which to know or measure superior results. *How can you measure what you have never seen or experienced?* And where do we find this context to define, know, live, and measure actual superior PMO? The short answer is, *"We find it in the PMO organizational culture."* But that answer is insufficient. Why? Because that answer makes the *invalid assumption* that whatever PMO culture exists is the correct culture—*and you must realize that no matter what kind, some culture always exists in any organization.*

I am here to report to you that there is for all intents and purposes a 0% chance the PMO culture that exists where you will be assigned or currently work will be the correct culture, the culture you need to deliver superior PMO.

> **The soul takes nothing with her to the next world but her education and her culture. At the beginning of the journey to the next world, one's education and culture can either provide the greatest assistance, or else act as the greatest burden, to the person who has just died.**
>
> —*Plato*

Setting aside Plato's lack of a correct understanding on the Trinity, heaven, the soul, etc., *Plato was on to something here.* Many centuries ago Plato recognized that your level of education alone is not enough to succeed. One needs education, which we have labeled here "the science side of PMO." But we need the science *and* culture. What is the culture?

> *Culture is the environement under which you practice the science learned through your education.*

THE RELATIONSHIP OF PERFORMANCE TO CULTURE

Great assistance to you—*or your greatest burden*—is the result of how you blend the art and science of PMO. Yet so many focus on acquiring knowledge and education—the necessary science of job skills in other words—*and completely overlook the role played by the art of creating organizational culture-building in influencing satisfactory results, much less superior results.*

More specifically, how does an organization's culture shape job performance? Is this a critical question to answer? Yes, very much so. Why? Because it does you no good as a PMO administrator to know what you are doing technically with the science, to have a fully trained PMO staff that in turn also knows what they are doing, if they are trapped working under a broken culture. <u>All the education and job-related knowledge in the world will never overcome being animated on the job by a broken organizational culture</u>.

Oh.

The first priority for the non-profit executive's own development is to strive for excellence.

—Peter Drucker

The culture is the invisible but critical organizational glue that binds everyone working in PMO to our common cause and goal: delivering superior PMO service. Far, far, too much emphasis is placed on training employees in the nuts and bolts science of doing their respective jobs, with little to no attention paid to the culture that exists under which people do their jobs. *The culture is what animates all employees while they are actually learning and/or performing any assigned daily tasks*. Thus, *culture always steers results*.

Sometimes we might mislabel organizational culture as "attitude," but culture is much more than mere attitude. How so? Well, of course first one must know what he or she is doing on the job, the science of the work in other words. Of course, one must know how to complete each assigned task. And it is precisely at this point the superior performance train jumps the tracks in most organizations. Why? The master role played by organizational culture, the overwhelming influence of culture on what, where, when, why, and how anything is done, *is not given proper context or understood by management.* And what is often substituted for an understanding of the influence of culture on performance and results? The as previously mentioned broken yardstick of observed "busyness." If people in PMO appear busy, well then, we must be producing superior results! *This is complete nonsense.*

Naturally you must be concerned with the characteristics and mechanics of your personal or PMO staff development—in other words, the science mechanics of PMO. This is necessary information that rightfully concerns you becoming a fundamentally competent administrator and/or leader, as well as to further the development of paid and/or volunteer personnel who may report to you. This is all well and good and necessary, *but to what end do we learn this particular nuts and bolts information?*

The obvious answer is to improve PMO delivery wherever we serve—but you don't need to read this book to learn the X's and O's, the nuts and bolts of parish management, when such information is already readily available from other books and articles; just read the other books and articles. Therefore: *do not expect to find herein a restatement of step-by-step instruction you can easily find elsewhere.* However, note this well: you can read every how-to book on management ever written or that ever will be written, and still fail to produce and deliver superior results. And why would this be? This is why:

There is another question, *really the most critical question*, standing behind the first question in any organization. After we approach and master the science of PMO (or anything), the mechanics and principles of what we must do day in and day out on the job—and this part is not complicated in PMO—now what? Here is precisely where people mistakenly end their search for knowledge—because after all, they now know the mechanics of what to do—the science of the job. Yet, they go to work and wonder why things are not superior even though they, and everyone else, well know the mechanics of doing their particular jobs. The reason for this, "If I know what I am doing why aren't things improving" conundrum? They stopped learning before they correctly answered another critical question: *what else influences how well or how poorly anyone actually execcutes on the job, day in and day out?* The answer is expressed in six words: *the culture they are working under.*

Culture drives great results.
—*Jack Welch*

Establishing and maintaining the culture is the *art,* not the science, of practicing PMO. Therefore: I don't care how much "how to" knowledge anyone has about their job, any job. *If you do not set the organizational culture correctly, you will never deliver superior PMO or anything else.* Repeat: *if you do not set the organizational culture correctly, you will never deliver superior PMO or anything else.* This is why we can find both *consistently superior* organizations and *chronically broken* organizations in every sector; business, government, military, or religious—some get their organization's culture right, and sadly, some never do.

Organizational culture *is paramount to superior PMO*. Of course you must know what you are doing, but then what? Is that all there is to any job, of any nature, anywhere? Simply know what you are doing and you are good to go? No. There is one more organizational ingredient, the paramount factor influencing results: culture. Why is the culture where you operate paramount to effective PMO? This is precisely why:

You can have the entire budget, all the clock time, all the fully trained paid PMO staff and volunteer personnel, all the equipment, and all the higher authority approvals you need to fully execute your PMO mission under a well-crafted mission statement…*and still fail miserably to produce our goal of superior results*. Why? How? How is it possible you can have everything you need and still be mediocre—or fail miserably? Precisely this way: if your PMO culture is broken, corrupted, and dysfunctional—*and fully note your acknowledgment and/or recognition of this fact is <u>not</u> a requirement for it to be so*—what you and/or others do in PMO will necessarily be in whole or in part broken, corrupted, and dysfunctional. How so?

Notice you can touch your financial statement in the sense you can know your bank account balance in real-time, know your debt level, know your expenses, etc. You can read your personal schedule and know you have enough time allotted to devote to the tasks at hand. You can count heads in relation to the work that must be done and know you have enough personnel to do the job. You can talk to those who are tasked with doing the job and know they are well trained in their craft. You can see with your own eyes that you have all the necessary equipment you need to complete the work at hand. *But you cannot see in the same tangible ways the culture within the PMO department, and it is the culture that animates everyone involved in actually <u>executing</u> the above and much more.*

Oh.

The culture is akin to the air we breathe—you don't see it, you don't smell it (we hope), and you don't think about it. But unless it is perfect, you will pay a heavy price for breathing polluted air—and the more polluted the air, the faster your health erodes. The importance and impact of culture, in any type of organization, cannot be overstated. *Everything right and great about an organization is directly and inexorably related to its culture.* And the corollary thought: *everything wrong and mediocre about an organization is directly and inexorably related to…its culture.*

THE RELATIONSHIP OF PERFORMANCE TO CULTURE

There is no escaping the impact of culture on any organization. The culture of an organization is an invisible—*but imminently controllable*—working atmosphere that animates and motivates what people do, how effectively they do it, and with what level of energy and passion they put into their duties and responsibilities. *You will come to understand that a proper culture is your best and closest friend as an administrator or leader of any enterprise*. However:

Due to matters related to establishing, building, and maintaining the correct, or incorrect culture, in all organizational policy making and subsequent execution you will find there is a direct connection linking the culture of any organization to its success, or the opposite: *perpetual employee, volunteer, mediocrity, and institutionalized organizational stagnation*. You can have all the tangible assets you need in working capital, trained personnel and equipment, etc., at your disposal and yet still fail miserably in delivering robust, vibrant, and superior PMO services. Why? How is this possible? Because if the culture in your organization is broken, the work product of your organization will be at best condemned to mediocrity, or at worst, be a clumsy and disjointed mess.

> **Executives who make a really special contribution enable the organization to see itself as having a bigger mission than the one it has inherited.**
>
> —*Peter Drucker*

Now, it is far more likely than not you will be assigned to administer work *within an existing parish and/or Church organization* of some sort, as opposed to being given your own new parish to build from the ground up. In other words, although you arrive at your parish with no figurative baggage and a clean personal slate, *you will be inheriting an existing culture* as opposed to being afforded a blank culture canvas from which you can create the proper culture from the outset. As such, it becomes a fair question to ask: what task do you tackle first, second, third, etc., upon your arrival? Raise more money? Train your personnel? Hire more personnel? Procure necessary equipment? Replace obsolete equipment? Answer: none of these. This is what you do first: *you address the preexisting culture model first, because as sure as you are reading this, your inherited culture will be broken.*

CHAPTER 22

FUNDAMENTALS ON CULTURE

Whoever loves discipline loves knowledge, but whoever hates reproof is stupid.

—Proverbs 12:1

There is no try. There is only do, or do not.

—Yoda

How do you address your inherited "broken culture model"? First, some fundamentals on culture:

Everything you do is shaped by the culture that exists within your organization. How so? Like this: if you receive blood from a donor who is HIV positive, that's not good, to say the least. Why? *Because your blood assimilates the virus living in the donor's blood.* Or if you prefer a scriptural analogy:

Likewise, no one pours new wine into old wineskins. Otherwise, the wine will burst the skins, and both the wine and the skins are ruined. Rather, new wine is poured into fresh wineskins.

—Mark 2:22

What do you think happens within an organization with a broken culture that is given the budget they need? *The new money is misused just like the previous money.* What do you think happens within an organization that has enough personnel to do the job at hand? The job at hand is still done in a mediocre fashion because the problem within the organization was never about having too little or too much _____ (insert items of choice here). Mediocre performance—or worse—*is always, always, always, at least in part about having personnel animated by a broken culture.*

> **It's the economy, stupid.**
> —Candidate Bill Clinton to George Bush

Administrators and/or leaders who miss the above point/lesson will continue and forevermore fruitlessly drill down on everything but the root of the PMO underperformance problem—*the elephant in the room is their broken culture.* They will replace and train new personnel and volunteers—*to little or no avail to the core mission of PMO.* They will raise additional contributions and donations (aka: working capital)—*to little or no avail to the core mission of PMO.* They will purchase and/or upgrade capital equipment—*to little or no avail to the core mission of PMO.* They will—as we have already examined, "look busy" and indeed, actually be busy—*and all their efforts will not fix a doggone thing in terms of producing superior results for the core mission of PMO: bringing souls to Christ*. Why? Because they are not addressing the HIV in the workplace's bloodstream. They continue to pour old wine into new wineskins. They are failing to address the root of their problem. And what might that be?

It's the culture, stupid!

Culture is the force that animates and motivates people, thereby creating a correct working environment and now bringing us to this important additional insight: *it is a derivative of the correct culture that provides the PMO admin-*

istrator with the foundational framework *for accurately measuring all results*.

Forget "busyness" as an eyeballed performance yardstick and remember this connection: *a broken culture distorts your ability to accurately measure results*. Why? Because in a broken culture results are endorsed, enshrined, and measured relative to how things are done and have historically been done, *instead of how things should be done*.

Oh. That's not good.

> **For good performance, we give a raise. But we promote only those people who leave behind a bigger job than the one they initially took on.**
>
> *—Peter Drucker*

Culture provides the lens/optics and is the connection glue *between viewing job performance and correctly measuring the job performance you are viewing*. In other words, employee job performance is not only animated by organizational culture, but as PMO administrators, *we must only see and measure employee and volunteer job performance exclusively through the lens of a correct culture*, not the rose-colored glasses of a dysfunctional culture. *Note all observation is done through some cultural lens, whether or not the observer and the observed are conscious of their lens selection choices.*

When you connect the dots on the role of culture in the above manner you can now clearly detect how *working within a broken culture completely defeats all your efforts to improve PMO through any and all other means of improvement. No matter what you do, you will just keep pouring new wine into old wineskins when you are operating under a broken culture*. Further note you will never overcome a broken culture by ignoring it. If you ignore a broken culture, *you are just wasting your time.*

CHAPTER 23

CHANGE A BROKEN CULTURE?

So you have a broken culture and you want to change it—that's not news. But how do you change a broken culture? Oops, land mine! BOOM! "How do you change a broken culture?" is the quintessential *wrong question to ask*, and exhibits wrong-way thinking, which necessarily leads to a totally wrong solution approach to addressing a broken culture. The phrasing of that question, "How do you change a broken culture?" reveals I just stepped on a land mine. How so? Memorize this:

<u>***You do not change a broken culture.***</u>

You do *not* attempt to change the culture in any gradual or incremental fashion. The notion of "change" is an out of place expression in regard to "changing the culture." The very implication or notion of "change" in culture *is precisely the wrong imagery to apply here*. What is the correct imagery?

<u>***You kill and replace* the old culture in its entirety, and *you install a new culture*.***</u>

Repeat: you do not attempt to change the culture in any gradual or incremental fashion—*you must kill and replace the old culture in its entirety, and you install a new culture.*

<u>*The above point is paramount*</u>. There are no exceptions. Follow this rule on culture, or you will fail. You will waste your time. Never speak in terms of

"changing" the culture. It is a misnomer, a contextual misunderstanding, to say, "We must change the culture around here… The culture must change…." There is no such thing as "changing the culture." *You must **kill** the old culture, and **replace it** with a new culture*. You must think in these terms whenever you find a broken culture. Whenever you hear or read, "I have to change the culture… you must change the culture…the culture must change…" you can be sure of one thing: either they misspoke or, *they will fail to solve their organizational performance problems*. As such:

Perhaps you realize that things are going to become a wee bit personally challenging for the PMO administrator who inherits a broken culture, because once you have a look under the PMO hood, every trained PMO administrator in short order realizes in their heart they have inherited a broken culture—and nothing remotely close to superior results can ever be delivered by a broken culture.

Choppy waters are ahead, to put it mildly. Why? Read on.

CHAPTER 24

ON THE CULTURE KILLING AND REPLACEMENT HURRICANE

We have established that benchmarking performance, measuring results, making organizational and/or operational changes, etc., within a broken culture is just a colossal waste of everyone's time and energy. Only from a correct PMO workplace culture can we reveal another critical point: we can only derive a proper working environment, *and job performance measurement framework, from operating within a correct culture.*

Unless and until the culture is correct, *we are by definition in transition from PMO performance mediocrity to a state of superior performance, and the sooner we finish this transition, the sooner we will deliver the superior results we publicly promised in our parish mission statement.* This transition takes time (usually measured in months in a small enterprise, often but not always exponentially longer in a larger enterprise), and this transition timeframe within the organization correctly deserves to be labeled as a "bumpy ride"—or perhaps a hurricane would be more apt—as felt by those within the organization at the time. *Note this internal "hurricane" turmoil is almost always unavoidable, so consider it normal in that sense.* Why? And why does it take months, or longer, to kill the current culture and install a new culture? Two reasons:

1. People become stuck at the shock, denial, frustration, and/or depression of the transitional phases from the way things were, *to the way things must be.*

2. In general most people do not like change, accept change, or quickly embrace change of any kind—*much less the attention-getting type of change that is linked to either their ongoing employment, or dismissal.*

The fishermen know that the sea is dangerous and the storm terrible, but they have never found these dangers sufficient reason for remaining ashore.

—Vincent Van Gogh

However, also further note that *people fear risk, whether real or imagined—especially if the perceived "change" might impact their continued employment.* And what is the particular perceived risk for the PMO administrator? The risk in the mind of the docile, passive PMO administrator is that all the predictable transitional internal organizational turmoil caused by change will not be worth the effort in improving PMO service to parishioners. In other words, "Meh. Just leave things alone; too much personal and organizational stress, too much trouble. I'm not going there." After all, when mediocrity has been the PMO performance standard for years, you become acculturated to mediocrity. Mediocrity becomes your performance norm, your acceptable benchmark standard, and parishioners only come to know mediocrity—not that they necessarily label it as such—as their expected level of service (consider here the boiling frog metaphor). In other words, employees, volunteers—and out of ignorance, even parishioners—prefer things just the way they are and as they have been for many years. As such, *clear communication of your intent to kill the old culture and install a new culture is paramount.* (More on communication below.)

The intensity of the workplace bumpy ride/hurricane you must endure together all depends on the level of cooperation you receive as the administrator in charge from each person to whom you ultimately report, or who reports to you. Note the level of cooperation you receive, or lack thereof, to a high degree depends on *how you personally approach and communicate with the employee or volunteer, or your superior* (more on this point below). Clear communication will greatly help smooth the bumpy ride—but some bumps are inevitable, unavoidable, to be expected, and the price of admission to attaining superior performance. More specifically, you should anticipate three levels of difficulty associated with your organizational culture killing and replacement:

Hard to change: examples include any long-standing internal PMO processes, music selections, supported ministries, logos, and course materials.

Harder to change: examples include written job performance standards and expectations; changing publically expressed organizational strategies, objectives and philosophies. This point includes your efforts to enhance the parish mission statement to better serve your needs as the PMO administrator.

Hardest to change: any deeply held and embedded beliefs experienced as self-evident, and unconscious behaviors. In other words, without any deeper thought or reflection you are told, "That's just the way we do things here and the way we have always done things here."

At this point you should be beginning to sense that if you are not addressing your inherited broken culture, *you are stuck with mediocrity or worse until you do*. In other words, wallowing in mediocrity—or worse—is not only your lot forever, *you have also bequeathed mediocrity on those who report to you as well as those you were sent to serve. And that is not right*. Passing the broken PMO buck must end. It is irresponsible and immoral to knowingly kick the broken culture can down the road. If you have detected institutionalized, organizational, mediocrity—see it for what it is. Do not look the other way as the PMO administrator. To be crystal clear: we are not talking about job performance incompetence; *we are talking about deliberate gross negligence and dereliction of duty by the PMO administrator—not the employee or volunteer. The employee or volunteer does not know any better until you kill the old culture and install the new culture.*

Perhaps you have experienced such frustrating, institutionalized, systemic, organizational mediocrity before? Why is that? The parish, the diocese, (or whatever the organization—this point is portable) has been around for ten, twenty, fifty—even one hundred or more years. What's the story here? Why hasn't mediocrity and dysfunctional performance been sifted and sorted out by now? The reason institutionalized mediocrity exists is because of a broken workplace culture, and a broken workplace culture systemically exists *because the previous and/or current administrator lacks the intestinal fortitude and/or knowledge (usually both) to do anything about it.*

Is it just that simple? Yes, it is that simple.

At best, staff and volunteers may feel good about their contributions and efforts, but last time I checked "feeling good" about my contributions and efforts was not the proper yardstick for measuring the quality level of the *actual PMO results that should be delivered to parishioners.* When you can't make payroll try telling your employees, "Even though I don't have a paycheck for you on payday, I feel really good about my efforts at trying to make payroll." See how far that logic takes you. See what happens next. One could make a very strong case—and I am—that behind ignoring obvious PMO mediocrity and providing comfort food excuses for not addressing a broken culture, *the root cause of the problem is not incompetence, it is the sin of conscious and deliberate omission of duty.*

You are being instructed here and now that any chronic litany of, "I'm too busy…I'm too tired…I don't want to…I don't like this…I didn't ask for this…I didn't sign up for this…I'm not up for this…why me…" and all the other assorted derivative excuses are not acceptable for sidestepping, for ignoring, for failing to kill and replace a broken PMO culture. If not you, who? If not now, when? But how do you do it? We start by:

CHAPTER 25

EXPOSING THE GRAND ILLUSION

In terms of an approach methodology to confronting a broken culture, it comes down to one primary advisement: weak and timid is *not advised* when wearing your PMO administrator hat, as in: *all your weak and timid administrator efforts will amount to nothing more than singing Kumbaya around the campfire.* Be true to yourself, your own temperament? Absolutely. Never try to be somebody else. Follow your own inter-personal communications style? Absolutely. But at the end of the day you must address all issues that have corrupted the culture in a clear and precise manner. Whatever personal management style you choose to use, *you must kill the old culture and install the new culture, and you must do so immediately.* Simply stated, *you must attain results.* However, do not misread here. This is not to say in any way a "loud and aggressive" approach is being advised—*it is not.*

Be yourself. Use your God-given talent. But face these inevitable issues in advance: how will you handle individual confrontational pushback to your requests for changes? Because you will face pushback. How will you handle individual oblique—or not so oblique—pushback to your requests? How will you handle what is best labeled as "collective rejection" (aka: mutiny) to your requests? How will you handle those who agree to your face, then simply ignore your requests? You don't think any of these options are possibilities? That would be a mistake. One or most likely all of these situations are guaranteed when you begin to kill the current culture and install a new culture.

Failure to recognize the above circumstances leads to the regrettable condition whereby the administrator and those they manage *misunderstand and/ or defy your definition* of common PMO job performance-measurement yardsticks—*and your definition is now the only definition that matters in this context*. In the past and prior to your arrival, descriptive workplace terminology for measuring and subsequently discussing job performance with employees and volunteers, such as accuracy, effective, effort, opportunity, missed opportunity, initiative, prioritization, responsive, results, service, and speed *have not been equally and mutually understood by speaker and receiver.*

And what is the source of the administrator-employee-volunteer misunderstanding and/or defiance? *True north is corrupted.* Why? Because each employee or volunteer approaches the above word definitions with reference to their job performance from different points on the broken PMO culture compass—*instead of the same correct true north starting point as so clearly supported by the PMO related enhanced language in the parish mission statement.* Therefore, the outcome will be:

The PMO administrator, employee, and volunteer *must necessarily misunderstand each other <u>when using the same vocabulary</u>.* There can be no other outcome but miscommunication between speaker and receiver. Definitions of commonly used words suddenly become relative to an unknown standard, *which is to say the standard carried privately in each person's mind.* And why does this disconnect occur? *Because in a broken culture each person is unleashed to ascribe completely different definitions, actions, and levels of expected performance to the same job performance words.* Why? Because the well-oiled culture that you as the PMO administrator hold in your head, *does not align with the culture they in reality are currently working under that the* *employee or volunteer holds in their head.* This condition leads us to exposing the above-mentioned Grand Illusion, which is:

> In a broken culture all PMO employees and volunteers work under the Grand Illusion they are achieving superior daily results, because the untrained PMO administrator actively or passively encourages them to work under the influence of a culture that deceives them, a corrupted culture that not only gives false praise and tacit endorsement to mediocre or worse performance, but also never demonstrates what in fact does constitute superior performance. Why? Because you cannot give in job performance what you do not define and steer into existence through the correct results-oriented culture. Thus, *the Grand Illusion is a belief that all is well in PMO, when all is not close to being well.*

While an examination and living color visualization of the "actual employee results vs. expected employee results" gap might induce some laughter in a television sitcom plot (channel image of Lucy on the candy packing assembly line), living this image is disastrous in terms of an administrator and/or leader training and managing those who report to them.

As a further example, in a parallel manner notice how it is equally laughable that automotive companies rely on consumer survey feedback to inform them about the quality of their cars *that have already rolled-off their factory assembly lines and been sold to the customer.* And once-mighty automotive companies wonder how/why they went bankrupt? Yes, they went bankrupt. Why? Because they produced a mediocre product, yet upper management convinced themselves they were delivering a superior product. And predictably, what happened next? The marketplace spoke: buyers voted with their wallets and spent their money where truth was sold, not false promises. It is also laughable when a restaurant teaches their wait staff to ask customers *how their food tastes while the customer is already in the process of chewing it.* And the restaurateur then wonders why there are no repeat customers in their second year of business? Could it be they served slop, and expected the customer to tell them this was so *instead of them knowing it was so by their own honest self-measurement yardsticks, yardsticks that are the epitome of building the correct culture?*

> **We can ignore reality, but we cannot ignore the consequences of ignoring reality.**
>
> —*Ayn Rand*

If you are starting to sense here that proactively addressing a broken culture is paramount—but very hard work—you are on the correct thinking path. So where is the bottleneck in addressing all things culture? For most PMO administrators and wannabe leaders it is found in another dreaded C word:

Confrontation.

CHAPTER 26

THE ATTITUDE OF THE RECEIVER

We start by acknowledging that no rational person enjoys confrontation. But anticipating the inevitable personal heartburn and discomfort derived from confrontation *cannot be used as an excuse to ignore our duty as administrators and/ or leaders*. It is for this very reason—avoidance of potential confrontation—organizational culture is often allowed to remain broken in perpetuity.

Initially, addressing a broken culture is *face-to-face work. It is not phone work and not email work and clearly not, "I'll let the next person deal with this" work.* However, candid job performance conversations may—but not necessarily will—become confrontational. You can expect such conversations sometimes will turn confrontational, or at least be emotionally trying, due to the above comments regarding reluctance to acceptance of change, as well as the employee detecting the real risk of impending jeopardy to their ongoing employment—in other words, they might get fired. However:

All things being equal note that the reason why addressing a broken culture can become confrontational *usually has little to nothing to do with the administrator, who is simply acting as the messenger of news that should have been delivered a long time ago by his or her predecessor(s).* The messenger is blameless, provided he or she speaks with a charitable and understanding heart. If there is to be any confrontation over culture replacement, it most often stems from the stubborn minds of the receivers who do not want to finally hear what they must hear—the truth about their job performance. Thus, it becomes a fair question to resolve:

> Precisely what is the mental state of the receiver of the first fully honest and candid job performance review when viewed through the lens of a new and correct culture?

We can only speak here in general terms, but generally speaking when an employee or volunteer has been led to believe by a prior boss—either overtly or via years of passive acceptance and silence—that the quality of his or her work has at least been acceptable, if not been incorrectly labeled as exemplary, *how do you expect such a person to receive the news that his or her PMO work product is not what you, the new guy, want?* Do you think this person will be filled with joy hearing this news? Or is it more likely there will be initial confusion caused by your remarks because your remarks—although 100% accurate and necessary—*do not correlate and reconcile with what the employee or volunteer has been previously told for months or years?* Is it more likely or not—no matter how calmly and Christ-like you present the truth—that this person might ultimately transit from an initial state of confusion, eventually to anger and confrontation? Now, do you start to feel the temptation rise here for the current PMO administrator to ignore the culture problem, avoiding potential if not likely confrontation, and just pass the buck to the next administrator? Perhaps now you see why it is more likely than not you will inherit broken PMO—*it is far easier to pass the buck and dodge potential confrontation than it is to deal with it.* Well, too late now. You have been informed that option is not really an option at all for you—it is the sin of omission. Therefore:

Be prepared for anger, and let's be honest: why shouldn't the misled employee or volunteer be angry? *The PMO employee or volunteer did absolutely nothing wrong.* It is the prior administrator(s) who permitted the person to habitually operate within a broken culture, a culture that not only enshrined and reinforced mediocrity as the acceptable performance standard, but elevated mediocrity from what it truly is—unacceptable—to a higher label of performance than it ever deserved. This broken culture hid the truth of valid job performance measurements and performance reviews from everyone—*including the people actually doing the work who must now face reality for the first time in perhaps years of employment or volunteering.*

How in the world can the employee or volunteer initially be anything less than confused, and most likely angry, over being told his or her work product is not what you want, when up to that moment it had been declared—albeit incorrectly—as at least adequate if not exemplary? Thus, employees and volunteers may perpetuate the broken culture, *but the seeds of a broken culture are initially sewn by management—either by commission (proactive ignorance) and/or omission (inaction)—and subsequently watered by each management regime.*

Therefore:

> *Do not upon your arrival blame the employee or volunteer for any mediocrity you observe.* What's done, is done. *Look in the mirror instead, because it's now on you to remedy.*

CHAPTER 27

BREAKING THE CHAIN OF BROKEN CULTURE

Part of your job as an administrator and/or leader is to choose to break this chain of passing the buck of a broken culture from one administration to the next, or not—it's your call. Admittedly, the hard and narrow road is to displace the broken culture you inherit with the correct culture, but the much wider and easier road is to simply accept what you receive, as you receive it, operate within it, ignore creating a new mission statement that publically commits to providing superior PMO, and pass nothing better on to the person who ultimately replaces you. The former choice is to be our path; the latter choice is simply sin masquerading behind an invalid rationalization that, "things are just fine." (As Jesus teaches through the parable of the bags of gold in Matthew 25:14–30, the more knowledge you have the more bags of gold you have been given.)

All personnel come to know to what degree of excellence management expects in the quality of their work—or lack thereof—to remain employed. How do they know? *Via the culture that exists where they work.* Viewed from another perspective, in the culture that exists where you work, *how little does the employee or volunteer have to do to meet the currently enshrined standard of "superior" job performance?* <u>Rest assured employees know their answer.</u>

The answer to this question is animated by the organizational culture that is in place. That you might like to believe that those working in some capacity for the Church—or any organization—would be immune to such a weak formulation of attitude, *is to not only to deny the fundamental nature and attitude of the historically and previously poorly managed employee, it is to deny the influence of the existing workplace culture on everyone.*

There is no magic, no intrinsic inoculation, to displacing general human nature simply because the Church is the employer instead of the secular world. Working or volunteering for the Church does not supersede human nature. Over time the most outstanding PMO employees or volunteers will out of frustration either quit and move on to work under a more results-oriented employment yardstick—in which case you have lost their talents in your organization—or they will sadly succumb to the departmental drumbeat of mediocre job performance as exhibited by their peers, endorsed by their management through their silent acceptance, *and as demanded by the existing culture flowing through the veins of their workplace.* In the fight between "Broken Culture vs. Typical Employee," bet on Broken Culture—because Broken Culture usually wins. A broken culture gradually just beats people down, and the people who choose to stay in such a culture willingly accept mediocrity or worse as their performance yardstick— without even realizing it (again, channel the story of the boiling frog).

So, will you embrace proactive daily management of everyone who reports to you—*which does not necessarily imply a large investment of your time, but simply the correct and effective way to spend your time*—or will you defer to some other flawed notions of "management"? Will you embrace flawed PMO management practices found in other parishes? Furthermore, will prospective new-hire employees and volunteers, *obviously before a job offer is made during their interview process*, be read into your PMO culture—*the only culture the applicant will ever know—a results-oriented culture where it is made crystal clear before accepting a job offer that at this institution of parishioner service, the tail of mediocrity does not wag this administrative dog?* (More on this point in the chapter on hiring and firing.)

But note the good news: there is no need to gang-press everyone into achieving superior performance when the invisible hand of a correct culture inculcates within everyone *their free-will desire to perform in a superior manner, just as matter-of-factly as breathing.* Note this point clearly: once you have installed the correct culture, most people will naturally desire to conform to it. Why? *Because that's just how we do things here.*

This is a beautiful thing to behold but it doesn't happen by accident—*you have to build it.*

CHAPTER 28

THE PMO ORGANIZATIONAL CHART IN RELATION TO CULTURE

> **Man cannot conceive of an organization that some are not capable of subverting.**
>
> —*Russell Ackoff*

If you are not managing those who report to you while concurrently operating under the correct culture as your invisible but no less present assistant, *your staff is mismanaging you*—not "you" personally, *but "you" as in the destiny of your parish as a provider of superior PMO service*. The reality is that your PMO Org Chart pyramid is actually inverted—there is only the mere paper illusion you are the boss. The actual bosses are the names written in all the other Org Chart boxes. The proverbial tail is wagging the dog. No administrator should ever confuse employee and/or volunteer lip service given to following their instructions, *with personnel actually following their instructions*. Accepting lip service is the same as sailing in a fog. In a fog you can convince yourself you are anywhere from Disneyland to Paducah—but that does not mean you are where you should be.

Can you detect the difference between employee lip service and employees actually following your instructions and delivering superior PMO services? Will you? If your observed PMO services are not superior in every dimension, you will never be a superior service provider—and if you are not providing superior

PMO service in every dimension to your parishioners, *how do you look in the mirror?* Isn't that your job as a PMO administrator, to ensure superior services across the board are provided at every point of contact between PMO and the parishioner? Indeed, what is the point of even having a PMO administrator on the Org Chart if they are not going to proactively ensure superior service is provided to the parishioners? However, please consider this:

Where else can a parishioner go for PMO services, but the parish near them? Oh. Wait. *They do have other options.* If so inclined they *can* choose to go to another church denomination, or quit on their faith altogether—and many people do. Of course, on paper any number and quality of PMO services above zero is greater than no services at all. But the PMO administrator either exists on the parish Org Chart to provide parishioners with the highest possible depth, breadth, and quality of services, or the PMO administrator position doesn't need to exist at all. Just eliminate it altogether.

One must make up his or her mind to provide superior service—*and also provide all the services that should exist commensurate with your geographic area*—not only as expressed in words through the parish mission statement, *but also in concrete written employee policies, policies on job performance shaped by the correct culture that allows for management to manage employees and volunteers to that clear and written standard.*

If you are gradually building the impression that part of being a PMO administrator while most likely inheriting a broken culture is an intense, high-energy, servant-oriented turnaround job, you would be correct. But happily note the job is not necessarily "time intensive." *The job is knowledge intensive and perseverance-driven, <u>but not necessarily time intensive</u>.* PMO administration only becomes time intensive for those who do not know what they are doing, and/or refuse to engage in doing what they should.

If you don't like the PMO outcomes you are generating—which is to most

THE PMO ORGANIZATIONAL CHART IN RELATION TO CULTURE

accurately say the operation you are inheriting wherever you are assigned is underperforming—if you do not like the work product output in accuracy, quality, scope, speed, results, etc., of the personnel who report to you, does that mean you should change the culture? No. To repeat:

You do not change the culture—you kill the existing culture and install a new one.

Technically speaking, of course we can literally only do one thing at a time. But conceptually, *take the view that killing and replacing the culture is a holistic PMO exercise*. There is no pathway to greatness for *any* organization without installing a new, enterprise-wide culture that animates superior performance in everyone and everything they do. If a venture does not strive to greatness, an attitude reflected in and by its operating culture—not just in mere words but also in daily action—*you have a broken culture, and you are wasting your time until you recognize this truth*. No PMO Org Chart tinkering will make a significant difference. To take no further action is to institutionalize mediocrity, and to be honest, *there is no need for an administrator to oversee mediocrity if mediocrity has been enshrined by the culture as an accepted, expected, and sufficient PMO outcome*. Remove the administrator position from that parish Org Chart, save the payroll expense, and leave the position empty until someone is ready to do the job properly. Why? Because the worst thing you can do is occupy a box on the Org Chart—giving everyone the false impression a particular job is being filled—*when in fact the job is not actually being done right, only babysat by its current occupant*.

The only reason the "administrator" level of management should exist on the parish Org Chart is to—Shazzam!—*proactively administrate*. You defile the Org Chart and delude everyone—including yourself—by including an Org Chart box that designates an active PMO administrator position, *when in fact there is no such position except for it existing as a box on paper*. That's called a fraud, a sham in the secular world, and a sin in our world. It is nothing more than revealing the existence of a spiritual, future-robbing Ponzi scheme, whereby the growth of the Church in the post-WWII era continued is spite of poor PMO—not because of it. But when the music stopped, which is to say the post-war attendance growth stopped, the parishioner attrition epidemic began. One reason why: dysfunctional PMO. We simply took for granted the enemy was sleeping and the Mass attendance and vocation numbers would continue.

But our enemy never sleeps.

The Org Chart must reflect the way things actually are in PMO, not phantom reality or the way you wish for things to be in the future. Furthermore, do not accept the administrator role, do not place your name inside the "Administrator" box on the PMO Org Chart, unless and until all those you report to understand that if your name is in that box on the Org Chart, you intend to vigorously do your job, and a huge part of your job is to replace—not fix but replace—a broken culture should one exist.

And believe me…a broken culture will exist.

CHAPTER 29

PROVIDING FULL DISCLOSURE AND ADVANCED WARNING

Qui cum canibus concumbunt cum pulicibus surgent.
—*Seneca*

If you lie down with dogs, you get up with fleas.
—*Benjamin Franklin*

The dog we lie with in our context? A broken culture. The fleas we get up with? Mediocre performance, or worse. The contextual message here: if you operate within a broken culture, it cannot be a surprise to anyone that your results will suffer. And everyone above you in management on the Org Chart knows this—or at least they should. But what those you report to may not know is... *what happens if and when you ever decide you are tired of fleas? Before you take any action,* your advance input and notification is required to be given to those you report to. Specifically:

As the PMO administrator you must <u>in advance</u> make the above points crystal clear to whoever you <u>report to</u>, such that they are not only clear about the details, the who, what, where, when, why, and how of your PMO culture killing and replacement efforts, but you also fully read them into what was explained above regarding the projected, "PMO bumpy ride to...hurricane level turmoil"—which like white on rice inevitably travels with killing the old culture and installing a new culture. In other words, *expect employee and volunteer turnover, perhaps wrongful termination litigation, and so state to whoever should know these are possibilities in advance.* And let's not forget you can't stop the gossip train, so be forewarned once you begin the process of killing the old culture and creating the new culture: *the parish gossip train is likely to leave the station in a hurry.*

Your boss will hopefully accept your forecasted organizational turmoil as something that goes part and parcel with long overdue changes and improvements—*so long as they are not surprised* and they understand the reasoning and objectives behind your plans. *Bosses do not like surprises.* Bosses do not like fielding phone calls and/or reading emails or letters from angry long-time parishioners, PMO employees, and volunteers. Bosses do not like negative publicity in the media. *And bosses especially do not enjoy receiving phone calls from the bosses above them.* Make sure your bosses—and perhaps others—are made fully aware of the road you intend to travel, *before initially taking any action on culture.* Why?

A realignment of PMO in one parish is one thing, but the impact that such changes may have on the larger system of which you are a part is another valid consideration—maybe not for you, but at least for somebody. The PMO administrator is really informing the Pastor (unless they are the Pastor) and the Bishop that some complaints may be received as he settles into the work the Bishop is sending him to do. The PMO administrator might also do well to inform the other Pastors within their Deanery that they might hear some feedback and be in for ripple concerns from their PMO employees and volunteers. However:

If your boss ties your hands, if your boss explicitly limits or forbids your ability to replace the existing broken culture and install a new culture, at that point as the saying goes, "It is what it is." *You must act in obedience to valid authority.* But if you are able to articulate what has been presented here on the

PROVIDING FULL DISCLOSURE AND ADVANCED WARNING

impact of a broken culture on PMO—perhaps even hand them this book and identify certain chapters to read—with prayer we would hope you would be given the authority to do your job correctly and fully. Why?

Your boss should know—*and you must certainly know by this point*—that if you do not address a broken culture, superior delivery of PMO services to parishioners will never be achieved when it could and should be achieved, and absolutely not for some ego-driven reasons whatsoever, *but for the sole reason that those God has sent us to serve deserve to be served in a superior manner.* Since when do we enshrine mediocrity and mislabel it as superior service? Any service level less than superior must be viewed by any administration as an opportunity to improve what it does, not for its own sake, *but according to Scripture for the sake of those we are called to serve and for the glory of His Kingdom.* You must be able to clearly articulate this point so no one incorrectly concludes you are self-centered—*you are solely parishioner-centered, and everyone must note this distinction.* How?

By noting that "above and beyond average performance" is not really "above and beyond" anything whatsoever. *Above and beyond average is actually the minimally tolerable baseline for PMO performance—and to remain employed.* And should anyone think you are animated toward superior PMO for some self-serving, selfish, ego aggrandizing reasons, just carry on and go about your work. Kill the old culture, install the new culture, and gently but firmly educate such folks about our Scriptural-based commitment to serving those who need us in the most superior way possible, and that anything less than superior is simply an opportunity for us to show further improvement. Simple. Straightforward. However:

What if your superior—*having received the inevitable complaints about you*—becomes anxious, worried, and asks you for an explanation of your actions as the PMO administrator? Things are getting rough; complaints are being voiced. Because you discern this is a complicated matter to address, not to mention what you are attempting to do and the manner in which you are attempting to do it *is a completely foreign process to your boss and was a bit of a reach for him to approve in the first place*, you choose to ask if you can have a few days to compose a *written answer* to his concerns about the feedback he is receiving, what is actually happening in the office, why it is happening, what is true, what is false, and when things will get back to what he terms, "normal around here." You discern it would be wiser to write your response rather than spontaneously shoot from the hip and give partial answers to his many concerns, perhaps all valid from his perspective, because there is a good chance you would forget some critical component to a reasoned, cogent, comprehensive, informative, and well-crafted response. You realize that some of his concerns, if not all of his concerns, are animated solely by a lack of prior experience and detailed understanding of not only what you are doing, but why you are doing things in the manner that you are. Seeing things from the Pastor's perspective for a moment and walking in his shoes, he must be thinking—*were things really that bad here?*

Here is a sample response to address his concerns:

> Dear Fr. Smith,
>
> Thank you very much for taking the time to meet with me last week to share with me the concerns of the parish community as we transition into a better and more functional parish administration.
>
> At least we can affirm from our conversation that the community responded in the way I anticipated to you during my hiring interview, namely that a superior PMO administrator of the kind you have hired would necessarily need to address the brokenness that is bound to exist in any organization that has

not had a strong PMO administrator. It is for that reason you hired me, of course, and it is also for that reason that these complaints have come about. As Dante demonstrates in his Purgatorio, after all, all growth in virtue comes with some growing pains.

Specifically, though, you asked me to explain: 1. What I am doing. 2. Why I am doing it. 3. When the complaints will stop and we will start to move forward in a more routine way.

The answer to your last question is much easier than the answer to the first two, so I will begin there. I expect that we will start to move forward in a more routine way by the end of the upcoming calendar year. The reason is that it takes at least one year in the life of any organization to work through its normal cycles of operating and realign them so that they work in a superior manner. If you consider the various cycles of a parish life—ordinary time and the various seasons (Lent, the Triduum, Easter, Advent, Christmas) and the various activities done over the course of those times (summer camps, budgeting and auditing schedules, etc.) you can see that remapping them onto a new strategic plan requires retooling, even replacing the persons responsible for ensuring they are performed in a superior manner.

If you consider the strategic plan that you and I worked on together and agreed that it should be a practical rather than theoretical document, you will note that implementation of the plan requires some abilities that current staff do not presently have. Fine. For them, we provide new training opportunities to upgrade their skills where they have the capacity to be upgraded. If the persons responsible for implementation of the new plan, though, do not want to be retrained for whatever reason to do what their new job descriptions are requiring of them, then we need either to outsource the work or replace the person who would normally be doing it with someone who has the skill sets to do it.

This, in a nutshell, is why we are experiencing frustration on the part of those who have a vested interest in maintaining the status quo.

When my own administrative assistant refuses to be taught how to perform various administrative tasks that are essential to the superior performance of my office, for instance, I need to address that fact directly. I need to do with her what you are doing with me, namely ask her for an accounting of herself that goes beyond, "Because we've never done it that way," or "This is the way I've been doing it for thirty years." Don't get me wrong—I love Sr. Philomena like my own aunt—but there is a superior way of doing things that integrates into the work that other staff members and volunteers are doing, and if that integration process does not work for all, then the entire accountability structure you and I put together in the new organizational chart will not work. In essence, I am wasting my time because it is inevitable I will ultimately fail.

It so happens that all paid and volunteer staff are being realigned like Sr. Philomena to perform according to a new Organizational Chart and new strategic plan, so it's absolutely natural for them to balk at new operational methods required to bring this about. But their greatest concerns are not really the teaching, guidance and direction I have been providing, as much as it is what those things represent in their normal course of activities—namely, change. They realize they are being asked to stop doing what is "normal" in their routine for them and start doing something for which they have not yet gotten into the groove.

As to why they are complaining to you, I would say that we both expect that if a person cannot receive satisfaction of a concern from his or her boss, then naturally, that person will go up a level of administration and express those concerns to his or her boss' boss. That they're also expressing their concerns to the Bishop himself is a sign of desperation and of a lack of faith in your own ability to resolve the issue satisfactorily for them, which is namely to restore the parish to the way things were rather than to the way things need to be. They are seeking the pressure that can be applied to you from above to complement the pressure they are applying from below. No one works well in a pressure cooker, and their plan is to generate that kind of atmosphere in complaining to two levels of administration higher than mine.

There is no real substance, of course, to these complaints, but what is concerning is that, as part of the aforementioned resistance to change, the persons making the complaints are doing so poorly with half-truths, out of context statements and sometimes just plain false statements. When the gardener complained to you, for instance, that I was breaching subsidiarity by giving him direct instructions on how the front lawn of the parish should look—because he usually receives those instructions from Sr. Philomena—he didn't also tell you that Sr. Philomena was present at the time I was giving him and her the larger plan for the picture day ceremony, and how the flowers, if kept only near the staircase in front of the Chapel, would be blocked from view entirely during the photograph sessions of the parishioners who would be standing in front of them.

In short, what I'm asking them to do in examples like this assists in driving the strategic plan that will result in more parishioners attending weekly Mass, and greater efforts on their part for evangelizing those who do not attend Mass at all, both Catholics and future RCIA participants. You can see that the accomplishment of great plans requires implementation of small ones, so I am not being too demanding or unfair but being precisely what I need to be to ultimately create superior PMO.

Aside from organizing everyone to do things right, which is its own kind of reward, I believe we can address PMO employee and volunteer morale by showing them the fruits of their labors, which they will start to see as early as this Sunday's festival celebration, which will be filled to capacity. At present, they only see their work in parts because that's the way they're used to looking at it, but on Sunday, they'll see their work as a collective demonstration of what can be performed when working under a single organizational plan that brings all those parts together in a cohesive and superior manner.

Concerning complaints by persons other than the paid staff and volunteers, the fact that the paid staff and volunteers can mobilize other parishioners to also complain is evidence of their ability to organize at all if properly motivated. What you are receiving, though, is not an organized mobilization. Rather, it is several groups of persons coming to complain independently of one another on behalf of the concerns of one employee or other. It is evidence of the general mess that was in place when I arrived, rather than evidence of a new mess. Once that mess is cleaned up, after all, the complaints will turn to praises, not of me, but of you, and then you will have a different kind of problem to deal with, namely, that of living up to all the praise.

One group's concerns, namely those of the parish council, need to be addressed in a particular way and by you. Councils are always advisory at this level—that is, their input is consultative, not deliberative. This particular council, though, has developed over time a sense of entitlement, expecting that its decisions be binding, not only on the life of the parish itself, but also interpreted as marching orders for the Pastor. That is tail-wagging-the-dog kind of thinking, though, and it can be handled through a strategic reorganization of the parish council so that those responsible for its work begin to channel their energy in proactively supporting the new strategic plan, which they themselves endorsed, but cannot, because of the complaints they are now receiving, bear to implement. Of course, any plan that cannot be implemented by those responsible for its implementation is no plan at all.

In short, or at least a short end to a rather long letter for you on a Monday morning, I need you to both trust me and back me by referring all paid staff and volunteer concerns back to me. For my part, I will address them in a pastoral manner, and the most pastoral of manners—as you have often preached from the pulpit—involves telling people the truth they do not want to hear and moving them in directions they may at first, like St. Peter, not want to go. Those who remain with us after this first year will be the kind of superior paid staff (after all, we must also be wise stewards of parish money) and superior volunteer corps that we need to effectively fill our pews and events galleries for the purpose of realizing our mission to care for the spiritual and temporal needs of Christ's sheep in a superior manner.

In Christ,

Your name here

Just going through the motions of serving others is not why you are reading this book. Further note you simply cannot kill the culture of any organization and install a new culture, unless and until *you practice all the tenets of that culture yourself in every form of communication or personal interaction with anyone on behalf of the parishioners where you are assigned.* There is no hiding this, no dodging this, no denying this, and no deferring this fact to yourself even one more day.

CHAPTER 30

STATEMENT OF PMO CULTURE

How can the principle of PMO culture be informatively and succinctly stated? *First and foremost, as previously mentioned, organizational culture must be animated by and imbued with certain performance sentiments established within your public parish mission statement.* Without such brief but yet profound enhanced language within your parish mission statement, *you cannot create or support a correct "Statement of Culture.* (The details of why this is so will be fully explained in the chapters on hiring and firing.) Thus, a parish mission statement that neglects to publically profess the duty of the parish, to also address serving its current and lapsed parishioners through a superior commitment to PMO, *cannot lend itself to the creation or support of the proper superior service, results oriented, written statement on PMO culture that follows below.*

The following are sample Statements of PMO Culture derived from mandatory, additional, enhanced PMO support language placed within your parish mission statement. The essential objective of each sample statement below remains the same: to clearly and succinctly state the PMO culture. However, the specific language used to achieve this common objective *can vary to suit the personal temperament of the PMO administrator*. It is in this regard you will note significant differences in tone—but not objective—in the following five sample statements. Choose the statement you are most comfortable applying, or create your own, but no matter what exact language you choose, you need a written Statement of Culture.

Statement of Culture Sample #1:

At _____ (insert parish name here) we strive to make the correct PMO decision, or execute perfectly, every time. Superior performance is our only standard, and from this standard we measure our own performance and the performance of all those who report to us, whether employees, volunteers, contractors, or vendors. We further acknowledge that making the correct decision is absolutely irrelevant if we cannot or do not perfectly execute upon every decision ourselves, or convey immediately and clearly our instructions to those who report to us so that they, in turn, execute perfectly. This attitude cascades through every person in the entire PMO organization, because if it does not, the culture has not reached everywhere and everyone it must. This is known as a polluted culture, a broken culture, and we cannot tolerate a polluted and broken culture because we would be failing to fully serve those whom it is our duty to serve.

Training commensurate with any assigned task will always be provided, but then it is our duty as PMO administrators to further ensure those who report to us not only do what they have been taught and instructed to do, but they do so in the most correct way and by the date of completion that is never dictated, but always mutually agreed upon in advance, to be done in the manner taught and prescribed.

Mediocre performance by anyone cannot be accepted or overlooked in any way. Mediocrity will be immediately addressed, always face-to-face as the first communication preference, by phone as the second option, always and whenever possible. It is not our way to ever hide and communicate behind the facade of a digital screen and keyboard, except as a last resort, and no matter the method of communication used, we always immediately, whether by further training, re-

STATEMENT OF PMO CULTURE

medial corrective instruction, or termination of employment, personally address the issue at hand, or delegate to the person who is responsible and monitor their handling of the task through to full and proper completion.

Cultural indoctrination does not start at the bottom of the Org Chart and permeate up throughout the organization. Cultural indoctrination starts at the top of the Org Chart and permeates its way downward, throughout the organization. But you will achieve none of this culture if you do not formally teach these tenets to each current PMO employee and volunteer, A-Z one employee at a time, commit to begin teaching this culture as a matter of policy and correct interviewing processes to every new hire during the interview process, and simultaneously model the culture yourself to everyone in PMO, every day without fail.

The culture creator—which is to say you—further fosters an open-door policy whereby all employees or volunteers from top to bottom not only are most welcome to speak their mind, offer suggestions, criticize, etc., but further know this is true because they have been specifically taught that it is their duty to do so. This is not to say management accepts every suggestion or recommendation, but all employees know their input is most welcome and the only repercussions from commenting are none. At the least a gracious thank you will be given, and perhaps a bonus of some sort. All employees know this because thanks are always given, and bonuses are indeed witnessed as paid as warranted in relation to the value of the input received. We will in part know employee morale is high as built through this culture by observing current employees sending their relatives and friends to us to apply for work wherever we create this culture.

Those who do not accept this culture should not be hired in the first place, but if for some reason they are hired or already employed and by their own free will actions and choices choose not to fit in with our culture, they must be dismissed for their own good, the good of the organization, and most importantly, for the good of those we are charged with serving.

Everything must always be done in love and charity, but there is no love or charity found in enshrining and perpetuating mediocrity.

Statement of Culture Sample #2:

At _____ (insert parish name here) we practice stewardship: the grateful response of a Christian disciple who recognizes and receives God's gifts and shares these gifts in love of God and neighbor. We acknowledge Christ calls us to perfection. We cannot be half-grateful, nor can we partially receive His gifts. We must always strive to respond to God and share our gifts to the best of our abilities. We must be the good stewards who receive the Master's gifts and build them up. We cannot be bad stewards, lest we be cast into the darkness where wailing and gnashing of teeth await us.

The most visible aspect of our practice of stewardship in PMO is our service to God's people. God placed his Church on this earth to serve all of the needs of his people. We must all be good stewards of the gifts that God has given us; therefore, we must always strive for perfection in our service of God's people. Christ is the example and model of perfection in how we are to serve God's people. He loved His disciples, and valued them more than Himself. He communicated with them openly and honestly. He taught them what they needed to know. He corrected, and even rebuked them when necessary. He challenged them to go far beyond what they ever thought was possible.

If we are incapable of providing the service God requires of us for his people, we must take an honest, hard, deep look at ourselves. When we discover the cause of our inability, we must take any and all necessary actions to address the problem. We must remember that even though Christ exalted the smallest mustard seed of faith, he also condemned the fig tree that bore no fruit.

Be the mustard seed; don't be the fig tree.

STATEMENT OF PMO CULTURE

Statement of Culture Sample #3:

At _____ (insert parish name here) excellence is the only measure of success. We strive to do our best and put every effort in our work serving and reaching people. We work as a family, empowering one another. One should be responsible for his or her actions. Proper judgment is gained through training and wide understanding of the work. Thus, training shall be provided. Merits are gained through hard work. Consequences are brought by wrong judgment. As a family, we are stronger together and together we will make this parish great.

Respect begets respect. Know your superior. Speak your ideas and influence each other. Share your talent. Seek and you will find. Ignorance is not permitted. It is a pest that destroys the system. Knock and the door shall be opened. Be open to criticisms and have room for improvements. When you hear their voices, harden not your heart. Be ready to apply what you have gained from training and criticism. Do not work on your own ways.

And when things fail, justice shall always be served. Mercy shall follow. Together in our community, we vow our allegiance to the cross. Excellence is our goal. God is our guide. The people are our inspiration. We are the culture. This is our culture. In faith, hope, and love may our service prevail.

Statement of Culture Sample #4:

At _____ (insert parish name here) we are committed to provide everyone with the opportunity to encounter and gain a profound sense of the Sacred. We ultimately rely on the Holy Spirit for this to occur. However, in all parish ministries we strive to unobstruct the Holy Spirit by making correct decisions and executing them perfectly. We hold ourselves to this standard of superior performance as well as everyone involved in this organization. As a parish family, everyone, no matter what their position, is invited in charity to share their suggestions, voice their opinions and make necessary criticisms.

Everyone, both current staff and the newly hired, will receive the proper training to correctly fulfill their duties as described in their written job descriptions. Evaluations will periodically be made to assess job performance. Anyone not meeting the standard of superior performance will meet with their direct supervisor to discuss how they may better serve God and the parish community for the good of their own souls and the souls of all affected by the service they may be more suited to provide. If agreement cannot be made, the Pastor is then to determine what further course of action to take. This may include dismissal of a paid employee, or asking a volunteer to do another task at the risk of offending them and possibly seeing them leave the parish of their own volition.

Statement of Culture Sample #5:

At _____ (insert parish name here) we strive for superior performance in all facets of our mission. Superior is the measure of our performance, whether as employees, volunteers, contractors, or vendors. Fully acknowledging that no one is perfect, we respond to Christ's call "to be perfect as our heavenly Father is perfect" by always doing our best. This attitude, first and foremost, must be held by the Pastor who leads the parish, but must also flow to everyone in PMO. It is everyone's responsibility to hold each other to this standard while remaining charitable and understanding, for one must remove the beam from his own eye before removing the splinter from his brother's.

With the goal and standard of our performance being perfection, mediocrity is not sufficient. Mediocrity will not be accepted as our standard. Not only will tasks be completed correctly and on time, as mutually agreed upon prior, but also all tasks will be done in a superior manner, going above and beyond the basic requirements. If mediocrity does occur, management will address it in a timely manner, ideally face-to-face. While updates and normal communication may be done over the phone or via email, correction ought to be, if possible, done in person and never as a degradation of the person's value, but always as a means to ensure that mediocrity does not persist. This can be accomplished by retraining, adjusting responsibilities, reprimanding, or ultimately, dismissal. Ideally, the direct superior has this duty.

The Pastor promotes an open-door policy, so that the Spirit may move through all. While not all suggestions presented will be enacted, they will always be taken under advisement. The minimum response to employee/parishioner input will always at least be sincere gratitude and earnest consideration with potential for the payment of bonuses.

Those unwilling to take on this culture model should not be hired. If for some reason a current employee/volunteer willfully rejects this culture, they must be dismissed for their own sake and for the sake of the parish, but always in charity. To paraphrase Pope Emeritus Benedict XVI's *Caritas in Veritate*, truth without charity can be cruel and charity without truth becomes sentimentality and not truly loving.

Whichever Statement of Culture you choose, actually living the words daily is vital to achieving what the words actually represent. We must also concede that using ever-so-common culture-building boilerplate language such as, "We are committed to excellence… We provide world-class service…etc." can be demonstrated in an almost infinite number of ways as to be merely window-dressing and exposed for what it is: *hollow milquetoast declarations of no real consequence masquerading as statements of some consequence.* Such boilerplate language is just that—boilerplate. The DNA intrinsic to the correct culture is defined in the total Statement of Culture in the samples provided above. Therefore:

If you are not going to embrace the above culture, the reasons do not matter. Just know you can have the absolute best of everything in your PMO, but if your culture is just the slightest bit off you never become what you should be, both personally and organizationally. Remember, this PMO organizational greatness we strive for is *not* about control, ego, power, prestige, recognition, or anything like this. It is only about serving God by serving our parishioners—both current and lapsed—in the most superior way possible. The correct PMO culture is always asking: *is there any <u>more</u> we can do for those we are called to serve?* We either exist to serve the parishioner in a superior manner, or not.

Now, let's look at an "or not" example.

CHAPTER 31

EXPERIENCE A BROKEN CULTURE

We will now segue into a representative example of broken culture so that you may feel the texture of living in and under the effects of a broken culture, *and also consider the consequences of accepting the status quo of mediocrity—or worse—such a broken culture creates.* There is so much useful material here you would be hard-pressed to find a more costly example:

VW rocked by emissions scandal as prosecutors come calling

VW CHEATED—11 million times

Volkswagen has now admitted that it intentionally installed software programmed to switch engines to a cleaner mode during official emissions testing. The software then switches off again, enabling cars to drive more powerfully on the road while emitting as much as 40 times the legal pollution limit. The illegal software was made and installed in vehicles with 2.0-liter diesel engines during the model years 2009 through 2015, the EPA said. They include the Audi A3, VW Jetta, Beetle, Golf and Passat models. VW finally acknowledged installing the devices only after the California Air Resources Board (CARB) and the EPA insisted on a better explanation before approving its 2016 diesel models. "We met with VW on several occasions, and they continued to dispute our data, so we'd return to the lab. Over time, VW had no other explanations left, and it was our lab staff who actually got VW to admit that there was, in fact, a defeat device," CARB spokesman John Smith said. (Name changed.)

So, let's recap: the CARB folks continuously went back to their lab to "check their data"? Wow, there's an effective response to this major discrepancy—*said no one ever*. If the car passes your official tests but pollutes on the road *you know the car is somehow rigged*, and there's only one way you clandestinely rig today's software-controlled cars: through software cheats.

Buying the VW response—*for years*—is akin to believing all was well in the entire former USSR because on your pre-planned VIP driving route from the airport to the one and only decent hotel in the entire country, everything you saw looked clean and modern—just the way the Potemkin Village planners wanted you to see their fine dump of a broken national infrastructure. Who falls for that trick? What thinking person accepts such illusions? Obviously CARB did, among others, *but why?* Are you telling me employed in the entire state or federal government we don't have a single software engineer who can read a software code dump? And we don't employ the lawyer wherewithal to subpoena this suspected rigged programming code? There are teenage hackers living on pizza and sodas in a dimly lit basement who can read a programming code dump, but the government has no one qualified to do so?

The failure to expose this cheating had *nothing* to do with a lack of available talent and *everything* to do with the *poor management* of the talent and resources available. In other words, _for better or worse, working in a broken culture animates the behavior and thinking of all employees_.

Simply perform a programming code dump and read the code. That's it.

EXPERIENCE A BROKEN CULTURE

Read the code. Code doesn't lie. Code reveals, "Oh, Mr./Ms. VW software engineer, could you please explain this subroutine in your code that detects the presence of CARB testing equipment and subsequently jumps to this code over here that cuts engine power, reduces fuel flow, adjusts engine timing, etc., to pass our pollution tests? Can you please explain that?"

Eh, no, they can't explain that, at least not coherently—but nobody asked the question. Why? *Their broken culture did not allow, enable, encourage, or animate such thinking.* Why? Keep reading.

CHAPTER 32

WHAT HATS ARE ON YOUR HAT RACK?

Instead of discovering this ongoing VW charade, *what does the broken CARB culture essentially force CARB personnel to do?* These culture deficient "management" minds conspired with other bureaucratic minds to return people to spending *years* toiling in their very comfortable gulag of a testing lab trying to figure what could have been discovered in relative *minutes* by simply mentally switching from wearing their "Bureaucratic Administrator" hat to an "Entrepreneurial Thinker" labeled hat. CARB upper management should darn well have had this hat hanging on their hat rack and chose to wear it, *by so doing subsequently viewing the issue at hand through a different solution lens*. This figurative "hat switching" would be enabled and animated by *working within the correct culture*. And if you detect some passion here, chalk that up to the fact that my family and I live in California and we have all been breathing this additional pollution for years.

I am willing to opine you could ask every single person in upper management supposedly guiding CARB to bring us citizens to clean air Nirvana, "Are you culturally entrepreneurial in your approach to problem solving?" and you are going to receive a deer in the headlights look. Why? Because CARB did not have folks willing to operate while wearing the "Culturally Entrepreneurial Thinker" hat. The CARB bureaucratic "leadership" was mentally lop-sided, improperly constituted, and demonstrably useless in advising under certain crucial hats germane to the very core reasons their agency exists to protect the public. In other words, *owning and wearing but a single hat on your PMO administrator hat rack is not going to work for you.*

I am willing to further state there was at least one person working in the lab who at a gut level felt the above, but because the *culture*—there's that word again—within the organization was not correct, *they were afraid to speak their mind to those above them on the CARB Org Chart for fear of getting put in their place or getting their head chopped off.* So instead…they stayed within their safe zone—*as their broken culture prescribes*—*and said nothing.*

The above illustrates why military coups d'état are often led by colonels and other lower ranks, but not by generals. Why? Because the generals no longer see, or at least no longer care to see, what is broken while they maintain their status quo and live comfortably—*but the younger colonel walks with his eyes wide open and is willing to take the necessary action to improve a broken situation.* Thus, we have an environment where the collective mental horsepower of the entire organization is defeated, *simply by an incorrect, incoherent, and broken culture steering management personnel.*

And you want to know the absolute best-worst part of this VW story? *I know John Smith, the CARB spokesperson, and he knows me* because he purchased computer training from New Horizons Computer Learning Centers over many years, which means John Smith could have asked himself, "Hmm? Who do I have in my personal contact list who knows a deep thing or two about computer technology? Perhaps the founder of New Horizons, the place where I send our employees to be trained in…the use of computer technology. Yeah, I'll call him and run these odd circumstances by him, see if he has any thoughts, ideas, suggestions about this VW mystery."

Did John make that call? No. Why? *Because either that thought never*

WHAT HATS ARE ON YOUR HAT RACK?

crossed his mind, or if it did, he was afraid of the consequences of reaching outside his organization for help. Why? Because instead of switching hats, *which is to say switch the lens through which he viewed a problem or situation, as would be not only enabled by, but demanded by, working within a correct culture,* John chose to wear the one and only, safe and secure, hat enshrined on his culture rack, the hat labeled, "I'm a 'Spokesperson' only, that's my job. I don't have any other way of viewing or thinking about what is in front of me, *because never in my life did I have the good fortune to work someplace where this more expansive way of speaking and thinking was animated by a correct culture and allowed to become our expected behavioral norm.*"

Carry forward what a correct-culture-enabled simple hat switch made by just one person might have meant. Because we are dealing with a camouflaged 40X increase in diesel fuel emissions, people breathing in this pollution may have contracted various respiratory ailments and/or forms of cancer and died, *all because an entire gang of people did not switch hats and think outside their parochial little box worlds.* Why? Altogether now: *a broken and corrupted culture.*

If you find yourself not agreeing with this expansion of the article as I just described it, pause long and hard here because if you think you are for whatever reasons—emotional, intellectual, philosophical, etc.—going to behave like John Smith when working as the chief PMO administrator, you are in the wrong box on the PMO Org Chart. Further note:

The usefulness available to the VW CEO from the collective power of the minds of the VW Board members—in other words, minds that reside higher up on the Org Chart to assist those below—was soundly defeated because they were given the mushroom treatment. You are familiar with the administrative principle of treating people like mushrooms? And, pray tell, what is the function of a Board—or in our PMO world the Pastor or Parish Council—*if not to prevent such train wrecks from occurring in the first place?* But people higher up on the Org Chart will never be of any help when they, too, operate under a broken culture—they just become extended window dressing, their existence demanded by adherence to proper protocol as dictated by corporate or canon bylaws, *but functionally speaking they are a useless gathering of culturally silenced minds.*

And if you are asking here, "How could the Board have known about this issue?" look no further than the VW CEO who never informed them of the millions of cars under scrutiny for "emissions anomalies." If properly informed, do you think at least one VW board member might have ventured, "Eh, what emissions anomalies are you talking about?" But the correct culture that would have enabled and animated such a conversation did not exist. Imagine that. No fuel, no fire. The upshot: if you want the collective thinking power of the various parish councils and other advisors to be of service to you, you have to not only keep them informed, *they must operate within the riverbanks of the correct PMO culture.*

If the above sounds in any way too harsh for you to implement exactly as is, and/or if the above is not something that can be derived from and supported by your current parish mission statement, I invite you to start writing something other than the above sample Statements on Culture that is just as effective—or even more effective—in setting your mind to creating the proper PMO culture, but is worded to your personal liking. Note however, you do need a written Statement on Culture. Why?

Keep reading.

CHAPTER 33

EITHER YOU CHOOSE THE CULTURE OR THE CULTURE CHOOSES YOU

Culture eats strategy for breakfast.

—Peter Drucker

What has been written above in the example "Statements on Culture" are neither too harsh nor too soft, as the words themselves only convey the culture *but do not specifically articulate the manner in which you achieve what the words state when installing the culture and holding all personnel accountable to what the words mean.* However, note no matter how culture is approached, *at all times some form of culture exists in any organization.* Therefore, in the absence of any such statement articulating precisely what the PMO culture is going to be where you work, will any culture exist at all? Oh my, yes, absolutely—*a culture of some sort always exists because <u>you either choose the culture, or some culture by default will choose you</u>.* But what "culture by default" will you have without any deliberate written Statement of Culture informing and animating PMO behavior? Precisely this culture:

Just using simple numbers, if you have five paid personnel and ten volunteers working in PMO, you will have the *amalgamated sum* of their fifteen disparate, most likely conflicting, individual attitudes, subject matter knowledge, methods of operation, and subsequent uneven job performances derived thereby as your culture. Now isn't that just a lovely way to build PMO's foundational culture…*said no one ever.*

What kind of a Frankenstein operation are you managing—*or think you are managing—with a culture created like this?* How can you possibly know with full certainty what level of service parishioners are receiving from those who report to you, when fifteen different people *define for themselves in fifteen different degrees and ways* what, for example, a simple but profound cornerstone expression such as "level of parishioner service" actually means? Who in their right mind would allow their PMO culture to not only be guided by, *but be variably reset each transaction of every day,* by the collective whims of an essentially random and ever changing number of self-guiding, self-monitoring, self-grading, employees and volunteers? *This is a culture of omission and neglect.* Why? Because there is no such thing as "no culture." *Some culture always exists and this potpourri, this is the culture that will exist in any organization when you ignore creating the correct culture.*

CHAPTER 34

THE CONSEQUENCES OF WEARING THE WRONG HAT

The most common reason you may perceive taking the necessary steps to kill and replace a broken culture as being "too harsh"—especially in an inherited broken culture with established friendships, pre-existing relationships, historically low to non-existent job performance expectations, etc.—is very often rooted in the *corrupted perspective* of the PMO administrator charged with replacing the broken culture. How so? Over time, *the administrator has replaced wearing his or her administrator hat while at work with the wrong hat, such as the "I'm Your Friend" hat*. This is especially true when the PMO administrator is ordained, and instead of wearing an administrator hat when required to work in that role, *he incorrectly chooses to image-manage under the "Pastor/Pastoral" hat*. This dual-role quickly becomes an obvious untenable conflict of interest, not to mention a very confusing situation for the employee or volunteer: are you speaking to me as my friend, my Pastor, or my PMO boss?

Note any ordained person will always be perceived as ordained, so it is not that the ordained hat is ever removed—indeed, *the ordained hat cannot be removed*. But clarity while communicating is paramount when an ordained person has his name written in more than one box on the Org Chart. *You must always clearly present to the receiver you are wearing the hat that correlates to the appropriate box with your name in it on the Org Chart. Any receiver must always and in real-time know <u>exactly</u> what hat you are wearing whenever you are communicating in any form.

This point necessarily implies that all employees and volunteers understand the principle of "hat switching," so everyone knows "to whom" they are communicating can vary with the circumstances and topic of conversation at any given moment. Failure to achieve this clarity for any dual-role ordained person who is also working as the PMO administrator on the Org Chart makes for a very confused employee and volunteer. *You must be true to the precise hat you are wearing and imaging in whatever you do and whenever you are communicating.* For example, true story:

I sent Bill Gates via FedEx my copy of a *Newsweek* magazine with his photo on the cover with a "Hello Bill" note enclosed. I asked him to sign the magazine for me. We had met at a few Microsoft sponsored authorized training center conferences. I also, as a convenience, included a FedEx prepaid return envelope, and…*he used it.* Bill Gates, *one of the richest men in the world,* burned my money, not his, on postage—*not only as he should have, but as he must.* He. Must. Do. This. Why? Internalize this point: selecting the correct decision lens here *had nothing to do with the fact that Bill Gates is the richest man in the world.* The correct decision, *made only if viewing the matter through the correct lens and hat switching to select the correct hat at that moment* was to *of course* use my money, not his—and this is precisely what he did. *It is the only decision anyone animated by the correct culture and wearing the correct hat could produce.*

So long as you install the correct culture and wear the correct hat, there are very, very, rare and few exceptions to being fully animated and guided by the invisible hand of culture, and the necessity to clearly switch hats. Note how easy it would be for anyone to be confused, even disparage his decision, if either not aware of the hat switching principle in the first place, or not knowing which hat was being worn when a decision was made.

CHAPTER 35

ON THE PRIMACY OF HAT SWITCHING

Unless you already posses some very specific prior work experience, you probably are not yet fully dialed-in as to the *speed* of the administrative management or supervisory hat switching that is required of you in PMO. Five critical points might remain cloudy, muddled, jumbled, *but addressing these points is personal in nature and therefore you must sort them out for yourself*:

1. Nobody owns just one hat, so by definition hat-switching and communication clarity becomes a necessity. What is the *total number* of hats you own today?
2. No matter how many hats you own, do you own all the *different hats* that are necessary to be superior at your PMO administrative job? Owning a bunch of hats that do not lend themselves to the work done in PMO is clutter that must be sorted.
3. Do you recognize the need to *hat switch?* Constantly imaging to anyone and everyone 24/7, for example, the "I am your friend" hat, is going to create confusion and an unnecessary mountain of problems for you.
4. How *fast* can you switch from one hat to another? If the person(s) you are communicating with does not recognize you have switched hats, because in fact you have not yet done so in his or her eyes, you are just adding to the confusion and consternation.

5. Do you own the talent—not just the hat label but also the *actual talent*—required to operate under every hat that each of your respective responsibilities requires you to wear? If at this moment you know you do not know the answer to this question, stop. Look in the mirror. Find out, but do not try to fake it. If you need a basic accounting class, for example, find a book and/or an online class. But do not remain ignorant of core knowledge required to be a superior PMO administrator when it is your job to be a superior PMO administrator—make the time and go find the knowledge you need or do not occupy the box on the Org Chart.

The answers you provide to the above five points are paramount to observing a broken culture, then killing it and installing a correct one. Why? <u>*The hat you choose to wear controls the optics through which you choose to see.*</u> How so? When you grind beef, *do you expect to see pork exit the grinder?* No. So, what you put into the grinder is fundamentally, what comes out. As such:

> *You must first build in PMO culture what others with lesser skills need only manage after you and I are long gone from this Earth.*

Culture builders are extremely rare, but obviously, extremely necessary. In your mind if you visualize your parish too simply, just as "an ongoing operation," and believe what is written above is not applicable because your parish is in business accounting jargon, "an established, ongoing concern," I suggest you think again. You have bought into an illusion, for in all likelihood very little of serious consequence exists now as it should be or could be—you must build it. *And as you know, the foundation of building superior PMO is furthered by building the correct culture, and this is done in part by wearing the right hat at the right time, presented to the right people.* We call this hat switching. It is only when you put the correct culture into the PMO grinder—with all the other necessary ingredients—that you will experience the superior PMO results output you are seeking. However:

You will never be totally effective in your respective positions unless you accept and master what follows. I say, "master what follows" because it takes practice to hat switch, and much skill to operate effectively wearing a variety of hats—while still always wearing your ordained hat (if this applies to you). Is acquiring the science, the technical skills, our great challenge in this carousel of hat switching? *No, not even close.* What is the great challenge in this context? *The art of choosing the correct hat for the task at hand, then switching to the next hat...and to the next hat...and to the next hat...etc. This is the greatest challenge for the PMO administrator.*

The notion that you need encyclopedic knowledge of the science of PMO is simply wrong. Flush that thought from your mind. The science of PMO is relatively easy—*it is practicing the art of anything that is your greatest challenge.* This point helps explain why there are so many technically competent people in any field or profession, but so few have become superior administrators or leaders. Why? *Because they failed to master the art of practicing their craft, and intrinsic to mastering their craft is the art of hat switching.*

You must further develop the hat switch skill, *and further develop the art and science skills each hat represents that you do not own today.* For example, to the extent you must at times throughout the day wear the innovator hat and think like an innovator, are you comfortable with that innovator hat right now? Do you even mentally own a hat labeled "Innovative thinker"? Do you consider yourself an innovative problem solver, or a hidebound rule-follower who lacks both imagination and even the slightest willingness to take calculated risks?

Do not channel here images of childhood adolescent paper routes, or the adult-level equivalent of paper route problem solving, and lay claim to owning the PMO administrator innovator hat. PMO is more complex. Note the reason innovation in PMO today is critically lacking is because mostly *non-innovative people* apply the same tired processes as their "solutions" to chronic problems—with predictably poor results. Most importantly, do you know how to effectively operate while wearing any hat, or worse, *just think you do when the reality is vastly different?* Look in the mirror, check time.

It is this same line of questions and analysis for every hat on the administrator's hat rack, but what happens most often in PMO? The current PMO administrator is not hat switching, not to mention he only has one very well worn hat on his rack—*the default hat he wants to wear in every circumstance he faces, not the hat he should wear that corresponds precisely to the circumstance.*

Do not confuse what you just read with performing many and diverse daily tasks. Of course you do many and diverse tasks every day. But my point is that too many PMO administrators do these many and diverse tasks *primarily wearing the same thinking hat*, thus viewing the challenge or question at hand most of the time *through the wrong solution method lens*. Wear the wrong hat, get the wrong solution, imagine that? They put beef in their mental grinder and expect pork to come out. This one-hat same-hat error cannot help but render the wrong approach and solution to solving the problem at hand. Confusion reigns. At best, you tread water, one lucky step forward when your one hat fits the situation, one unlucky step backward when it doesn't.

While you might easily conceptualize the need to wear multiple hats as a PMO administrator, if you have not already been in an administrative and/or leadership role you may overlook—or not understand—a related challenge: *the speed of the "hat change"* itself, the lightning speed in which you must switch hats, the speed with which you first detect a hat switch is necessary, and subsequently, switch to the correct hat to engage the issue and/or person. As mentioned, this hat switch must be clearly communicated to the receiver. Initially, you may literally need to slow your conversation down in order to explicitly achieve the necessary hat switch clarity between yourself and the receiver(s), to deliberately pause the action or conversation to achieve the necessary communication clarity between all parties, until such actions become second mental nature for everyone. Further note:

Because of the nature of the PMO administrator's job, it is impossible for those in this position to concretely order the flow of their day, which is to say select the hats they must wear during the day in advance. Random order problem solving—*which is to say random order hat switching*—and interrupted planning is your daily norm. The administrator who can master the correct hat switch, communicate same to the receiver, *combined with owning the talent required to supremely wear the correct hat now on his or her head*, will become the superior administrator and/or leader.

Sadly, most people in management do not switch hats, perpetually switch too slowly, fight switching hats, choose the wrong hat to wear, or can't operate effectively while wearing the hat they have to wear for the task at hand. Their PMO results are predictably poor—which is to say those we are to serve are not served as well as they should be. Morale is also often predictably low in such environments, but people can't quite put their finger on the source of the problem. Why? *Because culture is an invisible, but no less critical force that is directly responsible for both internal morale and the quality of service provided by PMO personnel.*

Notice it is telling that when morale is low employees and volunteers are aware morale is low. Why? Because internally, they know they can perform better than they are—*they just lack the helping hand of a correct culture to guide them to a higher level of on the job performance.* Just imagine the boost in employee and volunteer morale when things are made right and run right.

CHAPTER 36

ON THE OPTICS OF PMO

From moment to moment the PMO administrator may be called upon—which is to also say may be viewed as a contract negotiator, department manager, entrepreneurial thinker, fundraiser, meeting chairperson, etc., and perhaps in your case, ordained clergy. *Therefore, it is absolutely paramount that you do not look at every decision to be made through your preferred decision-making lens. You have no default hat.* Why? *Only the correct lens, implicitly chosen by selecting the right hat to wear as defined by the circumstances you are facing, guides your decision-making style for each situation.* Do not resist this point. Look at it this way: if you see every problem as a nail, *the only tool you think you need in your toolbox is a hammer—and you can't get much more wrong in life than using a hammer on every challenge you face.*

But how in the world can you ever develop the senses and intuition required to do your job in a superior manner if you only see how to deal with situations through the same lens, as your preferred optic's first and last choice? What if just "one way, my way" is not only your default chosen way to view your PMO world, *but given your attitude it is also your only way possible?* Would you ever bother to stop and ask someone else for advice when you have already convinced yourself you know what you are doing and you are doing the right thing? No. It is for precisely this reason you will have PMO problems, not because the problems were hard to detect or the practice science hard to master, *but because the problems were hard for you to see correctly*, much less solve correctly if viewing all PMO matters through one lens and while wearing the incorrect hat. So, *how do you learn to hat switch faster, and operate effectively under each hat?*

It's the same three points you interview for in job applicants (more on this point later). *To learn to select the correct hat and to hat switch faster you must*:

1. Possess high intellect.
2. Be willing to subjugate your ego.
3. Be willing to take direction from anyone.

Let us assume you have high intellect or you wouldn't be reading this book. But are you willing to subjugate your ego? Are you willing to take direction? Clearly note: a willingness to listen and take direction is not the same thing as *actually doing what it takes* to move a broken culture in a direction that rubs against your current and perhaps sanguine temperament grain.

If there is no change in your behavior, you may have listened, you may have understood, *but so what?* Who cares? You didn't buy, you didn't internalize what was being sold—*you didn't truly accept direction and convert direction into changed behavior in yourself and others. But a broken and corrupt PMO culture will never be replaced unless and until you adapt to* new ways *of thinking and operating.* Why? *Because nobody can change direction unless they first accept new directions, and the hardheaded and stubborn by definition refuse new directions.*

These chapters on culture constitute recognizing a new perspective toward PMO in general. Thus, only you can decide to act on what you have learned here. It is gut check time: will you kill and replace your culture with the correct culture, or not? *Do you have the will for that task in you, or not?* My sincere recommendation to you here: think like the front desk person at a five-star hotel has been trained to think: *think yes first, then find a way to accomplish the mission.* How? That is up to you; ask more questions, challenge until satisfied, do whatever it takes to reach a level of certainty we would label as, "I am persuaded. We can do this." Why? An affirmative answer carries with it from the beginning a powerful personal call to change hats, learn the ways of the new hat, and learn to effectively operate under each new hat.

I can teach anyone holding points 1, 2, and 3 above how to be a superior administrator or leader. You have point 1, but do you truly have all of points 2 and 3, *specifically as it relates to the critical topic of killing the old PMO culture and replacing it with a new and correct culture?*

CHAPTER 37

LEAVE THE CULTURE DNA ALONE

Whatever you do, **_do not tinker with the DNA of what you are reading here on culture_**. What does this mean? Precisely this:

> *Leave the PMO culture you have in your parish in place just as you inherited it unless and until you fully understand and accept everything that is presented here on culture. And do not start the process of killing the old culture and replacing it unless you are ham 'n eggs pig committed to finish what you start.*

Are you familiar with a ham 'n eggs level of breakfast commitment and participation? The chicken participated, but the pig, *the pig was committed. You must be that committed, _or do not touch the culture wherever you are_.* And if for one second you think you will "make a few changes…make some improvements here and there" but not be all-in committed to what you are reading herein, *do not go there, do not fool yourself, do not change anything.* Leave things just as they are. Why? _Because the notion of an incremental improvement of a broken culture is a false paradigm_. There is no such thing. All you will do is akin to rearranging the deck chairs on the Titanic—*you are still going down, because your PMO will still have vestiges of a broken culture virus in its bloodstream.*

As previously mentioned, know in advance there *will be* the "bumpy ride to possible hurricane" turmoil associated with killing and replacing your current culture. Notify everyone above you on the Org Chart this turmoil is as natural as it is inevitable. *Do know that most of those who are already employed or volunteer at your parish may not climb on board with this new cultural model,* perhaps for philosophical reasons, perhaps because they just don't like you, but mostly because this model represents substantial and radical *change* from the environment that they are acclimated to and prefer to work in. This culture you bring is not the culture they were hired into, etc. Fine. To those folks we say, when we are reading you into the new culture and our teaching focus is placed on you, please make your call: *get on board, or move along to a new job somewhere else—because if you don't move yourself along, I will move you along.* Why?

Because your parish does not belong to them—or you—and quite honestly we cannot be held hostage by how someone prefers to work when stacked up against what we know is true, effective, legal, ethical, and most importantly, will stand up to any moral challenge. Challenge anybody to forecast a cohort of unhappy employees and volunteers read into this culture model from their very first contact with you, up to and through their hiring and ongoing employment. If you can make that argument, let me hear it. Indeed, I know from experience you will ultimately receive an overwhelmingly opposite reaction, a positive reaction from most applicants, who will tell you *they could not be happier hearing about and hiring into a performance-based, results-oriented, parishioner-centric PMO servant model.* Your greatest challenge in this regard is not in whom you hire, *but in whom you must inherit upon your arrival who stubbornly, resists change.*

We want superior employees and volunteers in PMO to deliver a superior level of service, and you will not accomplish that portion of your parish mission statement by allowing those who report to you to passively or aggressively dictate methods of PMO to you, all the while with little or no job performance and results accountability. Of course the word "dictate" reads too blunt for some, so the reality of an ongoing employee and/or volunteer dictatorship over current operations is sometimes camouflaged by euphemistic phrases such as, "we are protecting subsidiarity" and/or "we work collegially here." Do as you wish, but as a PMO administrator, I would want no part of that model, which is to say the current broken culture model in many parishes of hiding poor performers under the flag of "subsidiarity" or "collegiality," where the employee tail wags the administrator dog. But on the other hand:

If I were a current PMO employee or volunteer operating under a culture without accountability, if I were on the receiving end of enshrined autopilot pay increases and low/no job performance expectations? Oh my, yes! By all means, I want to stick with the current PMO culture model! Please, don't change a thing, new PMO administrator! I want the current deal and setup to continue in perpetuity! I want to be the employee tail that is wagging the PMO dog! Leave us alone! We know best! In fact, we have been working in this parish longer than you have been alive!

This is the culture choosing you instead of you choosing the culture—and it happens far too often. What you do about it is up to you.

CHAPTER 38

FACING THE JOB PERFORMANCE MIRROR

To replace the current culture and install a correct culture, the new PMO administrator must first be willing to endure a genuine look in the job performance mirror, subsequently accept what is seen as-is, and then make a firm commitment to fix whatever is broken or deficient (conjure here the 1945 film, *The Picture of Dorian Gray*). Sadly, in my experience, by far in most such situations the administrator's post-mirror look default position is an excuse-laden, do nothing, finger-pointing, entrenched stubbornness, misguided, time-wasting, disingenuously rationalized, refusal to accept reality, faulty analysis that moves PMO culture no further after looking in the mirror, than it was before. As such, two points remain:

1. Will you truly embrace everything that you are reading here on culture?

If your gut says no, fine. Say so and figure out where you will literally and figuratively go with that card now clearly on the table. *But the absolute worst thing you could do is pretend to embrace the points herein, but do so unwillingly, half-heartedly, and/or reluctantly*. Life is not only too short to live that way, but you will ultimately be unsuccessful anyway in trying to install a culture you do not, will not, and/or cannot choose to live yourself. Employees will reflect the values of their management *as they see those values reflected by their management*. If you cannot and/or will not embrace and build the correct culture, it is what it is. Leave things as they are. Do not tinker with your culture DNA.

2. But let's assume you desire to build a new culture. The next question: can you *execute* on what you are reading here?

Going forward you will find out, but also note the distinction that *embracing a concept is not the same as executing the concept* (more on this point later). It is paramount that you do not allow your desire to want to perform, *cloud your judgment as to whether or not you can and will actually perform in the manner described herein*. As you must realize by now, there is no path to providing superior PMO services that does not run through the name in the top box of any PMO Org Chart—and if that is your name there is either no escaping doing your total duty, or replacing your name on the Org Chart with someone who will.

Upon recognition that the PMO culture that exists where you are assigned is broken, upon gaining the prerequisite permission (if necessary) to kill and replace the current culture of mediocrity or worse with the correct culture, upon creating a statement defining the expected culture of your PMO, either by copying one of the above five sample statements or creating something equal or better of your own liking, upon accepting the personal challenge to quickly hat switch and wear the correct hat for the task at hand, *what will be your approach to the implementation and execution building your new culture?*

CHAPTER 39

COMMUNICATING THE CULTURE

Notice the above chapter title has not been framed as, "Where do I start first on communicating the culture?" because the number of ways a culture may be broken—which speaks to determining where to start first—is virtually infinite. However, without describing now the specifics on the ground in dozens of hypothetical scenarios, it is still possible to present how to approach a corrupted and broken culture in both general attitude—which has been addressed above—*as well as your chosen method of communication while wearing the correct hat.*

In regard to communications when killing and installing a new culture, there are three primary methods of communication and they are listed below in order of effectiveness and usage priority:

1. Face-to-face communication.
2. Telephone communication.
3. Digital forms of communication such as email and texting.

When you are ready to embark on the killing of your current PMO culture and install your new culture you have a specific challenge. What type of challenge? *Think along the lines of rebuilding an engine while it is running.*

Oh.

Just as is often the case in the business world, PMO services do not have the luxury of simply shutting down for some period of time while you build a new culture. As such, aside from the obvious point of knowing what you are doing before you start and 100% committing to finish what you start—akin to a surgeon knowing anatomy before starting surgery on his patient—communication becomes paramount to successfully terminate the current culture and install a new culture. How so?

Reading this far you should by now have an informed opinion and realize that, although every current PMO employee and volunteer you must read into the new culture could be joy-filled upon learning of these changes, as explained above, *that is not their most likely response*. Resistance to change, anger, confusion, disappointment, frustration, pushback, irreconcilable differences, etc., are all to be expected once you start this process—and killing the old culture and installing a new culture should be viewed as a process, not a one-time event. And what is the most common mistake made by the rookie administrator at this junction?

In anticipation of the aforementioned arguments against change and the subsequent predictable employee turnover and pushback caused by change, the administrator selects the path of least resistance, hides behind a glass screen, *and sends every employee and volunteer "corrective" or "educational" emails—an unending stream of annoying, useless emails*—attempting in his best and most collegial language to explain the "new" culture, etc. This is, among other things, *a monumental waste of everybody's time.*

This email approach accomplishes next to nothing, as the number of follow-up questions and concerns such an email generates in the minds of all PMO personnel only serves to compound whatever anxiety they already have. There is a time and place for digital communications, and this is neither the time nor the place. You cannot manage people remotely from the chair in your office via a keyboard. Well, you can try—but you will fail.

In circumstances where logistical challenges prevent the PMO administrator from meeting face-to-face with each employee and volunteer, telephone communication (including Facetime, Skype, etc.) is the best alternative you have available. But both telephone and digital communication *are distant second and third choices to the always-preferred choice of face-to-face communications.* It is much more effective for all parties that you speak to them in-person and answer all their questions and concerns—or at least make an attempt to do so. People may not like or agree with what you have to say for all the reasons cited above—especially due to the shock of hearing the truth on their actual PMO performance *for the first time*. But everyone will respect—or at least should respect—that you chose to speak with them face-to-face and were willing to listen to their concerns. Note listening is also paramount to the process of building a new culture.

CHAPTER 40

ON TURNOVER

The neutral news when killing the old culture and installing the new culture is you can expect employee and volunteer turnover. Why is employee and volunteer turnover considered neutral news as opposed to bad news? *Because the positive aspects of personnel turnover to the organization are misunderstood or overlooked, far too often being misconstrued as bad news when pruning is a prerequisite for new growth.*

The good news is that not everyone will resist the new culture. Some will be most thankful and consider the installation of a new PMO culture long overdue. But the best news is that those who embrace change will become examples to new hires and new volunteers, ready, willing, and able to indoctrinate and train new personnel in the ways of superior PMO service. Mediocrity and systemic brokenness will receive the permanent boot. This is as God intended. *Therefore, turnover can be a useful tool. Do not misinterpret the value of strategic employee and volunteer turnover.*

One mission of the Church is to be loving and charitable in everything we do. We understand this; we live by this code each day. However, by definition if you draw a payroll check from the Church or if you volunteer to work for the Church, <u>you must be held accountable to performance standards not of your own choosing</u>. PMO standards of performance are derived from the correct culture as drawn from language in your Statement on Culture, and as further supported by your parish mission statement. These points and others up ahead are integral and foundational to this interlocked, holistic system of PMO. If you neglect one point, by definition you are defeating the holistic nature of the system. And do not make the mistake of dismissing this material because you do not yet know where this material is already in effect. That few parishes you know, if any, operate in this manner is simply observing how things are in PMO—*not how things should be.*

CHAPTER 41

TO SHARE OR NOT TO SHARE

Now that we have a written PMO Statement of Culture, do we share it with all employees and volunteers? Or asked another way: who is the Statement of Culture primarily written for?

There are two schools of thought here:

A. Share the PMO Statement of Culture with employees and volunteers.

B. Do not share the PMO Statement of Culture with employees and volunteers; it was only written for its writer.

I fall firmly into the latter, B. school of thought for two reasons. Why?

1. It is very difficult—to the point of being not worth trying—to "explain" such a statement to every employee and volunteer. More specifically, we are talking about explaining the Statement of Culture to every temperament of employee and volunteer—and I can tell you in advance that is a 99% lose-lose proposition with this particular employee-volunteer cadre. This is a mountain I have no intention of climbing when I know in advance there are people, perhaps most people, who work and volunteer in PMO who do not understand business principles, *do not even want to understand business principles, as this is a core reason why they do not work in business*, have not had the benefit of reading this book. Such inherited employees and volunteers never will understand—much less

accept—the application of business principles in a Church environment. No thanks; I'm not going there.

2. See #1.

As such, in light of the above it is a fair question to ask:

If you are not going to share the PMO Statement of Culture, *why was it created in the first place?*

Now we have dug beneath the topsoil and reached the bedrock of culture creation and maintenance: the primary, and in my management world, the only reason the PMO Statement of Culture exists, is for *my* benefit as the PMO administrator, to keep *my* head on straight, to be *my* execution roadmap and touchstone, to guide *my* actions and to motivate *me* so that I personally model to everyone the behavior that the Statement of Culture describes and enshrines.

Please understand that words on paper are pretty much useless in the context we are discussing, that being the killing of a broken culture and installing a new culture. How so?

> *Killing your broken culture and installing a new culture is not akin to a contract. It is not a legal construct. It is a process. Culture building is not something that so much lends itself to being understood by reading about it as it lends itself to being understood by seeing the process in action via your daily personal demonstration.*

And who does the demonstrating of this new, correct culture? Who provides the action imagery that dynamically illustrates the correct culture? Who maintains the correct culture once it is enshrined? *The PMO administrator, not a piece of paper signed for the file.*

But you might say, "Why not both? Why can't I publish the PMO Statement of Culture for everyone, and also demonstrate it?"

TO SHARE OR NOT TO SHARE

Be my guest, but I know human nature and there are two problems with this approach:

1. It denies the truth and wisdom embedded in point number one above, which fundamentally renders it a non-starter, and;
2. It greases the skids for PMO administrators inclined by their own temperament to avoid necessary confrontation with failing employees and volunteers, by thinking that since employees have "prior knowledge in writing of what we are seeking in terms of job performance, etc.," another mere tacked-up, emailed, written word posting will be what you choose to lean on to build your new culture—instead of the only thing you should be leaning on: *your daily personal example of actually living and modeling the correct culture.* Remember:

> *The correct culture is installed from the top down, not the bottom up.*

Unless and until you are in a position that allows you to demonstrate the pieces of the correct culture face-to-face—not remotely via endless nanny, nuisance phone calls and/or emails—you will never appreciate much less fully understand *the singular power of what happens when employees observe their boss demonstrating in person what is meant by "working under the correct culture."* No piece of paper will ever come remotely close to this effect, so much so as to render publishing such a statement not worth all the derivative misunderstandings and problems publishing it will cause. As such, I am not publishing the PMO Statement of Culture. So, why was it written? It was written for my benefit alone; to keep my PMO administrator compass pointed in the right direction at all times, to keep my eye on the performance ball. *It was written as a promise to myself and as a permanent reminder: I will not skip this step.*

Eventually, gradually, after years not months, the behaviors that define and embody what we label as "the correct culture" will simply become a part of who you are, weaved into the fabric of you as a person—even beyond and outside of a PMO context. Only when you are living the correct culture because you do not know any other way, *only then* can you dispense with the step of writing such a statement in the first place, implicitly knowing that your actions always personify "the correct culture" in everything you do. But until that day arrives, you must write and subsequently live a Statement of Culture as further supported by enhanced language you have added to the parish mission statement. It is in this manner and for these reasons that I advise you to implement the PMO Statement of Culture—*but for your eyes only.*

The bottom line is this: as the PMO administrator, yes, you must create a culture statement in writing—but you do not have to publically share it. *You just have to live it and teach it and adhere to it*, whereby *you* define—not the employees and volunteers who come and go who work for/with you—precisely what defines and animates your PMO culture. As has already been made clear: as the culture goes, *so goes any organization*. All employee and volunteer performance, *or the lack thereof*, can be traced to your organizational culture, and the PMO culture creation, installation, and modeling starts with the person at the top of the PMO Org Chart.

In the revolving carousel world of constantly changing PMO personnel, *superior PMO service consistency and stability is maintained and sustained by the invisible hand of the correct culture.* This is a beautiful thing, once achieved. Until then, it is brutally hard work. What do you want?

Make your choice.

CHAPTER 42

WHY PLAN?

What do you want to achieve or avoid? The answers to this question are <u>objectives</u>. How will you go about achieving your desired results? The answer to this you can call <u>strategy</u>.
—*William E. Rothschild*

We have three pillars to our PMO foundation:

1. An enhanced Mission Statement that includes language publically promising our community superior PMO.
2. Knowledge that the "want" (aka: desire) to know, love, and serve God is *already* imbued by our Creator in every soul, and our job in PMO is to *discover and remove the suppression of want*.
3. Everything we do as the PMO administrator is animated and supported by our Statement of Culture, which itself is supported into existence by an enhanced addition to our Mission Statement language.

What's next? *We need the vision of what we want to be transcribed into a written strategic plan of action.* How do we accomplish this? The wise PMO administrator borrows proven and time-tested business tools that can be applied in PMO. One such principle and tool: *strategic planning* and its byproduct, *the written strategic plan.*

The reasoning animating this planning principle is succinctly (and classically) stated by the late Sen. Fred Thompson acting in his role as U.S. Navy Admiral Painter in the movie *The Hunt for Red October*. It is only nine words in length, but contains ninety years of wisdom:

Russians don't take a dump without a plan, son.

Oh. I guess planning is pretty important.

Must we be agile thinkers who understand the "Why?" animating the "How?" Yes, but just because we are agile thinkers able to hit the curveball, *that doesn't mean we can ignore all planning*. On the contrary:

If you fail to plan, you are planning to fail!
—Benjamin Franklin

We have been discussing facets of PMO that will, upon your arrival at your parish assignment—unless you are extremely lucky—require your immediate attention as an administrator. But where do you start?

You start where your strategic plan tells you to start.

What does that statement tell you? You must follow your written—*I must stress written*—strategic plan. You cannot take any substantial action in PMO—other than putting out immediate fires—*unless and until you have first created a PMO strategic plan*. In the same manner you just heard, "Russians don't take a dump without a plan, son," *you do not make any substantial PMO decisions or moves without first having created a written PMO strategic plan.*

Oh. Wait. Does that mean that unless and until I have in hand a written strategic plan, all my days as the PMO administrator—in other words forever—consist of putting out random fires, handling emergencies, and continuing on with the brokenness I most likely inherited?

Yes.

But what if you claim you don't have the time to create the PMO strategic

WHY PLAN?

plan? Well, I guess you better find the time *because you can't go any further in building and delivering superior PMO without one.* Wait. Let me rephrase: you could press forward without a written strategic plan, but that would be like living in a world of, "Ready, fire, aim!" If you were starting your own business my advice to you would be the same, but there is one key difference: unlike starting your own business without a plan and driving yourself over a cliff, *you don't have the right as the PMO administrator to operate in a parish without a strategic plan and drive your parishioners, PMO employees, and volunteers over a cliff.*

Therefore, when beginning your work as the newly minted PMO administrator, patience is paramount. It is critical you do not do anything substantial in/with/to PMO without first creating your strategic plan, which becomes the requisite blueprint that you will follow to address the who, what, when, where, why, and how of what must be done in "all things PMO." By following a strategic plan—*a written plan not simply a "plan" in your head*—the plan will lead your PMO improvements precisely where you want your PMO to go, provided your plan is correct *and you can execute* under the correct culture (a discussion on execution follows). But suffice it to say:

1. To merely have a strategic plan in hand is not enough, and;
2. To operate without a strategic plan, which is to say to operate without a blueprint, is as we have already stated unwise, not advised, and affords you only a 1 in 360° lucky chance of directing you where you not only need to be, but must be, in order to provide superior PMO services. That's right, luck can play a role in success. Do some parishes get lucky? Yes, but is luck what you want to rely on? No, or at least I don't. Therefore, you need a written strategic plan.

You've got to eat while you dream. You've got to deliver on short-range commitments, while you develop a long-range

strategy and vision and implement it. The success of doing both. Walking and chewing gum if you will. Getting it done in the short-range, and delivering a long-range plan, and executing on that.

—*Jack Welch*

It does not matter how dysfunctional you may find the state of PMO upon your arrival. Short of putting out the most obvious fires that cannot be ignored, *you do not touch anything until you finish your PMO strategic plan.* This point is paramount. The good news? The creation of a strategic plan in a PMO context is not as daunting as it may sound. But if you start tinkering with PMO without the benefit of a well-crafted strategic plan, you will at best just be reshuffling the mess you inherited, for a newer mess of your own creation. Why? Because broken PMO is always a *holistic problem solved via a holistic solution,* not a "If I just fix these one or two problems over here, then everything will be great!" type of problem. That is not the nature of why broken PMO exists in the first place, or how you go about fixing broken PMO.

If you do not have a holistic system solution at your fingertips guided by a strategic plan, by definition you cannot solve a holistic problem. Implementing piecemeal, catch-as-catch-can Band-Aid fixes do not truly solve PMO problems. In all likelihood, piecemeal fixes will only make matters worse. Why? Because every Band-Aid fix simply changes the current problems' DNA and now masks the morphing of a new problem of your own creation lurking beneath the surface. In other words, you create new problems with piecemeal solutions. Therefore:

If creating a strategic plan is mandatory before taking action and making improvements, *upon your arrival you must acknowledge that time is of the essence.* If you habitually push the creation, delegation, or completion of the PMO strategic plan to the backburner, chronic mediocrity—or worse—is the implicit byproduct of your decision to defer or delay. It is one thing to prioritize your other duties above creating your PMO strategic plan on an as-needed fire prevention basis. It is one thing to have your PMO administrator time siphoned away by unforeseen emergencies. But it is a guaranteed recipe for failure to consistently ignore creating the strategic plan because you conjure up any and every *excuse* to avoid this administrator duty. You do not have to like this task—*you just have to do it.*

Further note you will also waste the honeymoon effect and associated goodwill, the obligatory "new guy" margin for error vested in you by PMO paid staff and volunteers upon your arrival. Employees and volunteers will initially give you as the new guy the benefit of the doubt that you know what you are doing—until you prove that you really do not have a clue what you are doing, you are shooting from the hip, and you eventually have to start walking back your piecemeal implementation of "ideas" and "solutions." Why? *Because piecemeal idea implementation cannot resolve holistic and systemic problems. Holistic and systemic problems demand a holistic solution, and a holistic solution demands a holistic system approach to PMO as is being presented herein.* Here you are being provided the DNA of a holistic system and approach, but do not pick and choose from this system. Why?

Because there is no such thing as a little change to DNA.

We must also recognize that simply creating a poorly-crafted strategic plan for the sake of having a strategic plan "for our files," is just a waste of time and ensures absolutely nothing except that as you are making your PMO mistakes, you are at least following some written plan while you make them. Again, to have a strategic plan just for the sake of, "I must have a written plan to follow" is not the lesson or message here. What is the lesson and message here? You must craft a *brilliant PMO strategic plan* that is based on ideas and principles known to do what? *Produce superior results. Produce great and abundant fruit.*

Any plan created for the sake of checking a to-do list box just to have a plan at all, *will not do*. It is only with a *brilliant PMO strategic plan in hand* that you begin to tackle what must be done. Thus, your challenge is straightforward: *create or commission a brilliant PMO strategic plan—not just any plan—as soon as possible. Then—and only then—can you progress forward toward offering superior PMO services.*

CHAPTER 43

PMO STRATEGIC PLAN SCIENCE

> **Strategy without tactics is the slowest route to victory. Tactics without strategy is the noise before defeat.**
> —*Sun Tzu*

Perhaps you are thinking that if the strategic plan is as crucial to building superior PMO as has been explained above, and the Church certainly desires superior PMO, there must be something already in existence—some PMO strategic planning roadmap already created so you do not have to reinvent the wheel and start from scratch. Well, you are correct—*but only up to a certain point.*

The good news: yes, there are adaptable strategic planning tools currently available to you, flexible tools that will help you build a plan to address the precise PMO needs where you are. You will have to customize the basic PMO strategic plan outline to fit your exact scenario, but you do have access to tools that will assist you in the analysis and creation process. However, what you must also know is precisely, tactically, *how and why* to apply these strategic planning/helper tools within your parish. *No wise craftsman picks up a tool he does not yet know how and why to deploy for the job at hand.* As such, a word of caution:

Basic human nature dictates that due to a lack of familiarity and prior knowledge, *you will inevitably shy away from some very useful strategic planning tools because you have no prior experience with them.* This is precisely why those charged with PMO do not embrace strategic planning and create a strategic plan in the first place—they often have no idea what to do, and they have no prior experience with the tools of the trade.

This temptation to skip strategic planning is especially true when inheriting an existing but dysfunctional PMO operation—who has time for "strategic planning"? Or to borrow from the film *The Treasure of Sierra Madre*, "Hey! PMO already exists and is running here—what do we need a strategic plan for? Plan??? We ain't got no plan (badges)! We don't need no plan (badges)! I don't have to show you any stinking plan (badges)!" Such folks blithely proceed without a plan and achieve predictably poor results, unless and until blind luck intervenes, at which point something even worse happens: the people may be misled into believing they actually know what they are doing. Thus, PMO administrators arrive at new assignments and choose to either Band-Aid fix problems or just bumble along doing things the way they inherited them, the way things have always been done—with predictably, chronically, and perpetually poor results.

Note that strategic planning *tools* and strategic planning *knowledge* are two distinct components to solving broken and underperforming PMO. How so? Imagine a carpenter's toolbox, or the many rollaway drawers of a mechanic's tool chest filled with their respective tools of the trade. Imagine a hammer, for example. A hammer may require varying the applied force to properly use in some situations, but that's it; not much if any formal training is required. And further note if one can't really figure out how to accurately swing a hammer…*the hammer has a way of providing the user with some immediate and painful feedback.* The inept hammer-swinger learns, and learns quickly from his or her mistakes.

But what about some of the other tools in our imagined toolboxes, such as a carpenter's square or the mechanic's micrometer? Do we just hand someone either one of these tools and tell him to get crackin'? No. Could you simply get to work building a spiral staircase or rebuilding an engine without initial training? No, not likely. Would you know how to use a mariner's sextet just by looking at it? No, not likely. Training on the tools of your trade is a precursor to using any tool for the purpose intended.

And so it is the same for us: we must learn more about the strategic planning tools before we can use these tools to create or improve anything—*but that does not infer learning such tools are difficult.* The good news is we have adaptable and straightforward PMO strategic planning tools, which are really roadmaps meant to help us organize our thinking and put our thoughts in writing, made available to us from various sources. To highlight two of those strategic planning tool resources:

1. Visit the United States Conference of Catholic Bishops (USCCB) and the Catholic Standards for Excellence website. Word search "strategic planning."
2. The Catholic Standards for Excellence Leadership Roundtable. The Catholic Standards for Excellence Leadership Roundtable (TLR) website states the following regarding their mission and organization:

> The National Leadership Roundtable on Church Management is an organization of laity, religious, and clergy working together to promote excellence and best practices in the management, finances, and human resource development of the Catholic Church in the U.S. through the greater incorporation of the expertise of the laity. We are a Catholic 501(c)(3) nonprofit organization that brings together leaders from the worlds of business, finance, academia, philanthropy, nonprofit organizations, and the Church to serve the Catholic Church in the United States.

The Leadership Roundtable serves the Church through our Standards for Excellence program; ChurchEpedia, our collection of best practices; and consultancy services, which have assisted several archdioceses, dioceses, and religious communities across the country.

In particular, TLR has some very useful strategic planning tools for PMO administrators, labeled as "Education Resource Packets" in TLR website parlance. These planning tools cover a wide range of PMO and strategic planning topics. To be able to download these tools simply register with the TLR website. Topics include:

1. Developing and Revising the Mission Statement for Catholic Parishes
2. Ministry Program Evaluation for Catholic Parishes
3. Ministry Program Service for Catholic Parishes
4. Ongoing Planning by Advisory Bodies for Catholic Parishes
5. Compensation and Employee Evaluation for Catholic Parishes
6. Advisory Bodies' Composition for Catholic Parishes
7. Conduct of Advisory Bodies for Catholic Parishes
8. Conflict of Interest for Catholic Parishes
9. Personnel Policies and Employee Orientation for Catholic Parishes
9A. Model Handbook for Catholic Parishes
10. Volunteer Policies for Catholic Parishes
11. Financial Planning and Monitoring for Catholic Parishes
11A. Financial Planning and Monitoring for Catholic Parishes Supplement
12. Reporting Financial Improprieties for Catholic Parishes
13. Financial Policies for Catholic Parishes
14. Legal Compliance Checklist for Catholic Parishes
15. Legal Compliance—Liability Issues for Catholic Parishes

16. Openness for Catholic Parishes
17. Fundraising Costs for Catholic Parishes
18. Fundraising Practices for Catholic Parishes
19. Solicitation and Acceptance of Gifts for Catholic Parishes
20. Employment of Fundraising Personnel and Engagement of Fundraising Consultants for Catholic Parishes
21. Public Policy Advocacy Promoting Public Participation for Catholic Parishes
22. Efforts to Educate the Public for Catholic Parishes
23. Implementation of the USCCB Charter for the Protection of Children and Young People for Parishes
23A. Parish Charter Implementation Supplemental Resource Packet
24. Information Technology Planning for Parishes

Through the TLR website you now have access to one source—but not the only source—of PMO strategic planning tools and information. There are many other sources of information written specifically for business use, but with little to no change required are equally useful in PMO; simply word search "sample strategic plans" or similar phrases. But what remains to be addressed are the two challenges mentioned above:

1. Where do you start the PMO strategic planning process?
2. How do you use the various strategic planning tools?

CHAPTER 44

OBSERVE, QUESTION, LISTEN THROUGH THE CULTURE LENS

Plans are only good intentions unless they immediately degenerate into hard work.

—*Peter Drucker*

Be it large or small or somewhere in between, you will have some administrator role upon arrival at your assignment. Something, someone, and/or some group will report to you. The results they produce—or lack thereof—are by definition ultimately your personal responsibility. However, you must resist the tendency, resist the desire upon arrival to live the cliché, "Let's roll up our sleeves and get to work!" Why? *Because you are not ready for that step yet.*

Aside from putting out random emergency fires as mentioned above, you have only to *make the time* to complete the following step-by-step tasks to begin the strategic plan creation process. Building your strategic plan is a step-by-step process, detailed for you here. Follow these steps:

Step 1. *Keenly observe* everyone who reports to you as they go about doing their job(s) *operating in and under the present culture*. That's all, just observe, but note: *the culture that preexists your arrival is the culture animating everything that you see—or don't see that you should*. That means physically observe people at work, doing their job—but not like a mindless camera. You must "observe, question, and listen" specifically through this exacting PMO culture-building lens:

*You do not simply observe and process things as they are like a mindless camera. You always see, intake, and mentally process things as they are in relation to who, what, where, when, why, and how **things should be**. We do not look at where we are in relation to where we started. We look at where we are **in relation to where we should be**. This is your intake measurement yardstick, and no other. You observe and process what you observe through this mental intake lens.*

What are the practical effects of observing in this manner? Think of it this way: when you grind beef, *why would you expect pork to exit the grinder?* What goes in is fundamentally, what must come out. Therefore: if you observe work being performed in a mediocre fashion, *why would you expect anything better than mediocre service to parishioners?* In other words, you are not simply observing that something is done—*you are observing and asking yourself if whatever you see being done is being done* in the most superior way. However:

If your standard for PMO performance is merely mediocrity, or if you really have no standard of measurement, or if mediocrity is allowed to become your PMO target, if by commission of error or omission of duty through default you select "mediocrity" as your cultural "how things should be" observation lens, *then mediocrity—not superior performance—is what you will install everywhere you go.*

The notion that you observe personnel at work and subsequently insert into your strategic plan that, "more training" or any other pithy job performance bromide is required, *is absolute nonsense.* Mediocrity is not erased solely by "more training." The lifeblood of mediocrity is an apathetic and/or incompetent PMO administrator onsite, pumped daily through all employees and volunteers working in a broken culture as personified by the person nominally in charge. If

OBSERVE, QUESTION, LISTEN THROUGH THE CULTURE LENS

you do not break this cycle by starting your journey toward superior PMO as an educated and informed observer with a critical eye for detail, who will?

Likewise, if your mental observation lens is set to a higher performance standard, *you will necessarily install and instill that higher standard in your PMO culture via your strategic plan creation, content, and implementation.* This correlation is absolute; it can be no other way. This is why there is no such thing as participating in a generic form of "observation." *All observation is done through some cultural lens, whether or not the observer and the observed are conscious of their lens selection choices.*

During this critical observation phase/step, the PMO administrator is observing employees and volunteers through, hopefully, their own correct culture lens held in their mind as defined via their Statement of Culture, which is supported by their correctly formed and enhanced mission statement language. Further note the reciprocal is true: the employee or volunteer will *view the observing PMO administrator* also through the correct culture lens—eventually, but not upon your arrival. Therefore:

It is when we have a mismatch in culture lens choices that we have problems—and this is precisely where you are at this point when you inherit broken PMO. *You know* the culture you want, *but the employees and volunteers do not yet know the culture you want.* That's the bad news. The good news? Given this reality, *simply choose a higher standard—superior, and you will attain the superior standard—provided you can model and execute by personally demonstrating this standard to others.*

Do you see this simple but profound truth that begins with intelligent and informed observation?

> **Choose a higher standard—superior, and you will attain the superior standard—provided you can model and execute.**

Most employees and volunteers—but sadly not all—*intrinsically desire to do their job the way the boss wants the job to be done*. The catch? In the absence of clearly knowing what the boss wants, *each employee or volunteer is free to define what "superior performance" means, which is another way of saying that each employee is free to define the organization's culture*. This is the basic recipe for mediocrity in PMO, or worse. However:

What can be said with 100% certainty is that if you observe those who report to you while in a state of mental oblivion and through the wrong culture lens, or in naïve state of mind, or in apathy, you have failed. *To properly build a strategic plan you must begin with keenly observing through the correct cultural lens, which to stress again is*:

> *You do not simply see things as they are, you see things as they are in relation to who, what, where, when, why, and how **<u>things should be</u>**. We do not look at where we are in relation to where we started. We look at where we are **<u>in relation to where we should be</u>**. This is your intake measurement yardstick. This is the beginning of the raw data collection process, data that feeds the creation of the PMO strategic plan.*

Make no mistake here, you will most likely find yourself in a PMO turnaround situation, or in other words, things will not be superior upon your arrival. You will have much work to do. I can tell you in advance, applying the above performance intake measurement yardstick will be new to most people, if not all people who report to you. People have been led to believe—incorrectly, by those before your arrival—that in so many words their backward historical reflections somehow matter, all while heartily backslapping each other: "Look! Look! Look how far we have come! Isn't it wonderful! Great job!" I point this out because such rearview mirror thinking, although perhaps formed innocently enough, is an obstacle you must anticipate and overcome. Certainly, for the purposes of discussing *individual* employee performance as part of a salary and job performance review, acknowledging the progress an employee has made is mandatory. But for the purposes of observing and measuring *collective and overall* departmental PMO progress, this "look how far we have come" measurement yardstick is a gravely flawed and useless yardstick. Organizationally speaking, *nobody cares how far you have come from where you have started— what matters is where you are in relation to where you should be*. When you can look at where you are and know that where you are is where you should be, *then you can celebrate*. Otherwise, on to your next integral step:

Step 2. *Question.* As necessary while you are observing people working through the correct culture lens, collect data for your strategic plan by *asking questions* of anyone who reports to you—especially any "Why?" formatted questions. For example: "Why do you do _____ that way?" You must ask a question any time you do not understand (or perhaps think you understand but still want to check yourself) the who, what, where, why, when, or how of anything or anyone who reports to you. Assume nothing, especially as in: do not assume you understand anything if there exists the slightest possibility you may not understand. When in doubt, ask questions. However, this is paramount: *at this data collection stage offer no comment, feedback, or criticism of the answers you receive*. Poker face at all times. Reveal nothing. Just listen and appear to accept whatever you are told. Why? Because employees and volunteers tend to *extrapolate and speculate toward the negative*, and all such speculation does is fire-up the internal rumor mill, spreading needless trauma throughout the organization. Other than putting out immediate fires, you are not ready at this time to answer any questions, and you must decline and defer to answer questions posed to you at this stage (other than common sense, must-know-now questions i.e. "What time do I start work? Is tomorrow a holiday? etc."). At this stage you observe, you question, you listen, you gather answers and information to be used to guide the creation of your strategic plan—but you do not at this step fix or replace or teach anything except to address the most glaring brokenness. Why? Because you are not ready? Why? *Because you don't yet have a written strategic plan to guide you. You are in the process of building a plan at this time, and building the plan starts with acquiring information through observation and questioning.*

Also, you must take notes as you ask questions. *Do not rely on your memory.* You can either write notes as you make your observations and ask questions, or you can write your notes immediately afterward—*but either way you must document this PMO information collection and observation process.* Why? First and foremost, you are creating a picture of *what is*. You need the *exact* answers as they are given to you in order to analyze what to address when creating your PMO strategic plan. And if you want to discuss anything with a colleague you also need more than foggy recollections—*you need accuracy and precision in the collected information.*

But there is also another important reason to document as a habit of PMO administration: *documentation is the precursor ingredient to employee or volunteer praising, salary increases, terminating employment, or dismissing a volunteer.* Most critically note: no documentation, no termination—*and why in the world would we want to allow a personnel file void of the truth inhibit terminating an employee who is not a fit?* (More on this important topic in the chapters on hiring and firing.) Therefore, you must learn the habit of personnel documentation when any personnel report to you on the Org Chart. Again, you do not have to like the process—*you just have to do it.*

Step 3. *Listen.* Listen to the answers you receive from paid staff and volunteers, and as you listen, *listen intently for coherent, defensible, efficient, and logical answers.* Specifically, when you ask "Why _____?" something is done in a particular way—and you must ask this question even if you know or think you know the answer, *be especially attuned to answers that amount to*, "I'm not sure why we do it that way," and the wildly popular but terribly flawed, *"We do it that way because that's the way we've always done it here."* Nothing will anchor and condemn you more firmly to mediocrity in life than, *"We do it that way because that's the way we have always done it."* That answer is as corrosive to the speaker as it is stupid for the receiver to live perpetually under.

> **What's the use of running if you are not on the right road.**
> —*German proverb*

Further note you cannot observe PMO, form questions based on what you observe, ask your questions, and then "listen intently" to the answers...*with your cell phone ringing and an assortment of other distractions and interruptions pulling your mind and body in various other directions.* If you are going to do your PMO administrator job well, when you are wearing your PMO administrator hat you must give it your full and undivided attention or you are wasting your time and everyone else's. This is most especially true during the three discovery steps described above. Success at this stage is not about spending an inordinate amount of time on this task, it's about intense concentration and a laser focus on discovering exactly what you have in PMO—the good, the bad, and the ugly—while completing this task. Fighting through an assortment of distractions that can literally and figuratively be controlled via an "On/Off" switch makes no sense. Respect the importance of these tasks by giving them the undivided attention and focus they deserve.

To recap: 1. Observe. **2.** Ask Questions. **3.** Listen. **4.** Document. **5.** Analyze. But how do you analyze this fruit of your work, the collected information?

CHAPTER 45

THE GOOD, THE BAD, THE UGLY: ORGANIZE AND PRIORITIZE

> **Following the rules of your industry will only get you so far.**
> —*Max McKeown*

After completing the above steps for everyone and everything in PMO who reports to you as the administrator, *it is now time for you to organize and prioritize the information you have collected for input into your strategic plan.* How do you do this? You start by separating the data into three self-categorizing containers labeled with the self-explanatory, simple, but powerful nomenclature: The Good News, The Bad News, and The Ugly News.

The Good News

When viewed through the correct cultural lens of "Superior," what did you discover that is already truly superior in the PMO performance realm? For whatever and whoever reports to you, what/who did you discover that is already superior upon your arrival? Create a written list of your findings under "The Good" heading *knowing that whatever you include on this list will not be addressed in your PMO strategic plan.* But also further note:

How can you possibly know "The Good" if you don't personally kick the PMO tires? And even if you have a thorough look, *how can you interpret what you discover if you don't already know what the texture of truly superior PMO performance looks like?* This appears to be a Catch-22 situation: you will know something when you see it, but how will you recognize what you are looking for if you have never seen it before? Thus, once again we return to the paramount importance of organizational culture, as it is only by observing through the mental lens of an *imagined* superior culture—*in other words what you should expect to see in performance and not necessarily what you do see*—that we can detect brokenness and install a superior culture wherever we go.

And why do we bother with this process? *As always, so that we can serve greatly those we are called to serve.* If something were worth doing at all, why wouldn't it be worth doing in a superior way? Are the barriers to superior performance too tough and too high for you to overcome? No. Never. You will come to realize and understand, if you do not already, that simply adjusting employee and volunteer *attitudes* more often than not fully bridges the performance gap between mediocrity and superior performance. It does not take more money, more equipment, more manpower, etc., it just takes training and an attitude adjustment. *As the PMO administrator you will provide both via installing the correct culture.*

Attitude is often the only difference standing between mediocrity and greatness. But attitude adjustments can become confrontational, difficult, challenging, and it is for these predictable reasons many administrators shun their duty and choose to wallow in mediocrity—and gut-wrenching personal frustration, for which they only have themselves to blame. This is how strong the influence of the gene that causes a man or woman to avoid even the possibility of confrontation. They would rather wallow in brokenness and mediocrity than do what it takes to serve the parishioner (or customer in the secular world) in a superior way. It is not that they do not know what is broken or how to fix it—*it is that they rationalize a reason to refuse to pay the personal toll to fix it.*

And if and when your attitude adjustment efforts fail to improve someone's performance, then what happens? What now? Are you condemned to mediocrity because those who report to you are unwilling and/or unable to change, to improve? No. (More on addressing this elephant in the room in the chapters on hiring and firing.) Now, after The Good you must face:

The Bad News

The title is self-explanatory: pull from your notes and list all the bad you discovered through your observing, questioning, and listening. You must list everything, whether or not you have the immediate resources at hand to do anything about the problem. Separate your Bad News items and place them under the following PMO topical categories as listed below in **bold**.

To assist you in this process I have included some hypothetical reasons to list items in each category based upon your PMO observations and employee/volunteer questions. Also note how the following topical categories can also serve as your personal guide to what PMO conditions to observe, and what questions to ask employees and volunteers. Listed alphabetically:

Equipment: broken, outdated, hazardous, insufficient quantity and/or type

Facilities: crumbling infrastructure; carpet, flooring, fencing, walls, gardening, statues, roof, parking lot surface, lighting, church sound system, painting, heating, plumbing, air conditioning, pews, kneelers, organ, alarm, door security

Financial: no/low cash reserves, unstable monthly cash flow, low collections in relation to size of registered parishioner base, Mass collections not safely and/or securely handled, no financial reporting formatting standards, no firm financial report due dates, no daily at-a-glance administrator financial summary, insufficient accounting software, unreliable providers or sources of critical information

Management: no parish Org Chart and/or no PMO Org Chart, no parish business manager, lack of management presence, lack of leadership, job performance standards set by each person rather than management, no/low energy

Marketing (aka: revelation of want): little/no marketing and promotion of parish ministries, retreats, website, etc., little/no social media presence, little/no understanding of basic marketing principles by PMO decision makers and ministry leaders, overall marketing is misunderstood, decision makers confused that marketing is even in any way applicable to PMO duties, no marketing budget, no ideas, no/low energy

Personnel: overstaffed, understaffed, overpaid, underpaid, untrained, undertrained, no written job descriptions for every employee and/or volunteer position, low morale, no Org Chart, no personal accountability, no formal job performance review process, no formal employment termination process, no hiring methodology, no understanding of how to interview employees, volunteers, and/or vendors, multi-cultural overrepresentation, multi-cultural underrepresentation, insufficient number of ministry volunteers, unorthodox youth ministry activities, use of unapproved and/or unsound teaching materials

Physical plant operations: nobody in charge of physical plant maintenance, current plant maintenance personnel untrained, undertrained, and/or unqualified, personnel do not know the scope of their job, no written preventative maintenance schedule for all equipment, no budget for equipment preventative maintenance, no forecasted replacement dates and costs for all major equipment, safety hazards present

Organizational: no or outdated Org Chart, too few ministries in relation to the number of potential ministries, open ministry leadership positions, untrained and/or unqualified ministry leaders, dormant ministries, abandoned ministries, open seats on parish council, no finance council, open seats on finance council

Reporting: little/no formal reporting structure, little/no reporting input data collection, little/no administrative support reports, no routing tree for report distribution, no timeline for report delivery, incomplete and/or inaccurate personnel files

THE GOOD, THE BAD, THE UGLY: ORGANIZE AND PRIORITIZE

Training: little/no job training of employee and/or volunteer personnel, no one known to be responsible for training, no time allotted for training, training not formally acknowledged and/or recognized as a need in PMO

Technology: broken computers, outdated computers, outdated phone system, outdated parish server hardware and/or software, outdated anti-virus/malware protection, frequent system crashes, no scheduled backups, poor understanding of software, poor website design, poor ISP service, poor system maintenance, lack of procedures

How do you think you are going to discover the above if not by keen observation, questioning, and listening? *Are you going to make the fatal mistake of not checking and feed pure assumption or hearsay masquerading as factual data into your strategic plan?* Or assuming that because where you have been assigned has been in existence for ten, twenty, fifty or more years, all of the above must certainly have been sorted out by now? Do not fall into these traps. Follow the above guidance. Give yourself a *reasonable but not excessive timeframe* (i.e. weeks, *not months*) to discover answers to whatever PMO area(s) report to you, and only then proceed to the next step of actually writing your strategic plan.

The Ugly News

From all your items listed under THE BAD you must now create a high-priority sub-list of, THE UGLY. What is "THE UGLY," and why do you need this separate list?

Note something has to drive the priority for taking action for whatever is listed in your strategic plan. THE UGLY are those items on THE BAD list that you deem *cannot wait another minute to be addressed*. Yes, you are going to address everything on THE BAD list within your strategic plan as soon as possible, *but not all problems are created equal. Some problems will give you far more grief than others. Your top priority items are THE UGLY items.*

You will notice there are going to be some items that are not only killing you today, but you will never improve your PMO—which is to say you will never serve the people you are called to serve in the superior manner they should be served, unless and until the items on THE UGLY list are successfully addressed. *Therefore, items on THE UGLY list are what drive the prioritization of all the items ultimately to be addressed by your PMO strategic plan.* Side note: better finish creating THE UGLY list ASAP so you can then move on to creating the strategic plan that will address these issues.

THE UGLY are the items that provide critical shaping direction to your strategic planning as to what you should address first, second, third, etc. In other words, you address the most ugly item first, etc. The key to a well-crafted strategic plan will be found in the comprehensive strategy that drives the plan, and in part, the strategy you deploy is derived from answering precisely this question: from the universe of all THE UGLY and THE BAD items you must address, *now animated by your Statement of Culture, precisely which items and in what order will you address them?*

This decision is not something left unanswered or left to chance. Indeed, there are two words for working hard but without factoring in the *priority* of the work to be done: chaos and stupid. There must always be a conscious and deliberate hierarchy and prioritization applied to any work you do, and at your discretion that prioritization of work may be a collaborative effort, but note this well: *you are absolutely not obliged to take on tasks in the order they are presented or suggested to you by others.*

> **Any change is resisted because bureaucrats have a vested interest in the chaos in which they exist.**
>
> —*Richard M. Nixon*

Speaking of those administrators who master this work prioritization task

THE GOOD, THE BAD, THE UGLY: ORGANIZE AND PRIORITIZE

the best, how is it they are able to do so? It is because the best PMO administrators are able to view PMO services not from their perspective as administrators, *but from the perspective of the consumer-parishioner, the perspective of the soul who is on the receiving end of each service.* Thus we see in the world at-large:

An average administrator is mainly concerned with whether or not the trains run on time, *without giving much if any consideration to the actual experience of riding the train.* But superior administrators step outside of themselves and imagine what it would feel like to ride an on time PMO train, but can't because of receiving such poor PMO service from each and every item on THE UGLY list. *Superior administrators mentally ride on the parishioner's train; they imagine the experience of being on the receiving end of poor service.*

From this emotional, introspective, and sadness-filled point of view the superior PMO administrator determines—and notice this effort is more art than science—which item(s) in an informed opinion inflicts the most unwarranted and unnecessary anxiety, disappointment, pain, punishment, and/or suffering upon the parish/parishioner. For example, *they share the pain of the spouse when a request for a Mass on the anniversary of a spouse's death was lost or forgotten.*

CHAPTER 46

HOW THE UGLY DRIVES STRATEGIC PLANNING WORK PRIORITIZATION

Perhaps a specific aspect of your parish office organization becomes a strong candidate to be addressed first in the strategic plan, or perhaps facilities management, or perhaps, etc., etc. Only you will know precisely which items fall into THE BAD, and subsequently are deemed to be so bad as to qualify for placement on THE UGLY sub-list category. Specific details will necessarily vary from parish to parish. But to provide you with a working mental framework for your strategic planning order of work/prioritization:

The following list has been copied from the above hypothetical list of THE BAD broken and dysfunctional items that you discovered. At this point the question we must answer as we start to build our PMO strategic plan is: which of these items fall into THE UGLY, the *"I cannot wait another minute to address this issue"* classification, and which items can wait as lower priority problems to solve? How do you make this decision? Pay particular attention to which items are to be immediately addressed when you execute your strategic plan, and the rationale animating why they are addressed in the priority 1, 2, 3, etc., order given below. Actually fixing what is broken is the science of PMO—but the *discretionary ordering* of what to do first, second, third, etc., *this is practicing the art of PMO.*

Equipment: broken, outdated, hazardous, insufficient quantity and/or type

Judgment: Bad, but not Ugly. With the exception of anything deemed hazardous, do not address at highest strategic planning priority.

Facilities: crumbling infrastructure; carpet, flooring, fencing, walls, gardening, statues, roof, parking lot surface, lighting, church sound system, painting, heating, plumbing, air conditioning, pews, kneelers, organ, alarm, door security

Judgment: Bad, but not Ugly. Do not address at highest strategic planning priority (but for the exception of unsatisfactory door security on the Church, Adoration Chapel, and/or Rectory).

Financial: no/low cash reserves, unstable monthly cash flow, low weekly collections in relation to size of registered parishioner base, Mass collections not safely and/or securely handled, questionable financial reporting, no report formatting standards, no firm financial report due dates, no daily at-a-glance administrator financial summary, insufficient accounting software

Judgment: The creation of a daily at-a-glance financial summary must be addressed in your strategic plan as **Priority #2**. You must know—immediately know each day—the financial state of the parish, but note you do not need to solve every accounting-related problem to receive this basic financial information.

Management: no Org Chart, no parish business manager, lack of management presence, lack of leadership, job performance standards set by each person rather than management, no/low energy

Judgment: No PMO Org Chart must be addressed in your strategic plan as **Priority #1**. A PMO Org Chart must be created immediately. *All employees and volunteer personnel—including you as the PMO administrator—must know to whom they report at all times*. Also, lack of management presence and no/low energy must be holistically addressed through the correct culture lens, and this will be addressed as a natural byproduct of performing other items listed in the strategic plan. *The more you are observed in action taking action, the more the old culture is killed and the new culture is installed.*

HOW THE UGLY DRIVES STRATEGIC PLANNING WORK PRIORITIZATION

When we speak of "killing the old culture and installing the new culture," this is how that is achieved.

Marketing: little/no marketing and promotion of parish ministries, retreats, website, etc., little/no social media presence, little/no understanding of basic marketing principles by PMO decision makers and ministry leaders, marketing in general misunderstood, decision makers confused that marketing is even in any way applicable in a PMO setting, no marketing budget, no/low energy

Judgment: Bad, but not Ugly. Do not address as your highest strategic planning priority. Why? *You do not develop strategies to drive more people toward PMO services already acknowledged and known to be broken.* There is a time and place to get your PMO marketing house in order, but you absolutely do not market into known brokenness.

Personnel: overstaffed, understaffed, overpaid, underpaid, untrained, undertrained, no written job descriptions for every employee and/or volunteer position, low morale, no Org Chart, no personal accountability, no formal job performance review process, no hiring methodology, no formal employment termination process, no understanding of how to interview employees, volunteers, and/or vendors, multi-cultural overrepresentation, multi-cultural underrepresentation, insufficient number of ministry volunteers, unorthodox youth ministry activities, use of unapproved and/or unsound teaching materials

Judgment: As per above, creation of the Org Chart is **Priority #1**, and **Priority #2** is gaining a daily snapshot on the financial state of the organization—just so you know you will not run out of working capital. *Priority #3 is the creation of paid staff and volunteer ministry leader job descriptions.* Implementing **Priority #3** will begin to install/instill personal accountability into each employee and volunteer ministry leader. You will speak with each employee and volunteer ministry leader individually, privately. Why? To present them with their formal job description. Why? Because you will be taking this opportunity to explain—

as their written job description now clearly states—precisely what their job duties and responsibilities are, and as importantly, what your personal expectations are. We are to be charitable, *but we are not running a charity in PMO—note this important distinction.* Draw a paycheck from the Church? Wonderful. Now, *do your duty.* Volunteer to lead a ministry? Wonderful. *Now you must proactively lead that ministry—not simply fill a box on the Org Chart.* You must understand: *these moments are the beginning of PMO culture creation. This is where you personally explain in the manner you are comfortable with, but nevertheless clearly explain, the previous "good enough to get by, etc.," is no longer a satisfactory standard of performance.* This is where personal accountability and *fidelity to the written job description* are explained. Why? Because unless you want to burn yourself out on the job, unless you want to dislike coming to work, *you must master the art of delegation to qualified personnel.*

You must know with absolute certainty that the people who report to you will do their jobs, and do them in a superior manner. However, unless and until you have qualified people to delegate to, you will have no choice but to do the work yourself—<u>*and that is a sure and proven recipe for burnout and falling to serious illness*</u>. Sadly—but in full accord with what was stated above regarding confrontation—some administrators would rather in perpetuity assume on their already full plates the work of poorly performing employees, rather than to confront the poorly performing employee and perhaps replace the poorly performing employee. *Such is the strength of the inner urge to avoid confrontation.*

Many PMO duties will fall to the parish business manager—but only if you have a supremely talented parish business manager. However: do not incorrectly conclude here you cannot afford a supremely talented parish business manager. Such people are available—even to work full-time for free. *Your job as a PMO administrator is to find personnel you can train to do any job the way you want it done—<u>but absolutely your job is not to do all the work yourself</u>.*

HOW THE UGLY DRIVES STRATEGIC PLANNING WORK PRIORITIZATION

The three personal "crash or burnout" formulas are really very simple:

1. Your Idealism + Inaction = Here, have some depression
2. You are Overworked + Underappreciated = Here, have some burnout
3. You Fail to Perform Your Job = You are dismissed

Physical plant operations: nobody in charge of physical plant maintenance, current plant maintenance personnel untrained and/or unqualified, personnel do not know the scope of their job, no written preventative maintenance schedule for all equipment, no budget for equipment preventative maintenance, no forecasted replacement dates and costs for all major equipment, safety hazards present

Judgment: Bad, but not Ugly. With the exception of safety hazards, do not address at highest strategic planning priority.

Organizational: no Org Chart or amateurish "spaghetti" Org Chart (same person reporting to more than one person), too few ministries in relation to the number of potential ministries (where we are is not where we should be), open ministry leadership positions, untrained and/or unqualified ministry leaders, dormant ministries, abandoned ministries, open seats on parish council, no finance council, open seats on finance council

Judgment: See previous on creating Org Chart. As for the remaining issues, the same logic that applies to marketing applies to these remaining issues. For the same reasons and following the same logic that you do not market into brokenness, you do not increase the number of ministries, fill open ministry leadership positions, fill open council seats, etc., until you have your core PMO team assembled, trained, and running smoothly.

Reporting: little/no formal PMO reporting structure, little/no reporting input data collection

Judgment: See above. Addressed by creating a proper Org Chart.

Training: little/no job training of employee and/or volunteer personnel, no one known to be responsible for training, no time allotted for training, training not formally acknowledged and/or recognized as a PMO need

Judgment: Part and parcel with the creation of employee and volunteer ministry leader job descriptions is to provide the requisite training associated with each position. In other words, the creation of a written job description is the beginning, not the end. Whether or not as the PMO administrator you personally provide the training or delegate this task to someone else, training must not only be provided—*it must only be provided under the correct culture*. Why? The obvious answer is so that people know how to do their jobs, you know they know how to do their jobs, *and the employee or volunteer knows you know*. But why is this important? Job training—and specifically how you train—*is part of the culture killing and creation process*. Providing written job descriptions and job training also eliminates people jumping on the chronic "dog ate my homework" line of, "Nobody told me…nobody taught me…I wasn't informed" excuses train. Furthermore, you cannot in good conscience dismiss people unless and until you know they have been properly trained to do their job the way you want their job done.

Technology: broken computers, outdated computers, outdated phone system, outdated parish server hardware and/or software, outdated anti-virus/malware protection, frequent system crashes, no scheduled system backups, poor understanding of software, poor website design, poor ISP service, poor system maintenance, lack of associated procedures

Judgment: Bad, but not Ugly. With the exception of outdated anti-virus/malware protection and no scheduled system backups, do not address at highest strategic planning priority.

To recap the above hypothetical parish scenario:

1. **Priority #1**: a PMO Org Chart must be created immediately.
2. **Priority #2**: creation of a daily at-a-glance financial summary.

HOW THE UGLY DRIVES STRATEGIC PLANNING WORK PRIORITIZATION

3. *Priority #3*: creation of paid staff and volunteer ministry leader job descriptions, followed by employee and volunteer training.

The above points drive the order of work to be performed as will be specified by your written strategic plan.

CHAPTER 47

WILL YOU TAKE THE ROAD LESS TRAVELED?

If you fail to plan, you are planning to fail!
—Benjamin Franklin

The net effect of creating a PMO strategic plan prioritizing your work along the lines as explained above, which is to say to begin the process of killing and replacing your broken PMO culture, will in almost all cases bring you here: *temporary but predictable internal organizational turmoil, ultimately followed by institutionalized, enduring, and great success—if you know what you are doing and can execute.* Why?

As previously explained, most people do not enjoy change—especially when "change" is being misconstrued in their mind as, "You want me to work harder for the same pay? You want me to do things 'your way' when my way has been working just fine for years? Eh, no thanks. I'm going to resist that. Go back to where you came from. And have a nice day." You might not have these words spoken to your face—and then again you might—but regardless, this is what people will be thinking and this thinking forms the foundation of an entrenched broken culture. Therefore:

You can expect turnover after your employees and volunteers have been given their job description in writing, having been trained to perform their duties in the manner you have described and in alignment with the correct culture—*and subsequently they decide they are unwilling and/or unable to do the job as it must be done.* It is precisely at this point you have reached a crucial decision junction in your strategic planning and execution efforts that will determine whether you will succeed or fail in installing superior PMO. How so?

The process described above is mandatory for creating superior PMO, *but it is also extremely challenging to achieve*—not necessarily mentally challenging, *but emotionally challenging for the person driving the process.* It is grinding work from the perspective that it can be emotionally draining until completion—the polar opposite of fun. No rational person enjoys this, "fix THE BAD and THE UGLY" initial phase of the administrator's job. Oh my yes, every administrator wants highly effective and smooth-running PMO, <u>*but very few are willing to do what it takes to actually create the smoothly-running highly effective PMO they desire*</u>. They agree to be the chicken in ham 'n eggs, but no thanks—not the pig, they are not that committed to the process. Most folks will simply choose to muddle along with the employees, volunteers, processes, and level of mediocrity they inherit and call it a day. This temptation is especially true when you know you only have to endure broken PMO for an agreed upon specific length of time before you are reassigned and this mess becomes somebody else's problem.

As such, a certain type of, "Why bother? The mountain we seek to climb is too high! It can't be done!" apathy or fatalistic attitude seeps in. The tendency in such situations is to rationalize that it is easier to endure the short-term pain and then move on to your next assignment, than it is to do what is required to fix the mess you have inherited. After all, you didn't create the problems you inherited them, so why should it be your job to fix them? Well, in this regard let me be direct:

You do not need anything presented in this book to simply inherit broken PMO and perpetuate the status quo as it was given to you. But if you desire to provide the superior PMO service/services your community members deserve and you were called by God to provide, you are reading the right book. The key—besides knowing what you are doing—is in your ability to execute and work your way through the early tough months, without giving up, without quitting once you start. Expect those who report to you will quit—*but you don't quit once you start this process*. If you think you are going to quit, *do not even begin to start down this road.*

For additional support in this regard:

> The appetite of the sluggard craves but has nothing, but the appetite of the diligent is amply satisfied.
> —*Proverbs 13:4*

> The slack hand impoverishes, but the busy hand brings riches. A son who gathers in summer is a credit; a son who slumbers during harvest, a disgrace. A wise heart accepts commands, but a babbling fool will be overthrown. Whoever walks honestly walks securely, but one whose ways are crooked will fare badly. One who winks at a fault causes trouble, but one who frankly reproves promotes peace.
> —*Proverbs 10:4-5, 8-10*

> Whatever work you find to do, do it with all your might, for there is neither achievement, nor planning, nor science, nor wisdom in Sheol where you are going.
> —*Ecclesiastes 9:10*

> Jesus said, *"No one who sets a hand to the plow and looks to what was left behind is fit for the kingdom of God."*
> —*Luke 9:62*

What awaits you now are many tried and true methods and tools for you to use as the PMO administrator. The mechanical application of the tools, the science of PMO, is relatively easy. However, insofar as you are willing to allow a culture of mediocrity to exist where you work, you will have no need for these tools. Thus, everything starts with your initial, up-front, personal resolve and firm commitment, your choice to see your way through the initial turmoil phase, the toughest phase, where it seems there is pushback coming from everyone, and little to no apparent progress is being made as you implement your vision through executing your strategic plan. The question here and now becomes: *Do you believe?* Will you persevere through this very tough, early phase? Do you have the courage to terminate employees who will not adapt to the new culture? Or will you make the mistake of implementing your PMO changes and making improvements in a piecemeal manner, in euphemistic and patently nonsensical "phases" where the second phase never happens. Or will you—as you must—deliver to the patient all the medicine needed to cure what ails this sick person? In other words, will you kill the old culture and replace it with the correct culture?

Nobody more profoundly and clearly explains why to choose wisely here better than Robert Frost:

> I shall be telling this with a sigh
>
> Somewhere ages and ages hence:
>
> Two roads diverged in a wood, and I—
>
> I took the one less traveled by,
>
> *And that has made all the difference.*

Again, keep your status quo and <u>*do not go down the road described here*</u> unless you have already resolved in your mind this:

WILL YOU TAKE THE ROAD LESS TRAVELED?

Prayer of the PMO Administrator

If I am not going to finish what I am about to start, then I will not start. There is no turning back and there is no quitting once I start this process. I will ride it out no matter if everyone quits—I will ride it out. No matter what lies and false rumors are spread about me, I will complete the mission of transforming the PMO I inherited from what it was, to the superior operation it was intended to be. I will do this not for my sake—<u>but for the sake of those souls we are called to serve</u>.

Amen.

CHAPTER 48

EXECUTION OVERVIEW

What is execution and why is it important to PMO? How do you attain superior execution from those who report to you? The discussion on the nature of execution is akin to discussing how the sausage is made—it is a real world, blunt, candid assessment of the importance of execution in achieving superior PMO.

Those not previously (or correctly) familiar with this subject matter tend to incorrectly assume—based on reading the straight talk that follows—that the methods of achieving superior execution run toward the uncharitable, toward the proverbial Drill Sergeant, mean-spirited, etc. *This takeaway would be absolutely incorrec*t, *and is in fact the antithesis of achieving superior execution.* No such harsh methods in PMO need ever to be employed to achieve superior execution. But the bottom line is this:

> The tension you feel between balancing organizational competence and compassionate management is never properly resolved **by allowing incompetence to remain in the name of compassion.**

That some people you meet may not understand this critical point on execution, *does not make it any less true.* So as you read below, *read nothing into how you go about achieving superior execution at this point.* Your focus while reading should initially be on understanding the purpose, importance, and place, of superior execution in PMO. Of course, logically we must cover what is meant by "execution" before we can discuss the *art of achieving* superior execution from the employees and volunteers who report to us. But in an era of hyper political correctness, so-called "safe zones" and "trigger word warnings" etc., doing nothing and ignoring problems stemming from an imagined fear of being labeled as abusive, mean, etc., is an easy trap to fall into. Therefore, recognize when you read below on the nature of execution we are not yet making any comments about methodology, practice, etc., on how you achieve what you are reading. *Make no assumptions about approaches or methods.*

How we attempt to achieve—*and "attempt" is the correct descriptor here because there are no absolute guarantees when dealing with human beings*—superior execution through our employees and volunteers is discussed below, but I can report to you this much now: *developing personnel who can execute at a superior level is:*

1. Far more an art than a science, far more intuitive in approach and variable per person, than rule-bound, formulaic, and static—as any successful coach will tell you. Developing personnel requires a logical approach, but not a formulaic "one size fits all" rigid methodology. We are not here to flatten or homogenize anyone's strengths as an administrator, employee or volunteer, but to lean on them. Life has too many moving parts for an inflexible approach to personnel management. People are too complicated to be managed in such a manner. Rigidity in approach is counterproductive and ultimately will bury you because you will not be able to delegate—*there will be no one to delegate to because no one will want to work with you.* Our core job in this regard: highlight the strengths of all our personnel—including yourself—while helping each to eliminate their specific weaknesses. Thus, a PMO administrator must

be flexible, and a pre-cursor ingredient to flexibility is high intellect—*you cannot correctly exercise flexibility without high intellect.*

2. Fact: developing personnel who can execute at a superior level is not always achievable in every employee or volunteer who reports to you *no matter what you do*. Why this is so will be explained below, and what to do about it will be covered in the chapters on hiring and firing. The point here is to recognize that if you are of the opinion, not to mention temperament, that "everyone can be trained" to do their job, you may be right—eventually, given infinite time. And although you may have infinite patience, do you have the gift of infinite time?

Neither do I.

CHAPTER 49

THE NATURE OF EXECUTION

Whatever you do, do from the heart, as for the Lord and not for others, knowing that you will receive from the Lord the due payment of the inheritance; be slaves of the Lord Christ.

—Colossians 3:23-24

What is the nature of execution?

ex·e·cu·tion

noun

1. the carrying out or putting into effect of a plan, order, or course of action; "He was fascinated by the entire operation and its execution."

What is missing from the above definition? Acknowledging the elephant in the room that accompanies any discussion on execution: quality, as in the *quality* of our execution.

We start by facing this reality:

Q. What is the point of you and I and everybody else engaging in all this work if it ultimately ends with poor execution, poor delivery of PMO services?

A. There is no point. Poor execution can be achieved without the presence of any administrator or additional knowledge.

Whenever I have encountered organizational brokenness, "execution" has always been one of the most obvious elephants in the room. But execution is the topic many learners want to ignore, to sweep under the rug: "Let's just learn a bunch of stuff and call it a day. Forget about talking about the elephant in the room issue—*how well we execute the stuff we learn*. Let's just relish in the life of a learner, be a seeker of truth, blah, blah, blah." Eh, no. That position is not going to fly here. We are going to address the elephant in the room that answers to the name "Execution."

So what about you? Where do you stand on execution? Have you thought about execution in the context of applying this material and functioning in the future as a PMO administrator? Perhaps you have, but let's discuss execution through the more specific lens of "job expectations and job performance *of those who will report to you*."

> **In all toil there is profit, but mere talk tends only to poverty.**
> —*Proverbs 14:23*

As the saying goes "your mileage may vary," so we must speak here in *general terms*—because there are always some exceptions and who knows what the future holds. Nevertheless, the so-called "millennial" generation (generation Y) and "post-millennial" generation (generation Z) were raised by a generation of parents (either Baby Boomers or generation X) who often enshrined a performance doctrine best summarized as, "Everyone gets a ribbon!" First place, last place, whatever place, earned or not, Little Johnny and Little Susie have to get a ribbon, because after all, they tried, and merely trying, well, trying also deserves a reward! *So let me be very clear now for anyone so inclined to this line of thought:*

The "Everybody Gets a Ribbon & Co." attitude has no resemblance whatsoever to execution in the real world—the world of performance-based job reviews, merit-based raises and promotions, delegation of work to competent personnel, making payroll, paying all the monthly bills, dealing with litigation, etc. After the requisite training has been provided, superior execution of any and all PMO jobs must be done 100% correctly the first time—not merely, "I attempted to do my job correctly, therefore I did my job." The people we are called to serve *should actually receive* the superior service they deserve, and nothing less. This isn't T-ball. In the real world—which includes employment by the Church—*everyone absolutely does not receive a ribbon for trying*.

Does the above sound too harsh to you? Let me further explain:

Experience in execution is what you get when you didn't produce the expected results. Fine, *but experience at the expense of others is not what we strive for*. The parishioner *deserves* superior PMO service outright—*they did not agree to be recruited as an educational tool in your on-the-job training of PMO personnel*.

Recognize that superior execution is not defined as just showing up for work, and ultimately it is also not defined as "trying your best." All things being equal—meaning you *must* have been properly trained to perform the job at hand—the results you produce, or the lack thereof, *are directly derived from your ability and/or willingness to execute*. "Can you execute?" is not only the paramount question asked at this junction by the PMO administrator, *monitoring the answer to this question on behalf of parishioners you are called to serve is the reason you come to work every day*. Furthermore, and of paramount importance to your physical, emotional, and spiritual well-being:

Blessedly note here that I did not say you come to work so that you can do everyone else's job for them. Of course, everyone has a bad day. But the PMO administrator is not designated by intrinsic organizational design to be the go-to person to cover for the *systemic incompetence* of employees and/or volunteers who report to them. If you allow this condition to exist, you will cheat the organization you are charged to manage, while simultaneously burning yourself out. You will gradually become ineffective wearing any and every hat on your PMO administrator hat rack, exhausted at the end of the day but having accomplished very little.

CHAPTER 50

BUT I'M TRYING MY BEST!

Execution is what the PMO administrator monitors and measures. "Superior" is the standard of measurement for all execution, and this standard must be installed and then maintained organically by the correct culture—*but never literally some ham-fisted in-your-face efforts*. Note that once the culture is properly built, *a well-run PMO operation is a smooth running and self-sustaining operation*. People now intrinsically know their jobs and do their jobs as you have defined their jobs. It is truly a beautiful thing to be a part of. The hard part is the journey to reaching this thing of beauty.

Effort without accomplishment of the assigned task is at best the definition of mediocrity, at worst, abject failure. As the PMO administrator I can't tell someone seeking PMO services that even though we failed to serve them because we failed to execute, "Hey, look on the bright side! We gained 'organizational experience' and I learned more about our further need for 'programmatic cohesion' by utterly failing you, my dear parishioner. Thanks so much for helping us learn on the job—at your expense! And better luck next time—if we ever see you again!"

If for any reason the "everybody gets a ribbon" rationalization attitude is allowed to become your job performance standard of execution, either actively or passively, then as a PMO administrator mediocrity or worse will be your lot—and you don't need to read this book to be mediocre. Drucker didn't mince his words:

> **An effective nonprofit manager must try to get more out of the people he or she has. And that's decided by the basic people decisions: whom we hire and whom we fire; where we place people, and whom we promote. The quality of these human decisions largely determines whether the organization is being run seriously, whether its mission, its values, and its objectives are real and meaningful to people rather than just public relations and rhetoric.**
>
> —*Peter Drucker*

It can't be stated any better than the above. I would re-read this statement if I were you, and then reflect on what you will find when the person at the top of any Org Chart in any enterprise *cannot execute in a superior manner*. What does that organization most commonly deliver? Exactly what Drucker stated: nothing meaningful, just pro-forma public relations and rhetoric.

Now we are drilling down to the core reality of what happens when you are on the job and switch from your "Friend" hat to wearing the "PMO Administrator" hat: *it's about attaining superior execution from those who report to you*. It's not about Happy Meals, blue stars, mutual back-slapping recognition, ribbons just for showing up, or "trying your best.*"* If you allow your PMO workplace to permeate an, "anything we do is acceptable to the boss as long as we try" attitude, *you have just created a permanent refuge for mediocrity*. You have institutionalized mediocrity as your norm. As the PMO administrator, you might as well just not show up for work because even if you do, *what does it really matter, what difference does it make?* People don't need a boss to be mediocre—mediocrity is something that is perfectly achievable without your supervision.

And yes, "trying your best" does have a place in the correct culture—it will earn you a second chance to get things right—*but not infinite chances.*

Vision without execution is delusion.

—Thomas Edison

If superior execution is not a product of your PMO culture, and not the standard you are known to use to measure employee and volunteer performance, what is the point of having a well-crafted parish mission statement, or Statement of Culture, or superior strategic plan, or a tool box full of PMO tools at your disposal? *Why bother with any of that if you are not going to commit yourself to achieving superior execution?*

All of this and more are rendered into mere window dressing—and who needs more window dressing? *We need superior execution.* All things being equal, *the difference between mediocrity and superior service is ultimately found in the quality of execution.* And the greatest single influence on achieving superior execution by paid staff and volunteers? *Your PMO culture, which you set and maintain as the PMO administrator.*

As a PMO administrator, you might find the desk sign of President Harry S. Truman helpful, and from where this book draws part of its name:

The Buck Stops Here

Truman was the man solely responsible for granting permission to drop two atomic bombs on Japan. Clearly, a most profound and sobering expression of the execution buck stopped with Truman. Personally, the wisdom contained within Truman's desk plaque moved me many years ago, and his same words have also sat as a plaque on my own desk ever since. Why? *Because life is not an academic exercise.* Life does not issue letter grades. We are not here just to check boxes and go through the motions of life. Darkness feeds on apathy. *Life demands that those who choose to serve others be able to execute and execute in a superior manner*, otherwise the people they are meant to serve are not served—or at least not served as they deserve to be. There is nothing Christ-like in conscious and deliberately poor execution. If you are aware of mediocre-to-poor execution, you have a duty as a PMO administrator to immediately and correctly address the situation. If you don't want to fight fires don't be a fireman. If you can't or won't do all the tasks of a PMO administrator, don't put your name in the top box in the Org Chart.

What you do after reading this book is your business and entirely up to you. But as for me, I accept the truth and wisdom that employee and volunteer good intentions…*never made a single payroll*. I don't praise—even faintly—abject failure in job performance. Why would I? *How is disingenuous praise helpful to the poor performer or the culture of the organization?* However, I do recognize that the failure of someone who reports to me is simultaneously somehow a failure <u>*also on my part*</u>. I need to face the mirror, too. Why? Because:

Somewhere along the line, something *on my watch* had to also go wrong for failure to execute to occur. *As the PMO administrator I must also own that failure to execute and do what is necessary to ensure it does not happen again.* A failure to execute by someone who reports to me is more than just cause, more than enough reason for me to also look in the mirror and honestly assess myself. But what I cannot do and will not do is embrace the "everybody gets a ribbon" school of management to avoid confronting the person who has directly failed to execute. To do so would be an abdication of a part of my duty as a PMO administrator—and I will not be an effective administrator if I choose this path.

CHAPTER 51

THE ART OF ACHIEVING SUPERIOR EXECUTION

> The role of the musician is to go from concept to full execution. Put another way, it's to go from understanding the content of something to really learning how to communicate it and make sure it's well-received and lives in somebody else.
>
> —Yo-Yo Ma

What the PMO administrator wants to achieve in others is precisely what Yo-Yo Ma stated. We want to communicate _____ (insert subjects here) to paid staff and/or volunteers, such that our message is well received by the receiver and they fully execute in a superior manner everything we have communicated to them. Sounds simple enough; you teach, the receiver learns, we move on. So why is this task so often difficult, and what can we do to improve our chances of achieving our goal of superior execution?

First, you must enable reaching the goal. What goal? How? *The goal is to always deliver every PMO service to your community in a superior way;* establishing the correct culture initially enables reaching the goal. This is also your publically stated goal. Stated where? *In the enhanced language of your mission statement.* Not mediocre service. Not good service. Not, "well, something is better than nothing, take whatever you get" service. *Superior service to everyone, all the time, is the publically stated goal.*

Our public mission statement enabled our Statement of Culture to say this is so, *but you must make it so through superior execution*. Putting policy words on paper is not the same thing, indeed not even remotely close, to actual execution. So many "managers" think their work is done when they send a perfectly crafted email or issue step-by-step instructions to be followed by subordinates. *This thinking is deeply flawed, because your work just started.*

Now, why is this task of "execution" so difficult and how can we improve our chances of achieving our goal? The quickest way to address this question is by investigating the answer to another question: why do companies use basic robots (we are not speaking of AI robots here) to replace human beings whenever possible? Let us count the ways—because the first order of business is for you to fully recognize the many layers of complexity and all the challenges associated with achieving superior execution.

The following list of ten points is *not* meant to be read as any general advocacy for robots, much less that robots can perform PMO functions. However, invoking mental imagery of a robot working in PMO can be useful and revealing. How so? In highlighting the relentlessly perfect execution of a robot, *by comparison we will one-by-one expose the execution weaknesses of mistake-prone employees and volunteers*. In this manner we will shine a spotlight on the challenges facing the PMO administrator attempting to deliver superior PMO. So as you read these ten points, stop and consider at each one that you must achieve everything specified in a superior manner, but through an imminently fallible human PMO employee or volunteer. *It is at this point the scope of your superior execution challenge is revealed.*

Regarding a robot:

1. You can electronically transfer knowledge of how to perform tasks to a robot, and also electronically transfer instructions from robot to robot,

THE ART OF ACHIEVING SUPERIOR EXECUTION

with 100% fidelity. Absolutely nothing is lost or misunderstood in this instructional and/or information transfer process. If anything is lost and/or corrupted during the transfer you would automatically and immediately be notified, allowing you to restart the transfer process and repeat it until it is completed with 100% accuracy. Indeed, the transfer restart would likely occur on its own.

2. The intelligence level, capacity, and capabilities of each robot are stable and known in advance.
3. Should you need to upgrade, a robot is easier to upgrade because the upgrade process is formulaic, mechanical, known, and predictable.
4. A robot does not have an emotional component.
5. A robot cannot lie, cheat, steal, or otherwise of its own accord act in an immoral or unethical manner.
6. Robots will without complaint of boredom complete repetitive and mundane tasks.
7. A robot never needs work breaks, pregnancy or sick leave, ever escalating vacation time, holiday breaks, salary increases, bonuses, rewards, insurance, and the like. To ensure constant uptime, preventative maintenance (i.e. adjustments, parts replacements) can be done on a robot during non-working hours.
8. Robots lend unsurpassed accuracy and precision to their work product. This accuracy and precision leads to less waste, zero or nearly zero mistakes, and lower costs.
9. Robots will never sue you.
10. Robots are expendable. They can perform dangerous tasks, work with dangerous ingredients, and lift heavy loads.

To allow non-performers to stay on means letting down both the organization and the cause.

—*Peter Drucker*

Now, to more clearly understand our challenge in achieving superior execution from all those who report to us as PMO administrators, let us examine each of the above points *from our PMO administrator perspective:*

1. You can electronically transfer knowledge of how to perform tasks to a robot, and also from robot to robot, with 100% fidelity. Absolutely nothing is lost or misunderstood in this instructional and/or information transfer process. If anything is lost and/or corrupted during the transfer you will be immediately notified, allowing you to restart the transfer process and repeat it until it is completed with 100% accuracy. Indeed, the transfer restart would likely occur on its own.

PMO administrator challenges to achieving superior execution:

The PMO administrator must personally train, or at least oversee the training of employees and volunteers who report to them. This training is provided through the lens of an established and correct culture; otherwise, *you are wasting your time.* Also, if the training is merely perfunctory or superficial, *you are wasting your time.* Employee and volunteer training is not something you do just to check a box marked "Completed." Superior execution, and therefore superior results, will forever elude the PMO administrator who in any way short-changes employee and volunteer training. While training is a mandatory step toward achieving superior execution, it is at the very least time-consuming at the start, and can also be arduous and tedious depending upon the pre-existing skill set and level of knowledge within those you are training.

2. The intelligence level and capabilities of a robot are stable and known in advance.

THE ART OF ACHIEVING SUPERIOR EXECUTION

PMO administrator challenges to achieving superior execution:

Upon your arrival at your assigned location, recognize you will inherit paid and volunteer PMO personnel. Who are they? What do they actually know about their job? What do they think they know, but don't? What are they capable of? How well do they currently perform their job? There is no operations manual you can read that will answer the above questions. Further note that it is likely one or more of the personnel you inherit will be unable and/or unwilling to learn and/or perform their job to your standards. Now what? Do you accept mediocrity?

3. *Should you need to upgrade, a robot is easier to upgrade because the upgrade process is formulaic, mechanical, known, and predictable.*

PMO administrator challenges to achieving superior execution:

When people who report to you have been trained and cannot or will not do their job according to your standards as set by the correct culture, you have the following options available to you: a. live with them and do nothing, or; b. find them a different job they can handle, or; c. dismiss them. Clearly, why read this book if your choice in this situation is to live with them and do nothing? And it is unlikely you will find an open but different job for anyone in this situation. This leaves us with option c: dismiss them. And it is precisely at this point the PMO administrators determine their own fate: *will you run PMO, <u>or will PMO run you</u>?*

If you are unwilling and/or unable to dismiss either paid or volunteer personnel who *after sufficient training* still fail to do their job, PMO will run you…and this aspect of your day, every day, will not be a happy or joy-filled experience. In truth, if this is your choice you should vacate the position of PMO administrator as soon as possible. Why? Because the worst choice you can make is to present everyone with the illusion that there is a PMO boss, *when in fact there is no boss*. At least when the position is presented on the Org Chart as clearly vacant, those at the top of the Org Chart will understand that the reason why their PMO is dysfunctional is because the PMO administrator position is empty. When you present the illusion the PMO administrator position is filled—but abdicate your duty—*the person at the top of the Org Chart is being misled*. Necessary organizational change does not occur. A false sense of security permeates—*but not forever*. You can hide problems, *but you can't hide problems forever*.

4. *A robot does not have an emotional component.*

PMO administrator challenges to achieving superior execution:

As previously stated, *a ham-fisted ogre of a boss will never work*. However, neither will apathy in the face of failing job performance. The art of the PMO administrator can be found in their ability to motivate and teach personnel <u>*in the manner each receiver best receives teaching*</u>. Note this is an art to master, not a set of "how to" rules to follow. As mentioned, there is no "one size fits all" approach to employee and volunteer management. Each person and each problem calls for a tailored solution that in part, *appeals to the emotional component of the receiver and utilizes the powers of persuasion within the PMO administrator*. Whereas for example one person appreciates the direct, blunt, "Just tell me what you want" approach, another person requires a softer, more circuitous inter-personal style. Fine. The PMO administrator must recognize the emotional dimension of each person before communicating with them, either in writing, telephone, or in person, and have the skill and wisdom *to adjust their approach to fit each receiver. This is the art of all administration*.

5. *A robot cannot lie, cheat, steal, or otherwise of its own accord act in an immoral or unethical manner.*

PMO administrator challenges to achieving superior execution:

THE ART OF ACHIEVING SUPERIOR EXECUTION

Sooner or later, someone in a position of trust will disappoint you. What you must do after-the-fact is usually self-evident and driven by common sense and the circumstances of the event. However, this point is about prevention, about vigilance, about establishing or following existing prescribed protocols for handling money, credit cards, gift certificates, expense reports, password security, server protection, office supplies, lost and found items, etc., that reduce if not eliminate the opportunities to fail in the above manner. You must also anticipate here the most obvious pushback elephant in the room: "I don't understand? What's wrong with the way we have always done things? Do you think we're crooks? Are you saying that we steal?" and on and on. All you can do is explain yourself and your decision. You cannot control how some people may choose to spin your motive away from what it truly is—proactive and responsible administration of resources—into what it is not. You especially cannot be paralyzed by the fear of being misunderstood, and choose to do nothing instead of the right thing. Not everyone is going to like you, so get used to it. Just remember the storm comes before the rainbow.

6. *Robots will without complaint of boredom complete repetitive and mundane tasks.*

PMO administrator challenges to achieving superior execution:

Rest assured the more boring and repetitive a task, the more likely it is that task will eventually be executed poorly. It's a known truism…*you don't want to buy a new car built on Friday afternoon.* Why? Workers' minds are everywhere but on the task at hand. You can't change the nature of a boring task, but you can sometimes rotate tasks so the same person is not stuck with the same boring duty. Simple recognition of an issue will many times win you half the battle. Regardless of whether or not a task is boring or dynamic, the PMO administrator is ultimately responsible that every task is perfectly executed. Or not. You can focus on improving the execution, *or habitually clean up the messes created by careless execution and perpetually deal with the consequences and fallout.* There is no free ride. Either you focus on perfect execution of all tasks—including the boring tasks—or you spend your time putting out preventable fires *because your broken culture allows for poor execution without consequences.* But note this well: a PMO pell-mell, helter-skelter, "Who cares?" working environment *will eventually burn you out both emotionally and physically—and certainly will not help spiritually.* You will eventually grow weary of personally cleaning up after people too _____ (insert descriptors of choice here) to care about the quality of their execution—if they ever cared. Perhaps then you will recall this advisement: *you don't have to enjoy confrontation, but sometimes you just have to confront someone.*

7. *A robot never needs work breaks, pregnancy or sick leave, ever escalating vacation time, holiday breaks, salary increases, bonuses, rewards, and the like. To ensure constant uptime, preventative maintenance (i.e. adjustments, parts replacements) can be done on a robot during non-working hours.*

PMO administrator challenges to achieving superior execution:

PMO is 24/7/365. Let that sink in: *PMO is 24/7/365.* Everything PMO is your responsibility as the PMO administrator, it never stops being your responsibility, and as the saying goes, "If it's not one thing, it's another." Translation: if it's not an unexpected employee absence for some reason, it's a pipe breaking in the middle of the night, or someone tripping over an uneven sidewalk, or vandalism, etc., etc. But no matter what it is, it will land on your desk—*unless you delegate. Delegation of work to competent and trained personnel is your best friend.* Until you have installed a competent parish business manager you will run yourself ragged. In this regard:

Do not necessarily equate having a competent parish business manager, or the lack thereof, with money and parish cash flow. I was a parish business manager, full-time, for five years, for free. Competent people can be found to work in His vineyard, *but only if you proactively seek them out.* This person may live outside your parish, but so what? Geography is not a deal breaker. The Pastor was the PMO administrator where I worked. In light of what you have learned in this book so far, do you think he was receptive to having me literally knock on his door and offer my services to the parish just before remodeling our 1950s construction era asbestos-laden Church interior? Yes, God will provide, *but you also need to do your part.* You need to be open to the idea of searching for a parish business manager. You might need to advertise the position, etc. Or not—it's your call. But if you do not delegate, you will burn yourself out. The catch? You cannot delegate until you have competent and trained people under you. It is a holistic system—one piece depends upon another.

8. *Robots lend unsurpassed accuracy and precision to their work product. This accuracy and precision leads to less waste, nearly zero mistakes, and lower costs.*

PMO administrator challenges to achieving superior execution:

The accuracy and quality of the work product produced by those who report to you is ultimately your responsibility. However, over time your level of oversight can be *substantially reduced* if you have installed the proper PMO culture. The proper PMO culture inherently lends itself to fostering superior PMO execution. Employees and volunteers will automatically self-check/self-correct their work if working under the proper culture. Why? Because just like every human cell, they obey the culture's DNA, indeed they relish this culture; they are a living part of the culture, a culture that by design can only endorse superior execution. Everyone who reports to you will come to know and understand this truth about execution, but only if the culture fosters this understanding. Note this well: if you do not already, you will come to know it takes no more time to do a superior job in PMO as it does to do a mediocre job—*so why not do a superior job in the first place?* This is not only the essence of the culture, *when properly implemented it is a time lifesaver for the PMO administrator.* Your best friend at work is the proper PMO culture.

9. Robots will never sue you.

PMO administrator challenges to achieving superior execution:

There is a process to hiring, there is a process to firing, and there is an art and science to both. In general, you must follow the hiring and firing process science as ultimately dictated to you by diocese policy. That said, you must also be wise and be aware of certain realities when it comes to hiring and firing in order to minimize the risk of litigation. However, it is paramount that you do not allow the fear of litigation to paralyze you into inaction, into accepting mediocrity. This topic will be further discussed in the chapters on hiring and firing.

10. *Robots are expendable. They can perform dangerous tasks, work with dangerous ingredients, and lift heavy loads.*

PMO administrator challenges to achieving superior execution:

There are ways to get hurt in a parish, everything from falling off a ladder to slipping on a wet floor to being hit by a speeding car in the parking lot. As a PMO administrator you should walk every inch of the grounds and buildings with a hazard-specific safety specialist, with an eye toward removing or mitigating all safety hazards. You should ensure all employees and volunteers know who to contact in case of an emergency, no matter the time of day, holiday, vacation schedule, etc. There are no guarantees, but if you minimize your risk profile you have minimized your potential for future problems and potential litigation.

CHAPTER 52

THE BOTTOM LINE ON EXECUTION

As a hypothetical discussion: at a glance and without stating a specific context one could argue robots are clearly better than humans when it comes to achieving superior execution—but this is actually an illusion in our PMO context. How so? *Because all that typically a robot lacks is precisely what we need in order to deliver superior PMO.* Specifically, we need creativity, spontaneity, and an emotional human-to-human connection with those we serve based on love of neighbor and the complete teachings of Christ. Thus, the PMO administrator seeks in their employees and volunteers the heart and spirit of a servant's soul, coupled with an internal desire to deliver the most superior service they possibly can to those we are dedicated to serving. No matter the size or importance of the task, we are looking for people who do not need constant supervision and oversight to excel, but if and when supervision is required we acknowledge the first line of "supervision" is not the voice of the PMO administrator, *but the silent and nevertheless ever present voice of the proper culture.*

You will find that establishing the proper culture makes your PMO administrator focus on superior employee and volunteer execution vastly easier. Whatever time you put into setting the culture will come back to you more than ten fold in decreased time spent focusing on solving execution problems that never should have occurred in the first place. But given this clear truth, *why do administrators eschew proven techniques?*

Because when poor execution is noticed, it necessarily triggers a duty in the administrator to correct the problem—and it doesn't take the proverbial rocket scientist to figure out that "correcting the problem" might not be the most fun, comfortable, conversation in the world. In other words, our PMO administrator rationalizes, "Eh, I'm busy over here right now doing such-and-such that is more important than addressing Sam or Susie about _____. I'll speak to them tomorrow." Of course, we already know how this story ends: *tomorrow never comes.*

So let's not sugarcoat reality here or pretend we don't see the real execution elephant in the room labeled: ***Caution! Potential if not probable confrontation ahead!*** Because when you break it down the bottom line of what we are talking about in achieving superior results is derived from achieving superior execution, and all things being equal achieving superior execution is simply a contest of wills: your will, or the employee/volunteer.

But only one will prevail.

Whenever I find broken execution after adequate training has been provided, I know one thing: *the will of the employee prevailed over the will of management, and any administrator who permits this scenario doesn't deserve the title—or the job.* However, those so inclined who desire to avoid the inevitable and unavoidable conversations with underperforming employees and volunteers should feel at ease here, no worries, under one caveat:

Anyone who does not want to deal with the confrontation that inevitably comes with rebuilding any organization, taking it from brokenness to superior execution, *as previously stated must decline the PMO administrator job.* Do not allow your name to be placed in the "PMO Administrator" box on the Org

THE BOTTOM LINE ON EXECUTION

Chart. For the good of the parish you must be honest with the person offering you this position and decline to accept for the various reasons cited above, but mostly: the worst thing you can do is accept a job, occupy the box on the Org Chart, *and give the illusion to those above you that the position is covered when it is not, and you know in your heart you have no real intention of doing the job that is required.*

That is not ignorance or on the job incompetence—*that is sin animated by dishonesty.*

CHAPTER 53

PURPOSE OF PLANNING TOOLS

> Technology is nothing. What's important is that you have a faith in people, that they're basically good and smart, and if you give them tools, they'll do wonderful things with them.
>
> —*Steve Jobs*

Regarding execution: we have established that a firm resolve to execute perfectly is a prerequisite to any holistic system of management. It is a wonderful sentiment, but now what? Execute what, with what? Who? When? Why? To what ends? Applying your willpower, your commitment to execute perfectly, and your strong desire to execute in a superior manner...*is utterly useless without the guidance and vision afforded to you by well-crafted plans.* Therefore:

We create various PMO plans in order to address a variety of diverse PMO issues, through both short- and long-term plans each customized to the issue to be addressed—but *not always* necessarily complex, lengthy, or overly time consuming to create. Do not cringe at reading/hearing the words "written plan," and do not equate by default "planning" with any specific page length, or specific amount of time to create. Further note, a handwritten plan is still a plan—no need to master using another piece of specialized planning software.

For every minute spent organizing, an hour is earned.
—Benjamin Franklin

What is "strategic planning"? Thinking, then writing it down. That's it. Why is strategic planning so important? The obvious answer is that your plan becomes your blueprint for execution in *comprehensively* addressing all things PMO. Your plan provides the overall direction, precise directives to named personnel, and an operating timeline to completing specified efforts. However, although this is the obvious answer *it is also the secondary answer*. What is the primary reason we must create a plan? Do we create a strategic plan because traditional thinking demands that we do so? No. Do we write a strategic plan because everybody else creates a plan? No. Why do we create a plan? We create a plan in order to learn and discover, *but to learn and discover precisely what?*

1. The obvious: we plan in order to discover and learn more about that which we do not yet fully know, that we must know in order to successfully complete the task at hand. In other words, we plan and in the process of creating the plan we will learn new stuff. Fine. But these are *secondary* motives to create a strategic plan. What is the *primary* reason to plan?

2. The primary reason we must use all available tools to always create a plan—and if you learn nothing else from this book, learn this:

It isn't what we don't know that gives us trouble, <u>it's what we know that ain't so</u>.
—Will Rogers

Did you catch the nuance in the above remark? Did you catch the wisdom? Of course we create a plan and in the process learn what we must know regarding the who, what, where, when, why, and how to complete the task(s) at hand. We want to fill in any gaps in our knowledge and understanding, so we create

PURPOSE OF PLANNING TOOLS

a plan—simple or complex, short or long or somewhere in between. In the process of creating our PMO plan, we learn. Fine, all fine. But relatively speaking, *this is not where our worst land mines or future problems are to be discovered, our worst nightmares experienced or avoided.*

The real nightmares—the land mines that will kill you and your PMO efforts—are not what you don't know subsequently revealed by the process of creating a plan. *The real land mines are what you think is so, that is not so, that in the process of planning you discover and reveal to your most inner self.*

A few headline examples of the consequences when someone thought something was so, that was not so:

> Hospital Settles Suit Over Removal of Wrong Lung

> Good Samaritan Shot By Police After Calling 911 to Report Location of Shooting Suspect

> Passenger Plane Lands at the Wrong Airport After Pilots Ignore Their Cockpit Equipment

> Man Who Thought Gun Was Unloaded Shoots, Kills Himself While Driving

> Fukushima Disaster Was Preventable, New Study Finds

Oh.

You mean it's not so much what I don't know and never knew that will give me the most grief? *It is what I think is so that is not so—that is what will kill me?* Exactly. *Assuming they "know" something to be true, accepting and believing what is so that is not so and subsequently failing to plan*—"Meh! Who needs a plan for that!"—this is precisely how PMO administrators drive themselves off a cliff, *along with all those who report to them.*

The creation of any strategic plan when done diligently and with an open mind—not with a "why bother I already know the answer" attitude—will reveal to the open-minded PMO administrator an item(s) that they thought was true, sincerely believed was true, thought they knew all about, *that is not really true at all*. What at first glance or even final assumption appears to be "the obvious answer" is not only not always the obvious answer, this so-called "obvious answer" might blow up in your face because your failure to use the available tools to create a plan, inhibited you from discovering a critical truth. And what critical truth is that? That something you assumed, believed, thought was true—pick whatever word you want, *was not actually true at all*.

> **The secret of all victory lies in the organization of the non-obvious.**
>
> *—Marcus Aurelius*

For example:

You green light the roofing contractor to start work on replacing the old and leaky parish hall roof. Halfway through the project you are served a notice by the city to stop work. Why? You did not request a permit. Why didn't you request a permit? Because:

1. You did not think a permit was necessary for this work, but even if it were necessary...

2. You incorrectly assumed the roofing contractor would apply for the necessary permits. The applied formula here: wrong + wrong = wrong. Why? *Because this contractor relies on the customer to pull all permits.* But you did not ask, which is not the point. The point is: *why didn't you ask?* Because:

3. At the last location you worked—in a different city, county, or state—that locale did not even require a permit for the same type of work.

PURPOSE OF PLANNING TOOLS

Oh. You mean what you thought was true, was not actually true.

Experience is what you get when you don't get what you want—but so are scars and I'm not particularly fond of acquiring those either. And so is the personal and organizational pain that often travels with its close friend, real world experience. You assumed you knew what was so and you skipped creating a simple and short plan, a process that would have forced you to ask and answer the critical permitting question. Instead of creating a plan because that is simply what must be done by default thinking, you allowed what you thought you knew to blow you up—and as is so often the case you will usually blow up others with you. Instead of advance planning you found out by stepping on an avoidable land mine what you thought was so, wasn't so at all. And your pleas to the city for an expedited permit process? They go unanswered. It seems the folks in the permitting department are not so God-friendly, much less Catholic parish friendly. Imagine that. And now you will enter the rainy season not with just a leaky roof, *but a completely missing roof.*

If you had created a plan and checked that what you thought was so was actually a fact—*because the accurate completion of the plan would have demanded you check this point*—you (or whoever you delegated this planning task to) would have discovered that in this city, *you need a permit for this work, plus your chosen contractor expects the client to pull all required permits.* Now you must stop work on your roof—torn up and the rainy season approaching—and wait at an indifferent city bureaucrat work speed for the necessary permit to be issued before you can continue. And if you think the city department that issues such permits cares about your missing roof in the rain problem and will expedite the permit process, think again. Oh, and as an added bonus you—well, not really you—your parishioners, will also pay a fine for beginning the work without having the required permit in the first place. Now, have a nice day, and remember this: this mess really did not occur because of what you didn't know.

This mess occurred because of what you thought was so, that wasn't—and you could have and should have, discovered this. The only reason there is a problem at all is because by failing to plan, *you created the problem.*

> **Time is a created thing. To say "I don't have time" is to say "I don't want to."**
>
> —Lao Tzu

Fortunately for us, once you mentally commit to planning, during the creation and implementation of the plan as well as ongoing daily PMO operations, we have various tools available to assist us with each phase. However, could you skip creating a plan? Yes, but you shouldn't. But what if you don't have time to make a plan? What if you are claiming to be "too busy"? *Too bad.* Find the time. Make a plan, or delegate the planning task to competent personnel—*but make a written plan*. No matter the size of the task make a plan—which loosely translates to: "Think, but with a pencil in your hand."

Do not move forward on anything significant in PMO without a written plan. Remember, not all plans are necessarily complex or take a great deal of time to create—sometimes just mere minutes of clear-headed, focused thinking. Further note accuracy does not necessarily improve with the length of the plan; there is no guaranteed correlation between how wordy a plan is and how accurate or useful it will be. There is also the unwise PMO administrator who makes the decision to view another parish from a distance, a parish that you know doesn't plan anything but yet is somehow flourishing, especially a parish that was formerly in some distress, and conclude: "Plan? They don't plan over there! Why should I plan? Meh. Who needs a plan? I'm not going to bother with writing a plan." The fallacy in this thinking? Just because Parish X might have been granted a miraculous turnaround without a PMO strategy or planning—*doesn't mean your parish will.*

PURPOSE OF PLANNING TOOLS

And the more often you use the planning tools—*starting with your mind and a pencil, and layering on only more tools if need be*—the less time creating your plan will consume. Planning knowledge = cumulative experience; and the more you do it the faster the process goes. Furthermore, the return on your invested time spent creating a plan will be well worth it in contrast to the time spent and potential money wasted from failing to plan and stepping on land mines—and as sure as you are reading this the hidden land mines are out there waiting to be stepped on.

Could you create a PMO plan to accomplish _____, without planning and/or using any planning tools? Of course—*but after reading the above, why would you want to?* Do you think you have the experience of the strategic plan toolmakers, such that you can create a plan in your head without the support and inherent step-by-step guidance such tools offer? Perhaps in your future, but probably not today. So for now you must become well acquainted with these tools.

Insofar as the tools support creating any plan, you might as well start with the Mother of All Plans: *the master PMO strategic plan.* This plan will drive input to smaller, less comprehensive plans necessary to achieve superior PMO, but they use the same underlying logic in their creation. If you create the master plan for PMO, you can easily create any sub-plan. And don't forget: if you align with other parishes—which is to say you are on the same holistic system page and speak the same PMO language and principles as articulated here—why reinvent the wheel? You can share the redundant workload and farm some of the planning work out in sections, each section done by a person best suited for completing that section. You can mutually share strategic planning tasks, not that the results may be used verbatim—although they might be—but they would provide some useful initial guidance.

To create a master PMO strategic plan recall we must start with enhanced mission statement language that recognizes PMO, at least giving a nod to the existence of PMO as being integral to the overall mission of the parish. Without such a statement, how do you support your existence? What is your purpose in PMO? On what basis do you claim any authority to do anything related to PMO? From where do you derive your authority? Let's resume here:

Upon arrival at your parish, all things being equal (i.e. no crisis, no emergency to attend to), as seen above this is your general order of work to creating and installing superior PMO:

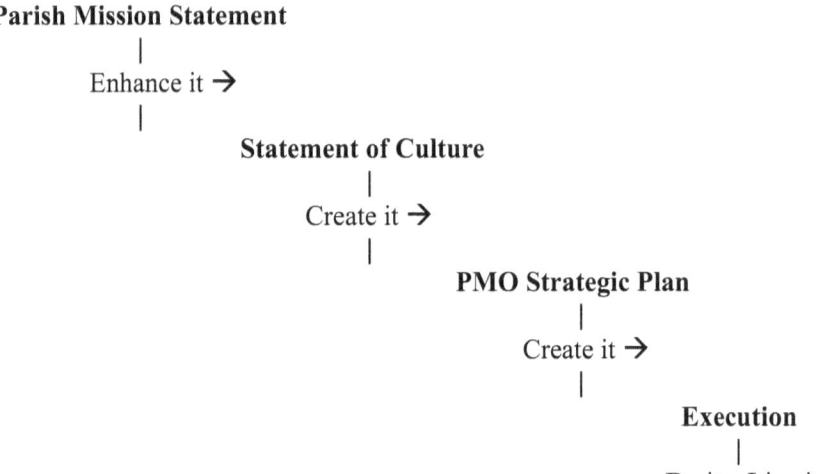

We have previously discussed the need for an enhanced parish mission statement. The PMO-related language in the parish mission statement essentially authorizes and enables PMO—indeed, legitimizes our duty to do our duty, and to create our Statement of Culture that animates *how* we will mentally approach everything we do in PMO. Now that we have a mission statement in place that declares providing superior PMO is a duty and obligation of the parish to its community, and we have a Statement of Culture that assists us in establishing the correct culture we need for superior PMO to take root and flourish, we need a PMO strategic plan—a roadmap upon which we will execute.

CHAPTER 54

TACTICAL DISCRIMINATION AND DELEGATION

If you are ordained what is unique to your vocation? Simply this: *through your ordination you have faculties enabling capabilities in the spiritual realm that the laity do not possess, and furthermore, will never possess.* That being the case, clearly we want our ordained clergy to spend as much of their time as possible working in the spiritual realm rather than the temporal realm, as issues in the temporal realm can be handled by the lay employees and volunteers working in PMO—*but this principled distribution of PMO work does not happen by accident.*

It becomes imperative that any ordained working in PMO practices the art of *tactical discrimination* when living the parish Org Chart on a day-to-day basis. What is "tactical discrimination"? Precisely this: as ordained clergy you must deliberately, proactively *maximize* your involvement in all *spiritual* realms, and *minimize* your involvement in the *temporal* realms of the Org Chart—but you must not do so to the detriment of managing both the spiritual *and* temporal realm issues in a superior manner.

Thus, the conundrum we must solve here is about time management, or time discrimination:

How do we maximize our time working in the spiritual realm, while at the same time ensuring that everything done in PMO in the temporal realm is concurrently done in a superior manner?

Working to achieve this balance between who works in the spiritual realm and who works in the temporal realm on the Org Chart is the essence of tactical discrimination. We are tactically discriminating as ordained where we spend our time between spiritual and temporal duties as these duties are presented to us on the Org Chart. In other words: which boxes on the Org Chart will be occupied by an ordained person, and which boxes will be occupied by laity? Ideally, we want every box on the Org Chart that can be fulfilled by laity to hold the name of a layperson in that box. But why should we care about our ordained being free to practice this tactical discrimination via the PMO Org Chart? This is why:

We want our ordained to spend as much time as possible working in the spiritual realm and doing for souls what only an ordained person can do. A major and driving factor in building robust and superior PMO is to reach a point whereby our ordained can spend most of their time each day on spiritual matters, *not temporal matters that can and should be addressed by laity*. But when the Org Chart is populated with incompetent employees and volunteers, PMO efficiency dramatically declines and this goal becomes impossible to achieve. Instead, every day our ordained are spending an imbalanced and inordinate amount of time on temporal matters that should otherwise be worked by competent laity.

Thus, tactical discrimination is a wonderful concept, *but it can only be achieved when the PMO Org Chart is finally fully populated with superior employees and volunteers*. Until such time, everything you just read immediately above was a waste of your time and the printer's ink. Sadly, our poor ordained will never be able to practice tactical discrimination. Instead, they will be gang-pressed every day into spending their precious time—an inordinate amount of time—handling issues that have little or nothing to do with the spiritual welfare

TACTICAL DISCRIMINATION AND DELEGATION

of souls, and underutilizing the precious faculties derived from their ordination. However:

The ordained must also do their part if tactical discrimination is to become a reality. What is the role of the ordained in this regard? As indicated above, superior employees and volunteers must be hired/engaged in every box on the Org Chart. But there still remains one more critical factor to master: the ordained cannot, must not, *waste their precious time by willfully meddling and micromanaging PMO personnel going about their daily duties.*

What is the point of filling every box on the Org Chart with superior personnel, *only for the ordained person to be poking his nose into every decision that must be made?* You think that is the definition of delegation? Do you think you can retain superior personnel without delegating the authority to them that they need to do their job, *and then trusting in them to do the task at hand without your meddling?* Meddling in the business of a superior employee or volunteer is the quickest way to lose that employee or volunteer. So, why do people meddle and micromanage?

The primary reason someone is unwilling and/or unable to delegate and stop their incessant meddling in the daily work of others comes down to a single principle: fear of risk, fear of failure. Those who cannot or will not delegate are overly fearful of risk. What risk? The risk of the fallout that is necessarily attached to the inevitable mistake someone will make. This fear of someone making a mistake—of course always exaggerated to the most extreme mistake imaginable—is enough to cause the risk-averse administrator to either constantly meddle in the work of those who report to them, or simply usurp delegated authority under some false pretense so they can do the task themselves and avoid that pesky risk of failure. Well, let me shed some light on such thinking now:

You cannot fulfill what your ordination promises in the spiritual realm, while simultaneously assuming the PMO Org Chart work of the laity in the temporal realm. This raises the very valid question: why did you become ordained in the first place if you are going to spend the bulk of your time either allowing yourself to be gang-pressed into temporal services, or willfully meddling in temporal matters that require no such ordination? Clearly you must delegate, but what about the risk? What about the risk that a lay employee or volunteer may blow something up, and you have to deal with the fallout and consequences? The answer is very simple:

> *When—not if—blow up happens you deal with it at that time. Period. End of story.*

I have known many a manager who out of an exaggerated fear of risk will not let go, cannot stop themselves from poking their nose into the realm of others whose job it is to _____ (insert task of choice here). Well, here is the plain and simple truth about risk: *you can never fully eliminate risk no matter what you do, so you better find a solution besides trying to do all the work yourself.* All you can really do is mitigate risk by having superior personnel reporting to you. But there is no free lunch: if you choose to mitigate risk the wrong way—by doing the work of others yourself—you are defeating the purpose of your ordination, wasting your precious ordained faculties, and are on the road to personal burnout. Therefore:

You must learn to delegate. Do not meddle and do not micromanage the personnel who report to you. Rather, in lieu of making these mistakes apply your ordained faculties to bring souls closer to Christ through the application of Org Chart strategic discrimination. Determine what Org Chart jobs can and should be performed by the laity, assign those jobs to the trained laity, *and then leave the laity alone to do their jobs.* Recognize that when something goes haywire—*and something always will*—you may need to become momentarily involved, you may even need to dismiss the employee or volunteer, *but what is not at fault or up for*

TACTICAL DISCRIMINATION AND DELEGATION

reconsideration is the essential principle: the principle of delegation of authority. Once you stop delegating you are dooming yourself to spend long and countless hours every day on temporal matters, instead of long and countless hours every day *on the spiritual matters that we need our ordained to be spending their time on.*

With the above in mind, from this point we are ready to proceed with creating the PMO Org Chart and writing the master strategic plan, or, maybe not yet. Why? At this point it only appears we are ready to begin writing our PMO strategic plan, but before we write a plan what do we need? We need something to act upon, to plan with and into. We need data; *we need information to feed into our plan.* Information is the raw fuel that feeds the planning process; *no data, no plan.* The complete PMO picture and story cannot be formed without the facts, or stated another way: *we need to paint the picture of the current reality facing the PMO administrator.* We need to see "all things PMO" as they truly are where we are, and not as we wish them to be. You cannot build anything without first having the facts of your situation. You must know the topology of PMO where you are. A building contractor needs architectural plans and blueprints before they begin construction. As such:

We already have an enhanced mission statement that enables us to write a Statement of Culture. The Statement of Culture animates us and will guide ongoing PMO personal, interpersonal expectations and relationships. Thus, we have our mandates in writing to begin our PMO strategic planning, but begin where? *You must begin by creating two Org Charts (handwritten is fine).*

Step 1: Create the PMO Org Chart where you work *precisely as it exists today.* Just sit down and write it out as best you know it to be, and;

Step 2: Eventually (not yet) we will create the Org Chart you want to install, *but that does not yet exist* where you work today. In other words, you must first know what exists as it exists in PMO (Step 1) *before you can convert what exists into how you want things to be in the future* (Step 2).

Perhaps there is an existing and up-to-date PMO Org Chart, but even if something is represented to you as up-to-date, *you must still verify what it illustrates is current and actual fact.* Most likely, expect there will be no up-to-date PMO Org Chart—if an Org Chart ever existed at all. Either way it is best at this stage if you literally start with a blank piece of paper and create your current Org Chart, box by box, connecting line by connecting line, just as you find it by inquiring from person-to-person, employee-to-employee: what is your job title? Who do you report to? Who reports to you? *You draw what you hear at this point, no matter what you hear and how incoherent what you are told may look on paper.*

After you create an up-to-date, all-inclusive parish Org Chart image that accurately reflects *all* current PMO personnel and volunteers—every single one, including their position title as they currently understand their title to be—you begin your thinking process with your Org Chart literally in hand, and specifically, *your Org Chart as it is,* not yet as you wish it to be. Sit down—because you will most likely need to—and take a hard look at what you have in front of you and then answer a few questions:

1. When asked, could each individual name his or her job title fully and accurately?
2. Could each person name, including full job title, who they report to, and who reports to them?
3. When you draw the lines connecting the boxes on the PMO Org Chart as it was reported to you to exist to the best of everyone's knowledge, is what you are looking at a coherent, logical, all-encompassing, accurate, functional picture of PMO? Does it look like a PMO Org Chart should look? Is it all-inclusive of every person and position you know should exist and work in PMO? Does it accurately portray PMO as it should be for PMO to serve the parishioners and geographic community? Is what

TACTICAL DISCRIMINATION AND DELEGATION

you are looking at functional and coherent as it is written, *or is it in fact a smoking gun indicator of precisely why your PMO is dysfunctional?*

For the sake of this discussion let's say what you have in your hand is an accurate depiction of current PMO. Now what? Your Org Chart reflects your PMO organizational architecture, all personnel and their managerial relationships—*but it is not useful to you unless it is not only accurately constructed, but just as importantly <u>correctly</u> constructed*. Odds are what you have in your hand now, though *accurately* constructed, in all likelihood is not <u>*correctly*</u> constructed—and note this critical distinction. Most likely what you have created as your current "PMO Org Chart" is actually to some degree an incomplete, incoherent, illogical, and useless Org Chart as the execution basis and foundation of your strategic plan, much less a highly successful PMO organization. However:

It was not a waste of time to create this Org Chart. Indeed, as stated above this step is mandatory. You must create your Org Chart snapshot v.1.0, an image of how your personnel currently perceive PMO to be constructed. Why? *Because you must know where you are in order to accurately map how to get to where you want to be*. Without Org Chart v.1.0 as your starting point, *you will have no strategic planning starting point at all*.

You need a starting point in the strategic planning process. It makes no difference if your starting point is a mess, because if you did the above correctly no matter the starting point mess you have, the Org Chart map in your hand is still highly useful to you. Why? *Because it is an accurate portrayal of your PMO reality*. Just because you might not like what you see doesn't make what you see inaccurate. At this point we want to know where we truly stand right now—not where we would like to stand.

Now that you have an Org Chart, what next? You begin by collecting data for your strategic plan. To do this simply follow your PMO Org Chart, literally in hand, where each box leads you. How? Specifically, you:

Observe, question, listen. How so?

What you observe, who you question, what specific questions you ask are based upon the nature of each box on your Org Chart. *You literally question and/or observe the person whose name is in the Org Chart box for each and every box on the Org Chart.* You ask germane questions of each and every person according to the job title of the box each person occupies on Org Chart. The Org Chart in your hand is your roadmap to learning what this person on the Org Chart—which is to say this box on the Org Chart—actually does in his or her job. And note this point in the back of your mind now very clearly: *until you know what each person is actually doing in their job, you cannot move forward with whatever retraining and/or remedial correction(s) must be done.*

> **In this world no one rules by love; if you are but amiable, you are no hero; to be powerful, you must be strong, and to have dominion you must have a genius for organizing.**
> —*John Henry Newman*

And as you question personnel, how do you listen to the answers you receive? *You listen, but you must listen through the filtration of the PMO culture you desire to have in place, as per your Statement of Culture.* As you listen to the answers you receive you compare and contrast the culture you *desire* to exist, *against the culture that actually exists as derived from the answers you hear*—in other words, the culture that exists in PMO upon your arrival. You take notes documenting the information you collect so that you know what specific items must be addressed—and in what order, as per the previously explained "The Good, The Bad, and The Ugly." However:

You are also in this process learning the PMO culture that currently exists. Remember, at this stage in all likelihood the employee or volunteer does not

TACTICAL DISCRIMINATION AND DELEGATION

know the correct PMO culture—which is to say the correct responses to your queries and questions. All the employee or volunteer knows at this stage is to report to you what they do, as you observe the manner in which they go about their work—both of which will be based on the current culture they operate under. *Very soon in this process you will be able to mentally map the deviation between the PMO culture that exists, <u>and the culture you desire to exist as expressed through your Statement of Culture</u>.* It is precisely during this process where you will reveal to yourself the scope of the PMO personnel challenge ahead, because as you know, *it is your current broken and dysfunctional culture that animates all employee and volunteer actions.*

You will note what you find during your interviews while building your Org Chart according to our three basic categories:

The Good, The Bad, and The Ugly. More on this labeling below.

At this stage, you will personally interview every person filling a position/box on the Org Chart that relates to PMO, *paying particular care to note positions that you know should exist on the Org Chart but are either totally missing, or; the work of Employee/Volunteer A is conflated and overlapping with the Org Chart box and work performed by Employee/Volunteer B, C, D, etc.*

Further note we return to a general theme: if you will not do this task as the PMO administrator, who can? Who will? In order to detect a missing box on the Org Chart—which is to saying missing task on the Org Chart—the PMO administrator must know what he wants his Org Chart to look like *in order to compare the Org Chart that actually exists to the Org Chart he desires to exist.* Thus, at the end of this inquiry process you will end up with two Org Charts: the predictably incomplete and insufficient Org Chart diagramming the reality of the dysfunctional organization you have inherited, *and the second Org Chart of the innovative model of PMO you must install.* Now what?

> *The variance between the two Org Charts, plus what you learned in the discovery process about your existing culture, defines, illustrates, and roadmaps the work you must now complete through your as yet to be created plan to move PMO from where it is, to where you want it to be.*

Many PMO problems exist not because of what the Org Chart indicates, *but because of what the Org Chart should indicate, but does not.* Missing Org Chart boxes translate directly to jobs that should be performed, but cannot be performed because the position required for the work to be done is non-existent. How can a non-existent job be filled, must less the associated work be completed? Example: parish business manager? There is none where you are? No such box exists on the Org Chart? Or there is an insufficient understanding of this job? As such, it's not what you see on the Org Chart—*it's what you don't see that you should that is going to give you enormous grief.* The missing parish business manager box should become conspicuous to you by its absence—*but only if you have created an Org Chart of PMO you desire that includes such a box.*

This Org Chart creation task is critical because it is foundational, but at the same time not an easy task for a variety of reasons:

1. Prior experience reviewing organizations and creating-rebuilding Org Charts is helpful. Why? *Because you know where the skeletons, the usual suspects, the common deficiencies and failures are hiding.* You not only know what questions to ask employees and volunteers, you know the art and nuance of asking them. This wisdom comes with experience and practice. If you have no prior experience in relation to Org Chart analysis, it's tough to identify "what should be there, that is not." Do your best, but you are not alone. Know you can ask for help. Like anything else, the more you do it the better at it you will become.

TACTICAL DISCRIMINATION AND DELEGATION

2. The people you speak with in PMO will tell you all they know. The problem is, *they usually don't know enough*. You could easily end up with your "Org Chart v 1.0" as a few floating boxes on a piece of paper, poorly defined, poorly labeled, and also not connected to each other in any way, or at least in any coherent way, not because the boxes shouldn't be connected—but because nobody really knows enough to robustly answer your questions. Is this your fault upon arrival? No. Are you stuck fixing it? Yes, because you are the PMO administrator.

3. After you have an Org Chart 1.0 picture of the current state of your PMO, you must be able to create a new Org Chart v. 2.0 picture of what you need to exist to become superior in PMO. Do you yet know what your PMO Org Chart should look like based upon *all the specific needs* of the parish and geographic community you serve? Who told you? How do you find out? Are you sure your information sources are correct? Finally:

4. Rolling out a new Org Chart is like parachuting out of an airplane—*you have two chances to get this right—your main chance, and your backup chance when you burn up your "new guy" goodwill after blowing your first chance*. As such, you must fully and truly conceptually understand PMO—what it is and what it is not, what it should do, and what is not within the role of PMO.

Fundamentally, a correct Org Chart is merely a reflection of how any organization should be constituted—but there's a catch. What catch? The folks operating under the existing Org Chart are often very happy just the way things are, thank you very much. If you are going to introduce the trauma of organizational change—and *trauma* is the correct word—*you better get "all things change" right the first time, but for sure the second time*. Otherwise, you have blown your credibility—and that's something very hard to earn back.

CHAPTER 55

INTERNAL AND EXTERNAL STRATEGIC PLAN TERMINOLOGY

We know the culture we desire; now as we create the existing Org Chart we will simultaneously document the responses we receive to our questions, and then compare and contrast those responses to paint a mental PMO cultural picture created by those responses. In this manner we will develop a picture of all things that report to us related to PMO, and we will undoubtedly discover the elephant in the room: *the current culture model is broken and nobody cares—much less even knows.* People working in PMO just go through the motions of their job, no longer seeing the larger context as they go about their work: *are we providing superior services to our community? And most importantly, are we providing all the temporal and spiritual services we should?*

From the action list we have built we know to give thanks for The Good that already exists, list but temporarily bypass The Bad, and immediately get to work on solving The Ugly. Our objective now is to discover where we stand, to learn how things operate, not necessarily as they should operate, but how things actually do operate in every aspect of PMO. This is the discernment process, or stated another way:

> **God, grant me the serenity to accept the things I cannot change, courage to change the things I can, and wisdom to know the difference.**

From this assembled list of The Ugly, we will now select the correct tool(s) to address each issue via a written strategic plan of execution. You will find here a *parish strategic plan shell format* for your use in your parish. This shell is essentially a strategic master plan-building roadmap for you to use in conjunction with the Org Chart you must implement, to address the PMO issues you are facing. No two parish PMO situations will be perfectly identical, so you can now clearly see what items and what order you are guided to address will be based upon the specific issues and problems you have discovered in your parish. Nevertheless, the strategic master plan shell will be helpful. Also note:

Internal to this shell document the strategic plan does not use our *internal PMO vocabulary* of, "The Good, The Bad, and The Ugly" we use to drive collecting and prioritizing the input to our plan. Fine. This is the distinction between addressing those who must make the sausage and who work with you in that world—*using our intermediate and internal PMO terminology as the sausage makers*—and the language of those who consume the final product. Many fields and professions have both an internal vocabulary and a public vocabulary to express the same thought, the former often consisting of acronyms and shorthand phrases. PMO is no different. Those who consume the final strategic plan need only be familiar with the traditional language as expressed within the published version of the parish strategic plan. The fact is, there are too many terms used in the field of "strategic planning" that vary depending upon which school you attended, books you read, etc. But since we are operating here within a holistic system of PMO, *we need to use internal terminology that will be understood and is in common with all other practitioners of this same system.*

Parishioners not a party to the creation of the strategic plan do not need to learn the internal language of PMO we speak of here in this book (i.e. The Good, The Bad, The Ugly), which we use to discuss and build the plan. In other words, *how we go about expressing in language the processes by which we define what*

INTERNAL AND EXTERNAL STRATEGIC PLAN TERMINOLOGY

should be included in or excluded from the strategic plan is our own internal shorthand; we are not using this same internal terminology as we will use in the final plan meant for a wider, public, non-sausage-maker community audience that is by definition unfamiliar with the content, principles, and terminology presented in this book.

All our community members care about are the services provided by the parish, not the internal methods, means, and vocabulary used to provide each service. No matter the formal or traditional language used in the final version of your strategic plan, you will find that the data used to animate the creation of the plan does fall under and well correlate to the common-sense category terms we have used in this book—The Good, The Bad, and The Ugly. However, in the final strategic plan for presentation to parishioners it makes sense to use category labeling, language, and terminology that speaks directly to such topics as "Evangelization, Facility Usage, Youth Ministry," etc., rather than our generalized internal-speak, umbrella categorizations of, "The Good, The Bad, and The Ugly." Why? Because we must speak the language expected by the receiver.

CHAPTER 56

ON THE ART AND SCIENCE OF STRATEGIC PLAN CREATION

The following primary category labeling (and further sub-labeling) for public consumption should be considered as a master-planning template, but subject to changes made at your discretion. Should you choose to use other topical labeling and/or topical report ordering from that presented here, feel free to do so as warranted by the circumstances of your community. What is important is not so much the exact labeling or terminology selected, or the order of topical presentation, or the formatting, or the plan length. *What is important is that the strategic plan must be accurate, thorough, and in writing.*

However, "accurate" and "thorough" does not mean over-perfectionism, so a note of caution:

> **The maxim "Nothing but perfection" may be spelled "Paralysis."**
> —*Winston Churchill*

Note "accurate and thorough" *is not meant here to imply perfection.* There is a time and place for achieving absolute perfection—and creating this plan is neither. *Do not dither over every word or comma, etc.* Given the likely circumstances of PMO that you will inherit you will not have time for absolute perfection in plan layout or content. If your innate temperament leans toward perfection, then in regard to creating this plan: get over it. Let it go. For example, no piece of significant commercial business software was ever released for sale in a perfect, bug-free condition—and deliberately so. Serviceable, workable condition? Yes. Bug-free? Heck no—*as a matter of design policy we let the end-users do the final debugging of our code.* You think you are going to perfectly nail this strategic plan by agonizing over every detail? No, you are not. Besides:

This is a living and working document—if you're not trimming the sails as you go, and if you're not revisiting the entire plan once a year, you're not doing your PMO administrator job. You have an actual parish and geographic community that demands serious PMO problems be solved right now, today. You are not engaging in an academic exercise for a letter grade where you are—your parish community is hurting in many ways. You don't have time to dither and delay while striving for perfection—which by definition you will not achieve anyway without feedback from your parishioners—and how can you get feedback if you don't ultimately roll something out? So stop wasting time, write the best strategic plan you can, and then get to work implementing the plan.

CHAPTER 57

STRATEGIC PLAN STARTS WITH COMMUNICATIONS

> What we've got here...is failure...to communicate.
> —The Captain, Cool Hand Luke

The final parish strategic plan category labeling (the public release version) is up to you, but as examples the following strategic plan category labels may apply:

Communications

Evangelization

Stewardship

Youth

Facilities

As an example of strategic plan creation we will illustrate the planning methodology and thought processes via the first category listed above, "Communications." Why communications? Without superior communications across all of PMO, all other strategic planning tasks become more difficult if not impossible.

We will first discuss the science followed by discussing the art of implementing the "Communications" strategy points. As previously mentioned, we will emphasize the art because the science is just not that difficult. When we explore the art of anything we mean we are exploring the thought processes used to arrive at decisions—in other words the "Why?" animating the "How?" Simply offering a strategic planning shell—the nuts and bolts science—without also including a commensurate understanding of the art animating the science of each topic, is at best ineffective, and could be dangerous. Also note a simple internet search offers many sample parish strategic plan formats from which you may choose. Nevertheless, no matter which plan format you choose, you must always understand the "Why?" animating the "How?"

Communications

Objective 1: To foster building a parish community that is collaborative, mutually supportive, and well informed in real-time about all aspects of parish life so that all parishioners feel empowered and informed.

Strategy 1.1: First establish a *Communications and Marketing Board* (CMB) that will be a resource to the parish and its ministries and support them in defining and achieving their vision, mission, values, and strategic plans.

The science:

The establishment of any parish volunteer assembly, board, group, ministry, etc., initially requires writing a brief description of the required tasks, including any desired or mandatory requirements, and an estimated time commitment. Broadcast this CMB description and member opening through the parish bulletin, website, all social media channels, personal connections, and word-of-mouth. Recruit, interview, and retain the superior CMB applicants. (More on this dimension of the process in the chapter on hiring and firing.) Fundamentally, creating a CMB is an exercise in recruiting volunteers who will work as an advisory body—the CMB—and report their recommendations to the PMO administrator. (Note this process is common to assembling any board, group, ministry, etc.)

STRATEGIC PLAN STARTS WITH COMMUNICATIONS

The art:

I've searched all the parks in all the cities and found no statues of committees.

—G. K. Chesterton

The keen reader of the above realizes we are looking at creating a "Communications and Marketing Board" to provide much-needed and critical advice on every marketing activity and ministry that exists—or should exist, in the parish. But I'm not a big fan of boards or committees. Why? Set aside committee members' "good intentions," etc. Most committees in relation to the task at hand are a collection of good-hearted but poorly managed, relatively low/no subject-matter skill individuals, so unless and until you are willing to proactively recruit, populate, and manage the CMB with superior personnel in this field, navigate through any member's petty parochial interests, stop bad ideas from becoming reality, weed out those with hidden personal agendas, etc., the guidance presented here will never work for you. Why? Because of all the subtle reasons embedded in the above Chesterton quote. *Unless and until you are a master of populating your committee in the first place, and subsequently running your CMB meetings, you will fail.* If that is your case, then the CMB is a superior idea. In other words, if you populate your CMB with good-hearted but nevertheless low/no talent personnel, and/or you do not know how to manage the CMB to achieve your plan goals, the CMB makes for fine Org Chart window dressing—*but it will never work as intended.*

With the above in mind:

Gone are the days we mentally build a drive-thru window and order-take for higher ministry participation levels, more volunteers, greater attendance at events, etc. We are proactive in our PMO efforts now. In populating the CMB exclusively with supremely talented volunteers we are hereby acknowledging the critical need for…marketing? Marketing, within a Church setting and environment??? *Yes, absolutely*—and internally to PMO we will now call it what it is: *marketing*. Why? *Because we are now involved in an internal sausage-making discussion, and in such discussions we speak plainly and we speak the truth to everyone sitting at this table.* We do not hide our purpose or intentions behind some euphemistic milquetoast language more suited for those outside PMO, such as "encourage, publicize, notify, foster, nurture, cultivate, boost, aid, stimulate, assist, help, advance, further, advocate…." Those days are over. Therefore, from now on in PMO we are here to proactively market, *and the art of marketing starts with the fact that internal to PMO we are going to so state our intentions to market parish _____ (insert item of choice here) in plain English.*

Once you acknowledge you are actually involved in *marketing*, once you explain that sound business principles can, should, and will coexist with PMO and within a "Church" context, *you unlock and unleash ideas people would have been too timid and too hesitant to have otherwise offered for your consideration when their minds are shackled to notions that "marketing" is off-limits and somehow contrary to achieving superior PMO, much less existing within the Church.*

Strategy 1.2: Define and implement a communication and public relations/marketing plan so that information and resources can be shared within ministries, between ministries, and between the parish and the community.

The science:

This point in the strategic plan addresses technology implementation:
1. Establishing internal digital communications means and methods between all members of the various ministries.

2. Establishing external digital communications means and methods between the parish and members of the community.

Regarding internal communications between all members of the various ministries, this is an issue that must be facilitated through the person solely responsible for the parish email server configuration and all social media platforms. Email and social media groupings that correspond to the membership list for each parish ministry must be created (and frequently updated) to facilitate immediate broadcast messaging to/from all members of the ministry group(s). Training must be provided to anyone not technically confident or competent in his or her digital media skills and associated platforms.

In terms of communications between the parish and the community, the parish Webmaster and Social Media Yoda must use their respective channels of communications to broadcast all parish news approved for distribution. This point of course assumes—often incorrectly—that each and every ministry forwards any news, event dates, etc., they wish to distribute in a timely and complete manner.

The art:

Social media is not just a spoke on the wheel of marketing. It's becoming the way entire bicycles are built.

—*Ryan Lilly, author*

Proactive, timely, vibrant, communications between people is, conceptually speaking, not new or news today. What is new? One extra but critical dimension: superior *execution* of proactive, timely, vibrant, communications *between PMO* and parish ministry members, as well as the parish community at-large. *This point—adding PMO-generated agenda topics into the conversation mix—will most likely be a completely new paradigm in most parish PMO settings.* How so? For example:

If you find that PMO personnel think that the use of email is "cutting edge" today, you know you have a paradigm change challenge in this regard. Note all such PMO initiated parish to parishioner communication is part and parcel in the DNA of the correct culture, a culture you must instill and install. The PMO idea generation and communications paradigm must shift in the receiver from, "Who are these guys? Why are they sending me this stuff?" to, "Where are these guys? I miss their information."

And who are "these guys"? we are speaking of? Sam or Susie, the PMO administrator? No. *We are here to institutionalize PMO where we are*, and to institutionalize something is to migrate our thinking away from the realm of the individual, to the realm of, "The **Office of** PMO." We want people to look for PMO in the parish as a *distinguishably named entity, not a specific person* we know will ultimately leave. *What we want to be memorable is the Christian action itself connected to the Church, not necessarily the individual who initiates it.*

The science of communications between parish ministries and the science of communication between the parish and the community is not a mechanically tough problem to address—just start communicating via the available and familiar channels and tools of communication. However, the art of installing, institutionalizing, and supporting vibrant communications in PMO is a different matter, and one that tracks back to the art of installing the correct culture, to imbuing in all PMO personnel and volunteers the acceptance that one dimension of their job among the many, *is to communicate as and when necessary, but in the precise manner and method preferred by <u>the receiver</u>.*

> **That which is received is received according to the mode of the receiver.**
>
> —*St. Thomas Aquinas, ST 1. q. 84, art. 1*

STRATEGIC PLAN STARTS WITH COMMUNICATIONS

The paradigm shift here is not the science of communications—*it's the notion that in order to market ourselves we must not only communicate a refined and targeted message, but today and forevermore we must do so in <u>real-time</u>*. You must part and parcel instill this understanding on the importance of *communications speed* at the same time you are installing the new culture and killing the old culture. Thus, establishing the importance of communications between people working within each ministry, or the parish and community, is not something you do when you write the strategic plan—*it is something you explicitly do as a byproduct of killing the old culture and installing the new culture*. As opportunities arise you must expressly teach this point, and you also personally model this point in all your own communications. To delay is to fail.

By the time you arrive at this strategic plan creation phase, the necessity for all forms of communication in and through PMO should already be well understood, all personnel should be receptive to it, and simply be waiting for button-pushing instructions on the science of how to mechanically communicate via the hardware and software platforms you have chosen to use. Those, for example, who are still proud they only check their email, "whenever they get around to it...whenever they feel like it...whenever they have time," and/or, "I don't have a smart phone...I don't use social media...I don't like the internet...the internet is bad for you...what is social media?" must immediately reset their thinking to the present day, or seek employment elsewhere. Why? Because information travels from person-to-person *at the pace of its slowest communicator*.

Strategy 1.3: Improve existing communication mechanisms, and create and maintain new methods of communication with, and among, parishioners and the entire geographic community we serve. Fully engage social media channels of communication.

The science:

Your primary and self-explanatory PMO communications channel options with parishioners and/or PMO personnel are:

1. In-person
2. Telephone
3. Email
4. Weekly parish bulletin
5. Parish website
6. Social media (i.e. Twitter, Instagram, Facebook, etc.)

Anyone confused about the technical working mechanics of any of the above points should seek technical support specific to their needs.

The art:

Any surprises on the above list of PMO communications channels? No. Anything conceptually new to you on the list? No, or at least there should not be as a PMO administrator. The challenge is not failing to know what communications channels are available, or the fundamental purpose of each particular channel. The challenge is twofold:

1. Do all of the above communications channels—which taken collectively form *the digital aeropolis* of communications today—fully and vibrantly exist in your PMO?

2. What do you actually *do* with all of the communications channels, and how *effectively* are they deployed to communicate PMO services provided to the community you serve? Are you just happy that such digital communications exist at all, *without due regard to their level of utilization and actual engagement?* Do you even know their exact levels of utilization and engagement—and if you do, as previously discussed, what are your measurement yardsticks? In other words, *is your utiliza-*

tion and engagement of these communications channels commensurate with the size of the geographic area you serve? Are you as engaged with the community through PMO as the size of your geographic community statistically indicates you should be engaged? Have you skipped answering that elephant in the room question in favor of pretending that any level of digital aeropolis utilization and engagement is the same as total utilization and engagement?

In case you have not noticed, the US Postal Service is slowly becoming irrelevant to most people. Why? It is not efficient. Why? Emails move at the speed of light. Postal mail moves at the speed of truck. Email is not only faster but also cheaper. It is hard to compete with speed of light delivery combined with cheaper, especially when "cheaper" usually means "free." You can't get cheaper than free, and last I heard you couldn't go faster than the speed of light (you can theoretically bend space but that's another subject). Email is particularly dying among younger digital media users—and practically all new users of digital media are by definition younger users. Each day a new wave of younger users are being allowed by their parents to enter the digital aeropolis, either through a smart phone, tablet, and/or laptop computer. Do they also engage the parish digital aeropolis? *How can they if there is no such thing as an active, vibrant, digital aeropolis originating in your parish?* And each day the geneation of people who eschew all things digital in favor of a postage stamp or landline telephone are literally…dying. In particular:

Why is email dying with our younger parishioner community? Too many junk emails, but mainly because other much more intelligent, selective, targeted, and efficient methods of communication have become highly nuanced in delivering tailored content to only those who are interested in that content—and often with revenue generating ads attached. This is known as the proverbial "Win-Win" situation—a win for the sender and a win for the receiver. Further note when someone with talent and high motivation has a vested interest in promoting Technology A (for example, all methods of digital communications) over Technology B (the legacy and less-favored analog methods of communication), *you really don't want your PMO to be heavily invested in Technology B methodology, thinking, and culture*. Translation:

As the PMO administrator you can expect social media channels to collectively represent a very important and fruitful communications channel, especially to and with your younger target audience. And what is "younger" today? That age is a moving target, but roughly anyone under age forty is "younger" with respect to their technological comfort and proficiency—and that number continues to rise (eventually the analog generations will no longer be with us). So, that's a lot of people, but…*do you see as many of the forty and under crowd sitting in the pews today as you should?* Maybe one reason is that your PMO does not embrace, or at least fully embrace, the forty and under crowd's *preferred method of communications*, and your message is not crafted to their perceived needs at this time in their lives. And whose fault is that? *Not the receiver's, I can tell you that.* So where does that leave PMO communications?

That leaves PMO to think/act outside the proverbial box to reach people. For example, pause here and visit YouTube. Briefly view the video, "Theology on Tap Silicon Valley—Masculinity and Femininity, The Beauty of Complementarity" by Fr. Mark Doherty. The point here is not particularly about the content of his talk, *but rather the venue where Fr. Mark is talking.* Fr. Mark is meeting people where they are—a dining and drinking area, not at Mass where he would clearly prefer them to be.

> **These young professionals who have moved into the neighborhood generally have no connection to the Church whatsoever, and more generally seem to have none or very little**

STRATEGIC PLAN STARTS WITH COMMUNICATIONS

religious experience or background to speak of. It means that engaging them is very, very challenging and it comes down to one-on-one encounters more than anything else.
—*Fr. Mark Doherty, Mission District, San Francisco*

The good news here: we do not have to invent anything new in terms of communications science to improve the effectiveness of our parish-to-parishioner communications. Perhaps life-sized holographic communications will come of age—but it is not up to PMO to make this so. *Our challenge is to most effectively use the channels that exist today.* All the information anyone might need is either available or can be created. We just have to be smarter in PMO in the art of communicating this information to our community—*our customer in business and internal sausage-making parlance*. In terms of PMO, the further good news is we do not have to create engaging, inspiring, motivational, topical content for our parishioners and community at-large—content already exists in abundance.

For excellent video motivation that sums up why the above thinking animates our communications duties in PMO—*especially in regard to seeking out those who have quit on their faith*—please pause now and view the short YouTube video "The Hound of Heaven: A Modern Adaptation," and then note this well:

You are the Hound's hands and feet.

CHAPTER 58

THE PMO COMMUNICATIONS CHALLENGE

What is our biggest communications challenge in PMO?

Our biggest challenge is not the science but the art, and the art is having the good sense to wisely choose Magisterially correct content to communicate from the tsunami of available material already published in books, articles, and/or on the internet, send it in a timely manner to precisely who needs it, via the preferred communications channel they wish to receive it.

However, what does "fully engage" mean to the receiver, specifically in a PMO communications context? To "fully engage the receiver" is really a euphemism for this starting point in the receiver's mind: *"Dude, don't bother me with anything I don't want to read or view."* Fine, but how do you accomplish knowing that? Imperfectly to start, and then you refine your message. What you don't do is give up and become satisfied with any current brokenness or deficiencies in PMO communications. Specifically, this is how you start:

In PMO we (aka: any PMO employee and/or volunteer) have the job of literally and figuratively becoming a micro-search engine working on behalf of every life-profile in our community—the young, old, active, lapsed, healthy, sick, married, divorced, homosexual, etc., member of our community. We do this proactively because it is our communications and outreach duty in PMO, *not because we are naïvely waiting to be asked questions by people who have already quit listening to us.* If you are waiting for apathetic and/or lapsed parishioners to help themselves in the spiritual awakening realm, much less ask the Church they already quit for anything, *you are going to be waiting a long time.* Specifically:

In PMO like the *Hound of Heaven, it is your duty* to digitally source solid and Magisterially accurate Catholic material relevant and helpful to the multi-faceted lives of our *active and lapsed* parishioners, across all levels of knowledge and interest. *We do this for them, and on their behalf—we do not wait for them to awake from their sleepy mental fog and finally "get it."* Why?

Because anyone who thinks their communication is confined to the available page space of the parish bulletin or parish website visitors…*needs to advance their mental clock forward several decades.* We do not even ask, much less expect or rely upon, the lost sheep within our geographic area to unilaterally seek out and find the information they need to grow deeper in their faith and closer to Christ, through the parish bulletin or website. If a parishioner or lost sheep does take that initiative, is a self-starter, and independent of anything we might send him (or her) in PMO, takes it upon himself to locate information pertaining to his faith-walk, *that is just a bonus*. But we are not going to implicitly demand by PMO omission of its outreach and evangelization duty that anyone, without our extending and helping hand, will spontaneously combust and become proactively on fire in their dormant faith. If an individual is not that far along in his or her faith walk, what then? *It is our duty <u>in PMO</u> to meet them where they are, not where we wish they were.* Therefore:

It is our duty in PMO to proactively communicate what is helpful to every person in our geographic area that God has—*or has not yet*, placed in our path. This is the art of PMO communications, and this is what it means to "help our brothers and sisters" in the digital era—*as we are never going back to the non-digital, analog, slow and inflexible era of communications—so as a Church we best get on-board with this much more proactive communications principle right quick.*

What parishioners do with whatever we send them is on them—but we will be proactively digitally communicating, as precisely and in as fine a granularity as possible in helpful content, whatever we discern/discover in the digital information aeropolis that will help current and/or lapsed parishioners in their faith walk. The communications science concerns the mechanics of *how* the information is sent; a technically competent professional covers this base. But the art of applying the communications science is in discerning *what* to send, *why* to send it, and *who* to send it to. However, we must now note:

You can't digitally communicate to your parishioners, the family and friends of your parishioners, or the lapsed and lost, unless and until you know:

1. Who they are in the first place.
2. Social media and/or email account contact info.
3. Precisely what germane topics/subjects they want to know more about.

And how do you acquire the above information? The old fashioned way:

> *Like the Hound of Heaven, you unceasingly and relentlessly and creatively and at every opportunity invite people to provide this personal contact information through every means available to you.*

For the sake of clarity allow me put achieving the above—*clearly not an optional activity*—in two contexts:

1. If you ever had to make payroll you know one truth: *missing payroll is not an option*. Make payroll, or shut down. Therefore: if you context acquiring the digital arena personal contact information you need in the same manner you would if you had to make payroll—in other words,

you must collect the required contact information or shut down—*you will be amazed at how this attitude colors your actions and efforts to collect the necessary contact information.* All of a sudden obstacles become something that by definition are simply, "things that must be overcome to reach my objective, because failure is not an option."

2. We strive to emulate what Jesus would do in our daily lives, which in this case translates to our PMO activities in sending useful communications to current and lapsed parishioners—well beyond the boilerplate parish potluck dinner reminders, notifications, etc. In particular, our example comes from Jesus on the cross when He said, "I thirst." Well, in PMO *we thirst, too.* Thirst for what? We thirst to serve the spiritual needs of every soul, but we can't serve them unless we know who they are and what they need, and we will not know what most of them need until we invite them to share with us how we might help them in a PMO communications context. As such, we must collect their digital contact information. But what is the *invitation trap* here?

> **Twitter is not a technology, it's a conversation—and it's happening with or without you.**
>
> —*Charlene Li, author*

Recall the old attendance roll call joke? "Raise your hand if you are not here." The same trap applies here. How so? As the PMO administrator responsible for communications, you want to better serve the temporal and spiritual needs of parishioners by inviting them to provide your office with the information requested in points 1, 2, and 3 listed above. So you place a request for this information in the parish bulletin. You know…*that same paper parish bulletin the audience you are seeking to reach already does not bother to read*, in part because this audience simply does not prefer to read via paper, but mostly because *they are not in Church in the first place to even pick up a parish bulletin.* How can someone read a parish bulletin he does not have? Clearly, you are not going to be nearly as effective as you could be—even when communicating with active parishioners—solely via the paper parish bulletin.

But how do you communicate with "parishioners" who have already quit on their faith? *Be kind, be patient, and show love, fundamentally that's how.* The Church has lost millions of people for a variety of reasons, *but she did not lose millions of people overnight.* Translation: those who left can return back through the same always open doors of the Church via the same free will that took them out. Your job in PMO is not to focus on how many people you reach; <u>*your job is to focus on how you reach people*</u>. If you do your part correctly, you know the Holy Spirit will do His part one soul at a time.

But in our "Hurry, hurry, faster!" society, how long does "one soul at a time" take? Wrong question. In PMO we are concerned with always doing the right thing in a superior manner—that's it. People are always looking for that single magic bullet—whatever the topic of discussion—which will totally change everything; instant success. *But there is no magic bullet in reaching lost souls.* It is better to think in terms of incremental gains—four singles equals a home run. It is easy to become discouraged if you do not accept or understand this point. Take for example the math of starting with a penny and doubling the amount every day for a month. Relatively speaking you have nothing to show for the first two weeks of your efforts. Sounds discouraging. But on Day 31? *You will have a staggering $21,474,836.46.* Clearly, your patience is paramount when building PMO. Gains will likely take months, not days or weeks. The problem?

The problem is—and has been for far too long—we accept the attrition of parishioners without a parish-centric, <u>*PMO-led*</u>, communications counter-strategy to bring each parishioner back by overcoming the reason(s) for their apathy or antipathy, not to mention better serve the composite temporal and spiritual needs of the parishioners who have not yet left—but might tomorrow. At the same time, we must acknowledge the avalanche of garbage accessible—not just on TV, but also for example via the ubiquitous smart "phone" we carry every waking moment in our pocket or purse. Therefore, we must answer:

Originating in PMO, what are your proactively delivered sound Catholic sources of targeted, timely, relevant, information to counter the avalanche of readily available secular garbage? When I am in the privacy of my mind, if not vocally, wondering what is wrong with moving in with my boyfriend or girlfriend, or what is wrong with IVF when we desperately want a child, or why homosexuals can't be married in the Church, note I have mostly long since stopped caring what the Church has to say about that. *Except for an interesting truth:* the prayers and petitions offered on my behalf by a loving family member, friend and/or total stranger that have by the grace of God pried open an ever-so-small window in my soul willing to listen. *If only someone would proactively send me something doctrinally correct to read or listen to that would answer my questions*. However:

Since I am no longer seeking communication with the Church in general or engaging my parish in particular—indeed in my mind I no longer "belong" to a "parish" or Church—how does PMO communicate with me when they don't know who I am, where I am, or what is on my mind? As follows:

1. Rome wasn't built in a day. Translation: be persistent, be patient, and never quit. See where you are in a year, in five years, in ten years, of relentlessly applying this PMO communications strategy day after day.

2. If you are looking here for a solution, a perfect solution to this conundrum of needing to communicate but not knowing precisely who to communicate with or what topic the receivers are most interested in right now, guess what? *Again, there is no magic bullet solution.* There is, simply, a solution as follows:

What did we already establish as our objective in PMO in general, and PMO

THE PMO COMMUNICATIONS CHALLENGE

communications specifically? To help people with their faith walk by leading people to Christ. And what is our specific challenge in PMO communications? To provide useful and timely information to current or lapsed parishioners in our geographic area, we need to know *who* to reach, their social media *contact information*, and what *topic(s)* they want to know more about. The low-hanging fruit in this challenge: our current and active parishioners. If someone is currently active in faith and parish, just ask him or her for their contact information—these are not hard people to find, nor usually reluctant to provide the details you are seeking. The more difficult challenge: those who have quit on their faith or were not catechized to begin with, and no longer participate in the parish. Which brings us back here:

If you are not here, raise your hand.

3. How do you communicate with people you do not know? As follows:

   Whenever you do not know precisely what to do, <u>you do everything you can imagine that is legal, ethical, and moral</u>. Even the ridiculous-sounding things? Especially the ridiculous-sounding things.

This brings us back to: what is the point of our efforts in PMO via the CMB? *We are trying to reach a critical mass.* Not every marketing idea succeeds, but every marketing idea that you never try is a 100% failure, 100% of the time. For example:

When I was in the education business we had a staff meeting, and one of the topics of discussion was directing first-time student-customers from the front door entrance of our large training facility to locate their specific classroom. Our problem? When students reached the T-junction at the end of a hallway they didn't know if they should turn right or left. Standard directional signage placed here for whatever reason was not always effective. People wandered the hallways trying to locate their classroom. What to do? How do we capture the attention of a lost, in a hurry, directionally disoriented, late-for-class new student-customer and give him or her clear directions to the classroom? Somebody in the meeting said we should paint a scarecrow on the wall, and of course everyone burst out laughing—everyone except me. That tongue-in-cheek scarecrow suggestion was actually a eureka moment.

I happened to know a superior artist. I knew him at all because I offered free computer skills training to people on probation, and this young man was on probation. What happened next? One month later what was on the wall at the troublesome T-junction in the hallway? *A larger than life-size perfect full-color rendering of the Scarecrow from the Wizard of Oz, both arms outstretched and pointing, with the yellow brick road and Emerald City in the background.* At the end of each arm were painted the large classroom numbers in each direction. Communication problem solved. How? By the painting of a scarecrow on the wall? Technically, yes, but in reality, not close. *You must first be wiling to think outside the proverbial box to solve your communications challenges.* The point:

Nobody—*and I mean nobody*—knows precisely in advance what will work and will not work in marketing and communications strategies. As such, nobody knows how to reach, both mentally and electronically, all those people in your parish's geographic area who have quit on their faith in God. But I know this: inside the box, narrow, timid, self-defeating, negative thinking will never allow you to paint a metaphorical *Wizard of Oz* scarecrow on your PMO communications wall. Hidebound, risk-averse thinkers unwilling and/or unable to allow for such ideas to be tried should not hold positions of authority when it comes to marketing. Another communications example:

Do you know what is on 24/7 display in front of the Holy Apostles College &

Seminary Cromwell, Connecticut campus, on the grass frontage area facing the road that runs past the campus? *Full-sized grave marker crosses.* There is also a large sign that all passers-by can read explaining that each cross represents 1,000,000 aborted babies since abortion was legalized in the Untied States by the Roe v. Wade Supreme Court decision. Skip for now focusing on the courage it took to approve building this display. *My point is about the outside the box thinking that was required to generate this visual communications display in the first place.*

So what is "outside the box" thinking in our communications context? For starters, it means: "Don't look for me to tell you the answer, *when I'm looking for you to tell me the answer.*" Translation: the first box you must learn to think outside of is the one labeled with your name on it—*because you don't have all the answers, and neither do I.* But God made sure that for every problem, *somebody does have the answer.* There is a key for every circumstantial block and lock. *Our job is to find it.* But you must be willing to try, to experiment, with what others are not. As such, what if you posted a street sign that directed people to your website to increase traffic? And what if upon visiting the website just one person of his or her own free will—just one—completed an online form providing social media contact information, and requested more information on some topic? Let's answer those questions with this question: what is the relationship of all your PMO communications efforts in this regard, *and the potential benefits to the soul of this one person?* Infinite. Incalculable. Beyond words.

> **A person who never made a mistake never tried anything new.**
>
> —*Albert Einstein*

You must be willing to try what others are not if what has been done to date is not delivering you superior results. Remember our performance-measurement yardstick is *not* to look at where we were in relation to where we are now—*nobody cares.* Our performance yardstick must always be to look at where we are, *in relation to where we should be.* If you are not where you should be—and you are probably not—you still have work to do. Doing things the way you always have in PMO will not get you to where you should be *or you would already be there.*

The Church/parish has lost people over time, one person at a time, and the parish will help return people to Christ in the same manner—over time, one soul at a time. And so we return to the *art* of PMO communications, and specifically how you as PMO administrator develop, how you establish traction, how you become trusted as a reliable source of information with both current and lapsed parishioners.

As mentioned, capturing the information in points 1, 2, and 3 above from active parishioners is relatively easy and quick—just ask them. But the superior PMO administrator should not be satisfied with only picking the low-hanging fruit. What about those souls who have left the parish, left the Church? Do we give up on communicating with them? Is that what Jesus taught? No. In PMO we just have to think in terms of how we creatively demonstrate and communicate, "be kind, be patient, show love" to people who are no longer looking at or listening to us—perhaps even mock and insult us. The only thing that works in this regard *is to try everything you can imagine in PMO communications that is legal, ethical, and moral.*

If at this point you are realizing the potential impact of superior PMO should deliver so much more to current and lapsed parishioners than ensuring the roof doesn't leak, events are properly scheduled, and the potluck dinner is covered—that is the intention. For far too long PMO has been misunderstood, viewed as a purely administrative function, a bureaucratic backwater that has nothing to contribute to the spiritual development needs of parishioners. *This notion is not only false it is detrimental to our mission of saving souls.* Therefore:

THE PMO COMMUNICATIONS CHALLENGE

How is PMO perceived in your parish, indeed, in each parish in each diocese? As a sleepy backwater of mundane administrative tasks? Has the PMO duties and responsibilities paradigm shifted yet where you are? Is the role of PMO correctly perceived as *far more* than stereotypical "parish office" work? The fact is:

> *PMO is the authorized, centralized, Org Chart-based responsible hub for your speed of light digital aeropolis communication initiatives and campaigns directed toward current and lapsed parishioners.*

Oh.

So that means...it is in the realm of PMO where creative and coordinating responsibility is placed for communications—and so much more? That is correct. Good to know that communications is not the vaporous, euphemistic, and Kumbaya sing-along, "everybody's job," but that actual responsibility for *producing good-fruit results commensurate with the size of our geography*—and not the Dr. Feel Good "Look how far we've come from where we use to be!" attitude—*is in fact grounded in personnel on the PMO Org Chart.*

Leaning on the printed parish bulletin, occasional website visits to check the Mass times and the like as a primary means of PMO communications today is totally absurd. Fundamentally, realize that if someone willingly and voluntarily subscribed to follow the maximum character limit of inane Twitter utterances by _____ (insert "celebrity" name of choice here—and I use that term loosely), that same person might, could, and certainly should receive a Tweet from your parish on a topic of this person's choice that will lead him or her closer to Christ—and perhaps out of mortal sin. However, if establishing such communications does not originate by, from, and through creative outside-the-box outreach thinking of PMO personnel, please: you tell me where such vital communications will originate to help the apathetic parishioner, a soul exponentially more in-touch with the latest celebrity gossip than the Gospel message of Jesus Christ.

And remember this clearly: it does not matter what topic a person starts to engage us with—any topic or concern that brings a person in contact with the Church is a good thing. Certainly, we will look at every parishioner contact that spontaneously comes our way, or we generate through proactive PMO communications, as being under the guidance of the Holy Spirit. And where this contact leads is between God and each soul. *But our duty in PMO is to serve the parishioner; current or lapsed it makes no difference.* We are in the service business—*God is in the results business.*

For example, active or lapsed parishioner topics of website and/or social media channel outreach might be:

- Abortion
- Annulments
- Bereavement
- Bible Study
- Books
- Car-pooling
- Crisis
- Children
- Events
- Divorce
- Employment
- Family
- Fellowship
- Financial
- Grieving
- Internships

- Legislation
- Marriage
- Ministry
- Music
- NFP
- Prayer
- RCIA
- Retreats
- Sacraments
- Spiritual Direction
- Youth
- Volunteering

If you review the above list and immediately jump to, "But many or all of those items are mentioned in the parish bulletin or website," *go back and reread the above comments on the parameters explaining how people prefer to communicate today.* We live in a digital world. My grandma reads the bulletin, maybe, if she can find her glasses. Furthermore, I can't read the bulletin if I don't have the bulletin to read. Lastly, even if I have a bulletin I'm not interested in scanning it for the one, possible, helpful nugget of information that I might find useful. Why? Because I am already mentally conditioned by how social media fundamentally works *to expect a filtered and customized level of service from my digital communication sources of information.* How so?

1. The sender must know what I want to know. Information I desire will automatically come to me, *I will not go to the information.* This is just how I prefer communications to work in my world today. *And if you don't want to conform to my communications preferences, fine, but you will remain shut out of my world—I really don't care.* And;

2. Whatever information does come to me, *I know in advance I elected to*

receive it and I will have some level of interest in it—or at least I did at one time. Therefore:

3. If the time between my need for information and receiving the information is measured in days, much less a comically mislabeled "weekly parish bulletin," this is most assuredly not the speed of delivery I have grown accustomed to in my personal digital world, and I will in all likelihood *learn to ignore* your PMO-supplied "communications" as a viable, much less useful, source of information and guidance in my life. Everybody in PMO needs to be onboard with this execution reality:

The communications speed limit today is 186,000 miles per second.

This point brings us back to a previous lesson on *execution*. If you can't/don't/won't execute according to the needs of the receiver, you are wasting your time creating a parish strategic plan. What is the point of having communication tools and channels that move messages at the speed of light, *if you don't take advantage of that fact?* After much work and trial and error efforts, someone informed you that they might be interested in something you offer at the speed of light, *but you are going to get back to them at the speed of whenever you get around to it? Whenever someone in PMO feels like it? Or the speed of the weekly printed "bulletin"? Whenever someone, "has the time"?* Don't bother seeking the return of this community of apathetic, lapsed parishioners and Catholics if this is how you intend to slow-play your PMO "communications." You are wasting everyone's time—including your own.

Furthermore, as you read the above list of communication topics do not think too narrowly in terms of serving any listed topic. For example, the topic of "Marriage" does not simply infer, "Contact the parish office at least six months in advance before your wedding date." PMO can go far beyond announcing prerequisite scheduling procedures and actually provide links to articles, podcasts, solidly Catholic websites, etc., *on all things related to marriage.* The reason this does not happen has nothing to do with a lack of useful information on Catholic marriage, *and everything to do with a broken PMO culture that dumbs-down the role of PMO to simply being the purveyor of marriage date scheduling rules.* Says who? Imagine the impact of receiving an article on some aspect of marriage you indicated of interest to you *from your Church.* You didn't have to go on an Easter egg hunt searching the internet for an authentically Catholic doctrine, Magisterially correct article on _____ (as if you could even know at this point in your faith walk what constitutes "authentically Catholic doctrine, Magisterially correct article"), because the proactive PMO communications in your parish did that information search for you and sent the information directly to you.

This proactive approach to engaging communications is the fruit of the new *digital* evangelization—*and it must be articulated within your written strategic plan or it will not happen.* You either get on board and become part of the speed of light digital content communications multiplatform solution, or continue the outdated ways of the past in PMO and remain part of the problem. It's your call, *but the digital communications train left the station long ago and PMO most everywhere was not a passenger on that train.*

If at this point you are thinking communications is not your job in PMO, you might as well stop reading here because you have failed to grasp that content is delivered via specific thinking that animates this paramount fundamental and foundational principle: *we meet people where they are, not where we wish them to be.* If we have to face a mountain of rejection just to hold one person's hand and spoon-feed them information others might find or have found for themselves, who cares—*that is your job in PMO.* We spoon-feed via a robust PMO communications effort. It is an intransigent stubbornness in fidelity to historically broken and über-passive PMO communications methods—methods that if they ever worked in a superior manner certainly do not work that way today, that contributes to the hemorrhaging of parishioners to the secular world—and our failure to return lost souls to the pathway that leads them back to Christ. Whether the outreach topic is administrative, apologetics, catechesis, or any other form of religious conversation, *it all starts with personal contact, and personal contact starts with communications, and communications starts with doing the spadework of discovering personal contact information.*

You will not find a romanticized version of the truth here concerning the typically ineffective, "potluck dinner planning…free donuts and coffee in the parish hall after Mass" PMO communications messaging content and transmission efforts so common to date. Ultimately, it is the difference between limply reporting the attrition of souls from the Church that we are already all too familiar with—"Gee, isn't it a shame Johnny no longer goes to church <sigh> but what can you do?"—*or doing whatever is called for in PMO communications to help stop it.*

Can you handle a heavy dose of rejection and failure to find an occasional victory over the enemy? Can you, will you, climb and conquer Mt. Rejection? If so, take the initiative and follow the communication advisements provided here, and/or create your own methods. The answer is out there—if you seek it. Create your own scarecrow story. Has anybody climbed this communications mountain? Yes. For example, an old woman by the name of Mother Angelica. Type her name into Google. Read her story. And then ask yourself why her communications story can't be your communications story on a local parish level. If not you, then who? If not now, when?

Strategy 1.4: Define new and enhance existing mechanisms that enable parishioners to provide input to parish leadership and receive meaningful and timely feedback regarding parish policies, programs and directions.

In Scripture we find an example of Paul providing rather direct feedback to Peter:

> And when Cephas came to Antioch, I opposed him to his face because he clearly was wrong.
>
> For, until some people came from James, he used to eat with the Gentiles; but when they came, he began to draw back and separated himself, because he was afraid of the circumcised.
>
> And the rest of the Jews [also] acted hypocritically along with him, with the result that even Barnabas was carried away by their hypocrisy.
>
> But when I saw that they were not on the right road in line with the truth of the gospel, I said to Cephas in front of all, "If you, though a Jew, are living like a Gentile and not like a Jew, how can you compel the Gentiles to live like Jews?"
>
> —*Galatians 2:11-14*

The art and science:

The essential part of creativity is not being afraid to fail.
—*Edwin Land*

In regard to the context of communications, you cannot "define new and enhance existing mechanisms . . ." *without also embracing the science of soliciting and capturing specific feedback from your current and former parishioners.* You need more feedback about what is working, what is broken, and what is somewhere in between broken and working—*and you need this feedback in as fine a granularity as possible.*

Of course, as the PMO administrator you have an idea of what is broken, working, etc. There are plenty of visual signs and indicators. There are also plenty of generic articles written on, "Why people are leaving the Church," etc., and of course PMO personnel working with you have some valuable feedback as well. But is that all there is to the science of communications? Just ask a few folks for their input? No. You must solicit and collect feedback from everyone you can—*but especially those who have quit on their faith in God.*

No matter the topic of discussion, your most valuable input does not come from repeat customers who are clearly drinking your brand of Kool-Aid. For such folks who fit this profile are already satisfied; just keep doing what you are doing to serve them. *What you really want to know is why former faithful voted with their feet, left the Church, and did not return. Of course* you should capture feedback from active parishioners. This requires the use of a feedback mechanism, a survey tool (many are available for download on the internet; simply edit the survey points to fit your specific needs). However, to capture the feedback you need you must reach out to everyone registered in the parish, *including those who quit.* It is in reaching those who quit that we accept our duty to do more than just serve the easy to reach low-hanging fruit—in other words, your typically dwindling base of active parishioners. But how to do this? How do we reach those who have quit? How do we find them?

Here is a list of superior ideas for reaching those who quit on their faith and Church to solicit their feedback:

CHAPTER 59

ON REJECTION AND FAILURE

Oh. Wait. You don't see anything above? No, "How to reach people who have quit their faith" list of ideas? Why is that? *Because to present you with a list of outside-the-box ideas not of your own creation is to invite the same eye-rolls, head shaking, rejection and ridicule many superior ideas first received.* Such a list of communications ideas will *predictably* be viewed as absurd, ridiculous, stupid, _____ (insert descriptor of choice here) by small-minded, risk averse people—of which there is no shortage in the world. Most people are not internally equipped to handle the ridicule and rejection of their ideas, so they quit trying and remain silent before they ever get started—*a deadly trait in any PMO administrator.*

But what would you attempt to do *if you knew you could not fail?* Have you ever looked at a challenge through this lens? Here's a key point: the man who chooses not to read *has no advantage over the man who cannot read.* The corollary observation in our present context: the man who cannot fail *is the same as the man who can fail but does not care.* What if you replaced dwelling on the "What if?" consequences of failure with, "So what?" What if you accepted the fact some ideas will not work *and failure is simply the price of admission to discovering ideas that will work?*

Actually, the dumbest and worst thing I could do for you is to supply here a list of communications ideas and initiatives. Why? Because the default position of most folks places such ideas in the trash bin of, "I categorically reject all non-traditional thinking! And I especially reject anything that I deem crazy, experimental, radical, ridiculous, and/or risky to the reputation I have slaved for years to build as someone who never fails, much less fails in a public or spectacular manner."

Such people will simply ignore what is on any such idea list anyway—whether presented here and now or later—as too stupid, too risky to their career, or too whatever to try. They choose to try nothing new instead of being compelled by a dark but objective reality—*the recognition their parish house is on fire and being decimated by attrition.* Overly cautious people utterly refuse to think outside the box to discover their idea—or their approval of someone else's idea—is actually a superior road to follow. But superior PMO administrators do not give a fig if they get knocked down and fail. They just get back up and try something else.

> **I don't believe I have special talents, I have persistence. After the first failure, second failure, third failure, I kept trying.**
> —*Carlo Rubbia, Nobel Prize-winning physicist*

Here is what I know: I know I don't have all the bright ideas or solutions about anything—especially when it comes to communicating with people who have quit on their faith and the Church—*but you might.* People in the neighboring parish might. People in some other diocese might. People on your CMB might. I have been down this road many times before, and the creative thinker and his or her idea is often dismissed by the small-minded person—unfortunately holding a position of authority over them—either for no reason at all, or one or more reasons cited above. However, this point is paramount:

> <u>The idea will be born if you insist it be born</u>—*and this is the first key: do not quit.*

ON REJECTION AND FAILURE

After you have an idea in hand that is legal, ethical, moral, and ready to implement, *you must insist on running with it over and through all obstacles and objections placed in your way.* The only person who gains when you do nothing is the person named "Status Quo." And how are the results of the status quo working for us in the Church today? What do the statistics show on Church attendance and attrition? What is trending? Do not allow eye-rolls, criticism, or the possibility of public failure to stop you. For example (listed alphabetically):

Mike Brinda—founded New Horizons Computer Learning Centers with ten dual-floppy IBM PCs in 1982, before the era of the ubiquitous personal computer, tablet, smart phone, or the invention of the internet. His immediate family and twelve banks refused to loan him a dime. He remortgaged his house to get started. Bankers, family, friends, and co-workers all told him he was crazy to quit a good lifetime job teaching at Sperry Univac. And then what happened?

Walt Disney—fired from the *Kansas City Star* newspaper because the editor said, "he lacked imagination and had no good ideas." He went bankrupt several times before he built Disneyland. In fact, the proposed park was rejected by the City of Anaheim on the grounds that it would only attract riffraff. And then what happened?

Stephen King—King's most first and most renowned book, *Carrie*, was rejected thirty times. King decided to toss the book, but his wife went through the trash to rescue it and convinced him to re-submit it. And then what happened?

Claude Monet—While alive, Monet's work was mocked and rejected by the artistic elite, the Paris Salon. And then what happened? Check the appreciated value of his works today.

Babe Ruth—His home run record is 714 during his career. But he still had a total of 1,330 strikeouts. At one point he held the record for strikeouts. He once said, "Every strike brings me closer to the next home run."

Dr. Seuss—Twenty-seven publishers rejected his first book, *To Think That I Saw It on Mulberry Street*. And then what happened?

Fred Smith—founder of Federal Express, received a "C" on his college paper detailing his idea for a reliable overnight delivery service. His professor at Yale—who should have immediately quit his job to back the plan—told him, "Well, Fred, the concept is interesting and well formed, but in order to earn better than a 'C' grade, your ideas also have to be feasible." And then what happened?

But wait, there are even more consequences to explore. Here's a fair question: what about the feel and texture of consequences derived from timid, wrong-headed decisions that lack the necessary and prerequisite vision demanded of decision makers? One example: Blockbuster refused to buy Netflix for $50 million. Netflix is now worth many billions. And where is Blockbuster today? And who drove them out of business? *Who* drove them out of business is not even the most relevant question here. But the root cause of *why they went out of business* is definitely worthy of your reflection.

All things being equal—if you have the time, talent, treasure, etc., under your management authority to give an idea a try with the only downside being that you might fail—*you must try the idea. You really don't have a choice*. Basically, people who are afraid to fail when failure is only one potential outcome have permanently closed doors that could lead to future success—not just personal success doors, *but global success doors for everyone in their enterprise, which they have no right to close.*

If you are the decision maker and you refuse to research any idea—much less try it—why this is so is basically irrelevant. If you and your temperament are unable and/or unwilling to embrace, endorse, and execute outside-the-box PMO ideas on any front, there is absolutely nothing wrong with personally holding to this position—*you just shouldn't be the PMO administrator who holds back giving new ideas a try. Immediately get your name out of th PMO adminis-*

trator box on the Org Chart. Either find another job, or find a way to green light and implement outside-the-box ideas—*but do not stand in the way of potential success solely because you are afraid to fail.*

It is what it is, meaning, if being afraid to fail is the reality of your temperament, *find another job that is a better fit for you, and one that actually rewards this character trait*—there is no shame in that. Just don't allow yourself to become trapped in a job-to-your-temperament mismatch and become an impediment to those who would otherwise become a fountain of ideas, but for the fact they know their boss reaches for the "**REJECTED**" stamp every time an outside-the-box idea is put forward.

The above does not mean you green light an idea you do not believe has any merit whatsoever—if you can articulate why. But here's the deal: <u>*you better be darn sure you are correct when you shoot down an idea before ever giving it a try*</u>. As such, your default position as the PMO administrator is "Must try _____." (Insert idea/suggestion of choice here, and also note this attitude will become an integral piece of the correct PMO culture.) It is also your job to foster and cultivate a culture of free expression of all ideas. There are no negative repercussions from attempted ideas that fail, only positive praise for anyone who proposes an idea—and a one-on-one private conversation with those *who never have an idea about why they never have an idea*. There are no eye-rolls to any proposed idea. Most importantly, you may reject an idea for explicit cause—*but there is no rejection of an idea solely because you are afraid of the potential fallout from failure. In and of itself, fear of fallout is insufficient cause for rejection.*

You must choose: inhibit PMO or enable PMO? Will you block the road or clear the road? It's as simple as this: if you cannot handle regular doses of rejection and failure *you should not be the PMO administrator*. Why? Because the difference between superior and average performance often comes down to an idea that Administrator A was willing to try, but Administrator B was not. And note this well: most ideas fail, but this fact cannot, must not, *be used as an excuse to not try new ideas.*

I was not the originator of every great idea I implemented, *but I know I would have never heard the next great idea from an employee if I wasn't willing to accept that many if not most ideas I try will fail.* Failure comes with the job. Accept it. Pay no mind to failure, *but foster a culture that is thankful for the idea anyway.* Here—and only here—I will turn to Friedrich Nietzsche:

That which does not kill* us *makes* us *stronger.

Basically, if you are not failing *you are not trying hard enough.* Failure is inevitable and consistently roaming in the lives of those who attempt to implement new ideas. The realm of PMO is no exception. Those who would use failure against you are sadly misguided and misinformed, *pay them no mind.* Indeed, one of the culture indicators I look for in an on-site visit are stories of failure—*of course not perpetual and systemic failure*—but stories of ideas that were tried, and bombed. If at this point you have to ask why I look for some signs of creative failure, why I would care about such things, you have not been picking up on the culture-building message being presented here.

The science of PMO communications is dully mechanical, and I will likely delegate the mechanical aspects of PMO digital communications (i.e. send this message content to this group on this platform at this time). Of course, be sure to use all the communications channels that are available to solicit feedback, but note this will gain you nothing or close to nothing if you do not embrace the core art of communications: *what* is said, *how* you say it, and *whom* you are addressing.

And where does this art of PMO communications begin? *Do not talk yourself or allow anyone else to talk you out of trying an idea to reach people and solicit their feedback—especially to reach those who have quit on their faith and the Church.* Why? Because:

> **Your most unhappy customers are your greatest source of learning.**
> —*Bill Gates*

CHAPTER 60

PEOPLE MAKE FOR SUPERIOR PMO

The chapters on hiring and firing are deliberately presented last. Why? Three reasons:

1. Role expansion. You must have been exposed to all the previous chapters in order to, hopefully, elevate your desire to deliver "superior PMO to current and lapsed parishioners." Indeed, the very concept of delivering superior PMO to current and lapsed parishioners had to first be defined and fully explained as a new paradigm to enable a shift away from incomplete, malformed, very low, etc., and self-limiting PMO performance expectations, *and on to our new reality of what could and should be delivered through PMO.*

2. This elevation in desire to deliver superior PMO—indeed, to even define it fully and correctly—has hopefully enabled you to see the importance of redefined and revitalized PMO in your parish and the Church as a whole, to such a high degree you are willing to battle through the inevitable barriers, obstacles, and roadblocks you will encounter along your journey. *Remember: do not start the process of building superior PMO if you might quit during the process.* But at the same time, you must know that delivering superior PMO, albeit enabled by a holistic system presented here, is in the final analysis something that is only achieved by

and through *the employees and volunteers working in PMO*. The system is just a tool.

3. In light of the fact superior PMO is, in the final analysis, something that is only achieved by and through the employees and volunteers working in PMO, it is logical that we to the best of our ability employ and hire superior personnel to gain superior results. Fine. Below we will discuss in detail how you achieve the goal that we only employ and hire superior personnel. However:

The following final chapters bring us deeper into the very heart of the sausage-making process, *so if you have read some uncomfortable things here to this point it might get even more uncomfortable for you now.* In other words, a factory tour of this phase of sausage making might generate some severe heartburn or nausea in some of our fellow tour members. Some might regret their decision to go on this tour at all. Why? For the same reason an unprepared viewing of how the hogs are butchered might cause discomfort: *some folks just don't have the talent for hiring, and especially, the stomach for even being around firing—much less doing the firing.* In this regard: *don't shoot the messenger.* I'm just telling you the way things are in hiring and firing—especially firing. I'm not saying you have to enjoy it—because no rational person does enjoy firing—*you just have to do your duty*. If you think you might fall into this reluctant tour member category, while this is certainly understandable, indeed quite normal that you are loath to fire someone—*it is also irrelevant*. How so? Why?

Suppose you want to be a pilot—but are afraid of heights. Suppose you want to be a surgeon—but the sight of blood and body part trauma makes your stomach turn. Suppose you want to be a soldier, but are afraid of loud noises. The list of "Suppose you want . . ." (or in your case perhaps, "Suppose you are *told* 'PMO administrator' is your new assignment . . .") can be very long—*but also very irrelevant*. Why? Because you don't have to choose to be that which you cannot be, but if you do choose it—or it chooses you as the case may be—*then as you develop the will and desire <u>you must also choose to do whatever it takes to overcome whatever is holding you back from taking all required actions</u>*.

You can either overcome what holds you back from becoming a superior pilot, surgeon, soldier, *or PMO administrator*—or not. It is your call, your choice. But if you are unwilling and/or unable to handle all aspects of the sausage making tour—and on our "tour" of PMO this includes hiring and firing—*why did you choose to go on this tour in the first place?* Did you not understand that superior personnel are the paramount raw ingredients to achieving superior PMO, and sourcing the right personnel in PMO is part of your job? Perhaps the message here for some readers is to strive to overcome their very understandable—if not also natural—desire to avoid firing someone. Regardless:

It was the deliberate intent of presenting all the prior chapters that fully defined and explained the benefits and purpose of PMO via an enlarged scope of service paradigm, achieved in part through practicing a holistic system, that might give those who need it a vision of your bright future with PMO. And perhaps also enough desire to endure the roughest part (in my opinion) of the PMO administrator's job/duty: *the hiring and firing necessary to build superior PMO*. In this regard:

> *Mediocrity, disinterest, lack of talent, and/or poor execution in hiring and firing will negate all your efforts in every other aspect of building superior PMO.*

Oh. That's not good.

That's a pretty harsh reality, but no less true. Therefore, what follows must be a very *necessary and candid* introduction into how you as the PMO administrator achieve and maintain superior PMO—*a goal that in the final analysis is always and utterly dependent upon the personnel you choose to keep and hire.*

In other words:

Sometimes the dragon wins.

How so? Like this: if you master and apply everything taught in all prior chapters in this book, but are unwilling and/or unable for whatever reasons to master hiring and firing, *you cannot by definition ever deliver consistently superior PMO.* It is impossible, thus the dragon wins. Why? Because ultimately it is *people* who deliver superior PMO. Yes, through a holistic system—but if you do not have the right people working in the Org Chart boxes, no system can or will overcome this deficiency. The dragon wins. Our holistic system of approaching PMO simply *enables* employees and volunteers; this system places all personnel *in the best possible position to succeed.* But if you do not have superior personnel in PMO in the first place?

No system in the world will ever overcome that deficiency; the dragon wins.

> ***Do not fear: I am with you;***
> ***do not be anxious: I am your God.***
> ***I will strengthen you, I will help you,***
> ***I will uphold you with my victorious right hand.***
> *—Isaiah 41:10*

> **And behold, Elizabeth, your relative, has also conceived a son in her old age, and this is the sixth month for her who was called barren; for nothing will be impossible for God.**
> *—Luke 1:36-37*

CHAPTER 61

HIRING—YOU JUST NEVER KNOW

We start with the topic of hiring, and let us specifically start here: nobody knew with any certainty—much less absolute certainty—that Abraham Lincoln would become a great President of the United States, including Lincoln himself. Given his record, how could anyone know this, and for that matter, how could he? There were a great many people on his own Cabinet team, influential and powerful people, who were opposing him and were certain Lincoln would fail as President—indeed, they were strategizing for his failure. On top of all this internal contention, add his former and new political adversaries waiting in the wings to defeat him in the next election.

And why didn't Lincoln, this self-trained country bumpkin lawyer, initially inspire hiring confidence? Let's look at some pertinent history, especially the twelve-year run-up before he was elected President:

YEAR	FAILURES or SETBACKS	SUCCESSES
1832	**Lost** job Defeated for state legislature	Elected company captain of Illinois militia in Black Hawk War
1833	**Failed** in business	Appointed postmaster of New Salem, Illinois Appointed deputy surveyor of Sangamon County

1834		Elected to Illinois state legislature
1835	Sweetheart **died**	
1836	Had **nervous breakdown**	Re-elected to Illinois state legislature (running first in his district)
		Received license to practice law in Illinois state courts
1837		Led Whig delegation in moving Illinois state capital from Vandalia to Springfield
		Became law partner of John T. Stuart
1838	**Defeated** for Speaker	Nominated for Illinois House Speaker by Whig caucus
		Re-elected to Illinois House (running first in his district)
		Served as Whig floor leader
1839		Chosen presidential elector by first Whig convention
		Admitted to practice law in U.S. Circuit Court
1840		Argues first case before Illinois Supreme Court
		Re-elected to Illinois state legislature
1841		Established new law practice with Stephen T. Logan
1842		Admitted to practice law in U.S. District Court
1843	**Defeated** for nomination for Congress	
1844		Established own law practice with William H. Herndon as junior partner
1846		Elected to Congress
1848	**Lost** re-nomination	(Chose not to run for Congress, abiding by rule of rotation among Whigs.)
1849	**Rejected** for land officer	Admitted to practice law in U.S. Supreme Court
		Declined appointment as secretary and then as governor of Oregon Territory

HIRING—YOU JUST NEVER KNOW

1854	**Defeated** for U.S. Senate	Elected to Illinois state legislature (but declined seat to run for U.S. Senate)
1856	**Defeated** for nomination for Vice President	
1858	**Again defeated** for U.S. Senate	
1860		Elected President of the United States

Or, let us consider another fellow:

- At age 5 his father **died**.
- At age 16 he **quit** school.
- At age 17 he had already **lost** four jobs.
- Between ages 18 and 22, he was a railroad conductor and **failed**.
- He joined the Army and **washed out** there.
- He applied for law school and was **rejected**.
- He became an insurance salesman and **failed**.
- At age 20 his wife **left him**. He became a cook and dishwasher in a small cafe.
- At age 65 he retired.
- He decided to **commit suicide** because he had failed so much. But:
- He realized there was still one thing he could do better than anyone: cooking.
- He borrowed $87, bought and fried up chicken using his recipe, went door to door to sell his chicken in Kentucky.
- At age 88 Colonel Sanders, founder of Kentucky Fried Chicken (KFC), was a billionaire.

Oh.

And finally, we have:

One Solitary Life

He was born in an obscure village, a child of a peasant woman.

He worked in a carpenter shop until He was thirty,

Then became an itinerant preacher.

He never wrote a book.

He never held an office.

He never did one thing that usually accompanies greatness.

He had no credentials but Himself.

While still a young man, public opinion turned against Him.

His friends ran away.

One denied Him.

He went through the mockery of a trial.

He was nailed to a cross between two thieves.

His executioners gambled for His only piece of property—His coat.

He was laid in a borrowed grave.

Nineteen wide centuries have come and gone.

Today He is the centerpiece of the human race.

All the armies that ever marched,

All the navies that ever sailed,

All the parliaments that ever sat,

And all the kings that ever reigned put together,

have not affected the life of man upon this earth as powerfully as that

One Solitary Life.

—Author unknown

HIRING—YOU JUST NEVER KNOW

All of the above is meant to install a bedrock point about hiring: *you just never know for sure what you are getting*. The "can't miss" hire with the "perfect" resume will fail, and the "I don't think he's gonna make it to the end of the month" hire…might one day become your boss. *You just never know*. As such:

1. Prejudge no one. And;
2. You must be willing to correct your mistakes in hiring because as sure as you are reading this—*there will be hiring mistakes to correct.* Maybe you did not make the hiring mistake in the first place, but fixing the mistake landed on your watch.

CHAPTER 62

THE PRIMARY HIRING FOUNDATIONAL PRINCIPLE

What else about hiring can be drawn from the, "*You just never know for sure what you are getting*" observation? Precisely this:

You may not know for an absolute certainty what you are getting when you hire someone, *but you better also have in your pocket some strategy or formula to increase your odds of hiring superior personal*. In other words:

1. Do not misinterpret the "you just never know" statement that all hiring is a dart-throw, a shot in the dark, or as some sort of quiet endorsement that there is no use trying to discern superior talent in the first place. And;
2. Do not believe that superior talent can be found through what you consider to be the "perfect resume."

Both premises are flawed and false. But this advisement is more about not being surprised or disappointed when you make the wrong hiring call—because if you are involved in hiring making the wrong call will happen. Here is what can be said about hiring and firing:

Hiring and firing are both an art and a science—no news here. But all things being equal, anyone can learn and apply the science of applicable labor law, terms and conditions of employment, follow all Diocesan-related employment policies, write a "Help Wanted" job posting, etc. But the art part of hiring is much different—vastly different. How so? *Memorize this*:

A-players hire A-players, B-players hire C-players.
—Steve Jobs

Full stop here to discuss <u>the</u> premier and foundational principle regarding hiring, courtesy of Steve Jobs. From time-to-time in life you bump into the perfect wheel. When that happens do not reinvent the wheel, *simply embrace the wheel you have been gifted to receive.* You will never in your life find a more insightful, succinct, useful, wise, and deceivingly simple piece of advice regarding the hiring of personnel—in any venture. What was Jobs saying here? *A whole lot more than first meets the eye.*

Most anyone can intuit an A-player is the overall best at their craft; superior, excellent, outstanding, etc. Since this definition is intuitive, nothing new here. But Jobs is also implicitly saying that B- through F-players must necessarily and by definition fall somewhere below A-players on the job performance scale. Fine. This point is also intuitively obvious to most casual observers. But is that it? Is that the entire message; there are superior applicants and less than superior applicants, end of message? No. There is so much more insight and wisdom embedded in what Jobs said that we must now unpack.

CHAPTER 63

THE A-PLAYER CONUNDRUM

Supremely talented people are characteristically, and notoriously, *supremely confident in their own abilities*. Yes, you want to hire such people—but you also better be able to manage them. Why is this point sometimes perceived as a challenge? Because superior and supremely talented people strongly desire, demand really, <u>to only work for and around other supremely talented people</u>.

Oh. That could be a problem. How so?

What if there are no or too few other supremely talented people in your PMO? That's not good. Bluntly stated, if you do not surround A-players with other A-player co-workers, and if you are not an A-player PMO administrator, *A-players will leave, they will run for the door and quit* (sorry, ordained, it is what it is for you. You can't quit so you can either improve, or endure). But lay A-players can't tolerate, indeed will not tolerate for long, working in the midst of incompetence and mediocrity. Indeed, another name for A-players could be, "organizational incompetence detectors."

Nobody promised you such folks would be a cakewalk to manage, but if you are looking for "easy to manage" stop reading this book, hire yourself C-players and place your PMO administrator job on cruise control. The truth is that A-players are an absolute joy to work around and easy to manage—*but only by*

A-player PMO administrators. But A-player pretender and wannabe administrators? *They are going to be in for some long days at work.*

Therefore, we conclude:

> *The creation and maintenance of a supremely qualified and staffed PMO department is forever dependent upon the person who is doing the hiring and firing, <u>and that person must be an A-player</u>.*

A-player employees and volunteers may be superior at what they do, but the PMO administrator is doing the hiring, *so the destiny of PMO is perpetually held in the hands of this person first and foremost: <u>the person doing the hiring and firing</u>*. You cannot, repeat, *you cannot*, deliver superior PMO results without superior people working in PMO. You can shout from the rooftops day and night, "We shall overcome our problems in PMO! We will serve in excellence!" Nope. Sorry. Not happening. Why?

> *No system or anything taught in this book or any book or any course is going to overcome personnel who are not capable or not interested in being A-players*.

You simply cannot ask/task a B-player to produce the results of an A-player; it is illogical and a contradiction in terms. And who benefits from this attitude/policy of hiring A-players, besides the individual hired and the person to whom they report? *The entire organization they work for benefits. Everyone they are meant to serve benefits.* Notice then that by logical extension the person responsible for hiring and firing PMO personnel must themselves be what? *An A-player. The PMO administrator <u>must be</u> an A-player to create and maintain superior PMO. Not a pretend A-player, <u>an actual one</u>.*

The above point raises a very valid question: *how do organizations (of all types) continue to exist when they are led by less than A-players?* Shouldn't they just run themselves into the ground and disappear? No. A simple but revealing answer: *such organizations simply get in the way of organic demand for their product or service.* They do not build demand—or in our case in PMO, unlock suppressed demand. *They exist only because of the fact some organic demand for their product or service will always exist.*

For example, some number of couples will always be married, children will always be baptized, people will always die, etc., and PMO can bumble along forever serving those organic core demands. But does PMO create greater interest in knowing Christ? No. Do they create greater demand for PMO services? No. Do they reach those who are suppressing their faith? No. Do they even believe these and many other actions are part of their duty in PMO?

No.

CHAPTER 64

B-PLAYER REALITY AND THE ROAD TO RUIN

We must now note the downward trajectory of any organization if and when *a B-player (or lower) is doing the hiring*. But why? What's the big deal? When you get right down to execution and producing results in PMO, really, what's so bad about delivering B-level results across the board? I mean, it's not superior PMO, but hey, it's good, it's okay, it's adequate. We get the job done.

Eh, no. Not acceptable. Why? Because besides not being acceptable on its face, there is a flaw in this logic. What flaw?

A-players by their nature choose only to hire A-players. They have no worries, no "turf" to protect, no parochial interests that hiring another supremely talented person might make them look less competent, outperform them and take away their position in the organization, inhibit their promotional opportunities, etc. No such shortsighted and petty concerns exist in the mind of authentic A-players. However, B-players? *A completely different mental paradigm, a completely different mentality exists.* How so?

B-players have unspoken, parochial concerns, *also known as the instinct for self-preservation.* B-players have concerns that A-players don't, and by definition will never have. B-players are worried—and rightfully so—that if they were to ever hire an A-player…perhaps they just hired their replacement, *and we surely don't need that, my fellow B-players, do we?* Solution? Just as Jobs stated, A-players hire A-players, but what do B-players do? Do B-players hire A-players? No. Do B-players hire more B-players like themselves? No. *What B-players do is domino down and hire C-players as a form of self-preservation insurance, as built-in job security, and/or because A-players will simply refuse job offers to work for identifiable non-A-players.*

You simply cannot attract A-level talent in your organization by conducting your hiring interviews through B-, C-, D-, or F-level interviewing talent. Notwithstanding A-players hiring A-players, *B- through D- players will always hire one or more talent rungs below themselves*—and who wants an organization built on that falling domino hiring effect?

CHAPTER 65

C'S LEAD TO D'S AND D'S LEAD TO F'S

Let us expand on the reason why some PMO came to be in terrible shape, by considering what happens to PMO when the PMO administrator…is a C-player. That's right, you guessed it: *C-players hire D-players for the same reasons B-players hire C-players.* In PMO performance and results terms, this is a death spiral. Why? Because D-players, try as they might—and remember we make no comments here whatsoever that such folks are "bad people, etc."—such folks simply cannot deliver in job performance and results *what they do not own* in job skill, attitude, temperament, etc. <u>One cannot give what one does not have</u>.

> **You look at Fortune 500 companies and you look at great CEOs, they don't go hire a CFO that's [considered] 50th on the chain. They go hire the No. 1 guy. They go hire the No. 1 guy. It's like they all go hire the best guys because, listen, they know those guys are going to help them be successful.**
> —*LeBron James*

Mediocrity is perceived as excellence when seen through the eyes of mediocre performers. If you want to condemn your PMO operations to perpetual mediocrity, just hire B- or C- or D-players, and mediocrity—or worse—is guaranteed to take root and flourish. Therefore, the point right now is to focus on how to detect A-player applicants. Specifically, if you do not know what questions to ask during an interview, *and how to properly value and weigh the answers you receive*, you will never master the art of discovering and hiring A-players. Instead you will incur a communication disconnect during your interviews and ultimately, make a B- through F-player hiring mistake. More on this point below.

Given the above, it appears we might have a conundrum, multiple dilemmas on our hands as an A-player PMO administrator charged with hiring PMO personnel. First, we may not be able to locate, interview, and/or afford to pay anyone we consider to be an A-player. Second, we may have inherited PMO personnel—longstanding personnel who are B-, C-, D-, and F-players. Now what? Are we condemned to mediocrity? *Yes, if you allow it to continue, no if you turn things around.*

Read on.

CHAPTER 66

ON HIRING THE BEST OF THE WORST

Let us first address any perceived inability to locate A-players to hire:

1. There are *always* A-players available to be hired, even if your budget is $0. In other words, "We don't have any money. We can't afford to hire this person" *is not a valid argument*.
2. See #1.

However, what happens in such situations is that the pressure to hire somebody, anybody, builds every day—if not every hour of the day depending upon the position that needs to be filled. Everyone in PMO is working extra hard, perhaps extra hours, perhaps performing duties they were never trained or hired to do, to keep the ship from sinking until a new person is hired. What happens next?

There is in such situations a tendency, indeed a very strong urge, *to hire the best of the worst* just to put a body in front of the problem and take the pressure off everyone else. Hire the best of the B-player applicants if no A-player is available. Or…hire the best of the C-player applicants if no B-player is available. Or take the best…you get the idea. *And merrily, merrily, down the PMO organizational performance scale we go.*

Remember, those who report to you are just seeking relief—*and they will look to you to provide it*. This internal pressure buildup is the quite understandable reason you might decide to hire somebody, anybody, to take the pressure off. Notice those who report to you are not necessarily thinking about the long-term damage done to the organization by hiring less than A-players—*managing the long term view is not their problem, it's your problem*. They just want relief now. All the PMO administrator hears in his mind—if not literally in his ears—from current PMO personnel is, "What do we want?! Relief! When do we want it?! Now! What do we want?! Relief! When do we want it?! Now! What do we want...."

So what does the PMO administrator do in such situations? Give up? Cave in? Hire a B-, C-, D-, or F-player? No. As difficult as it may be during this time—and believe me I know it is difficult—*never hire the best of the worst*. You just don't do this. What do you do? *You grind things out until you can attract and hire an A-player*. You do double duty, you work more hours, you pay bonuses, you pay overtime, you use a temp employment agency, you find volunteers—whatever must be done you do—*but you just do not hire the best of the worst*. You do not inflict long-term PMO Org Chart damage to satisfy and solve a short-term hiring problem. To hire B-players, or lower, over A-players to solve short-term hiring problems is a very poor choice, a bad deal. Make no excuses or exceptions. *Do not do it.*

CHAPTER 67

THE ART AND SCIENCE OF HIRING

Let us now discuss the two halves of hiring, the *art* of hiring and the *science* of hiring. Relatively little will be said here in regard to the science of hiring. Why? Because the science side of hiring is essentially rule-bound and formulaic. For instance, there is no argument that $2 + 2 = 4$. There is nothing approaching subjectivity here; just follow and apply the rules of math. Additionally, note another important point: even if two different people learn $2 + 2 = 4$ from two different teachers, the mathematical science not only demands, but also guarantees, *the student will come away with the same answer anywhere in the world, no matter who his or her teacher is*. However:

Suppose the same two students are learning to *paint the image of* "$2 + 2 = 4$." This task has clearly entered into the realm of art, not science. Whereas the science teacher is working with a subject that is objective, constant, universal, and is striving to ensure the students arrive at the same answer as everyone else, anywhere else, *the teacher of the artist has no such goal*. Therefore, notice when teaching the science of any topic you can separate the subject ($2 + 2 = 4$) from the teacher, and because the subject is science-based, *a completely different teacher will still result in the student producing the same answer as from any other teacher*. But can you see how the teacher of an art operates under different parameters? Therefore:

When learning an art in contrast to science, *your teacher's style* changes not just *how* you learn, but *what* you learn—the very message itself varies. Some teachers might push you to paint more dryly, objectively, limiting you to only paint precisely what you see, while others may push you toward more Monet-like Impressionism. This suggests, unlike science, an important distinction to any actions taken or words spoken under the rubric of learning hiring and firing as an "art." Specifically:

When learning the *science* of hiring and firing, *the content of the subject is objective and constant.* The goal of the hiring and firing policies is to ensure that any PMO administrator reaches the same understanding as everyone else, literally, when operating under the same employment and labor laws. The content of the subject and the actual PMO administrator are separable regarding the science aspect of hiring and firing. In other words, *anyone* who knows what they are talking about can tell you what forms must be completed by the new hire, explain employee benefits, health insurance, working hours, vacation policy, retirement plan, etc. But when learning the *art* of hiring and firing, the content of the subject (i.e. hiring and firing strategies, techniques, wisdom, etc.), the PMO administrator in training and his or her teacher are not separable. Therefore:

The teachers who teach the art of anything differ enough that choosing from whom you learn also determines, to a large extent, what you end up learning—if anything—about practicing the craft of the art under discussion. But to go even further, who really believes you can at all teach the fundamental essence of how to render in Impressionistic style the image of a castle, forest, ship, sunset, or really, anything? It is possible to discuss, to demonstrate by example, but at the end of the teaching, *the teacher is no more certain the student has mastered the art of Impressionistic painting than on the day he or she started, except by demonstration*. Grab your brushes and show me you can do it.

To distinguish between the art and science of anything is paramount. If you have personally tried to convey something that would be considered the "art" of anything, you know this to be true. Your way of conveying different strategies, styles, details, experiences, wisdom, essences, etc., is different from someone else. This point is not only important here, but equally important *when it is your task to train someone who reports to you.*

What do you think will happen if you delegate such employee or volunteer training? Or applicant interviewing? One must recognize when teaching adults that to simply drone on and on and on…about the science of the topic is by and large, doomed to fail with most adults in most situations. Likewise, in hiring one must know the mechanical science of the processes, *but also master the art of delivering the science in actual PMO work scenarios, such as asking an applicant to respond, and then listening with a trained ear.*

With the above in mind this brings us to our first art form to master: when interviewing applicants, how do applicants respond when given a hiring interview scenario to solve?

> **The typical applicant has already overstated the volume and/or relevance of the prior work experience in his resume, and is now in over his head during the interview.**

Is this typical overstatement of experience by the PMO applicant important to the interviewer during the job interview? No, not really—a point which may seem counterintuitive to you. And why isn't this issue important? *Exaggerating and embellishing their prior experience in both nature and duration is what applicants do.* It's like breathing. And why do applicants do this? Job seekers do what they are supposed to do—*seek a job and be hired.* There are no perceived interview rules for the applicant, save one: *get yourself hired.* As such, *it is not incumbent upon the job seekers to void themselves by un-*

derselling their past, or to withdraw themselves from consideration for a job. Indeed, just the opposite is their goal—to build themselves up grandly such that they gain any job they are seeking—*even if they are not qualified*. The fact you were fooled and hired a B-player or less? That's not their problem—*that's now your problem.*

Note the playing field is level during the interview process because both parties—the job seeker and the person conducting the interview—know the score:

> *You are here as an applicant to convince me you are the most qualified candidate in the world, <u>and I am here to discern if you are what you think and say you are</u>. To discern correctly is where we ply the art of hiring.*

Therefore, it is incumbent upon the *job interviewer* to determine the true qualifications of any applicant. And how do you do that? As has been previously explained, that answer is in the realm of practicing an art, but the hiring science is the easier part and comes down to this:

> *You must first know the right questions to ask the applicant before you conduct any interview.*

If you don't know the right questions to ask—shazzam! You will not gain the answers you need to determine if the applicant is a technically proficient fit for your PMO needs. In other words, do they know the science, the "How to" of the position they are seeking? Note forming and asking the right technical performance interview questions for any position is not the art of the interview process, *as such technical questions just form the science portion of any interview*. Make a list, work from memory, whatever you are comfortable with—the science of forming questions to ask on technical competency and proficiency is the easiest part of any interview process. You have all the time in the world before the interview begins to formulate (or delegate) creating such a list of technical and skills-related questions. Therefore:

Speaking in general, given unlimited time it is not difficult in advance to write a list of opening questions to ask a job applicant. But regarding the additional questions to ask *during the dynamic and unpredictable give and take flow of an interview,* how does one know the right follow-up questions to ask *if one has never interviewed for that position before*—or for that matter never interviewed anyone before, much less a search for A-players only? And here's an even better question to ask yourself: how does one know the right questions to ask, *if one thinks they already know the right questions to ask and the associated answers, but are wrong?*

Oh. That could be a problem.

Do you see now that any PMO administrator living life as the proverbial "know it all" is the administrator most prone to hire B-, C-, D-, and F-players? How so? Until you hire an A-player *you are doing something wrong in your interview process.* Do not doubt this point. Accept it and ask, "Now what? How am I supposed to hire an A-player to fill this open position, when I don't know what an A-player for this positions looks like?" Answer: *seek applicant interview help from someone you know that you know knows how to hire A-players for the position you are attempting to fill.* And who might that be? I don't know, but if the answer is "nobody" you better not hire anybody until you either find interviewing help, or personal coaching.

Your ability to master the art of interviewing only grows through gaining experience in the PMO interviewing trenches, *but at your wise discretion also supplemented by an advisor offering you A-player search interviewing assistance.* Why would you or anyone want to learn the art of hiring by risking, when acting completely alone, making a hiring mistake? Have you thought through the consequences of making a single bad hire in such a small enterprise as PMO?

What percentage of your total number of PMO employees constitutes even just one bad hire? You really cannot afford to absorb even one bad hire in such a relatively small operation.

There is no shame in admitting you are not sure if you should make a job offer to an applicant until he or she interviews with someone else. This is often the wise choice and indeed standard practice at many employers—but still not a sure-fire guarantee of hiring success. And what is "hiring success"? Hiring an A-player. The question is: who is your go-to "someone else" to assist you, and do they truly know any more about interviewing than you do? Most importantly, *do they know the art of interviewing to detect an A-player?* How laughable and ridiculous it is to run applicants through a multi-person interview gauntlet, yet no one in the interview chain knows how to define what they are truly seeking, much less how to query for it. Thus, it is the *applicant interview chain-builder* who is initially paramount to creating a successful A-player hiring process.

If you are armed with the correct questions in the first place to interview for the PMO position you are trying to fill—and also recognize some of your questions are universal and some must be specific to each job description—where does the art portion of the hiring and interview process come into play?

> *The art portion of the interview is in interpreting the answers you receive to the questions you pose.*

Notice how quickly you must make the *transition from science to art* during an interview: when you form and ask your question, that is the *science* part of the interview, the easier part, the premeditated part. But when you are *listening* to the applicant answer your question, *in that instant you are now engaging in the art portion of the hiring process.* <u>Notice there is no announcement of this transition from science to art and art back to science</u>. It is incumbent upon the person conducting the interview to realize and recognize, "Now is the time I must listen intently to the answers and analyze, answers to questions that have no pre-ordained or predictable responses." *The analysis of the applicant's answers in relation to the question asked and A-player profile is an art, not a science.*

You have no idea what a person might say in answer to your question, except you do know that you will now in an instant invoke the sum total of your accumulated knowledge and wisdom to date when listening to the answer. This reality forms the heart of the art of hiring: to listen to the answers given and make a judgment call—yes, *we do judge in this process*—as to whether or not the answers you receive make cohesive and holistic sense in relation to the question you asked in search of an A-player. Does it pass your own, personal, smell test? In this manner one can clearly see: *the more interviews you conduct—and the more mistakes you learn from—the more A-player positional hiring wisdom you will accumulate.*

Your ability to *align and correlate* the answers to your questions with what your instincts, your nose, your gut—use whatever imagery works best for you—is telling you, "That answer rings true to me" or, "That answer rings false to me," *this "feel" for the answer to your question is the essential art of the A-player hiring and interview process*. Yes, there are applicant testing software tools available to you for certain job categories and positions, but a quick cross-referencing look at the PMO Org Chart to available applicant tests will reveal that there really are no position types on our PMO Org Chart that will be helped by such applicant testing tools. In PMO, we are a relatively simple, but vital, operation. Therefore:

The art of asking job applicants the right questions is hard to do well. Why?

1. *Time pressure.* We do not have *unlimited* time during an interview.
2. You must know what questions to ask that are *specific to detecting* A-player potential, not simply technical competence and proficiency (more on this point in another chapter).

3. You must know how to *interpret* the answers you receive from any applicant for any position that reports to you on the Org Chart. This does not mean you can perform their job, *it just means you know how to hire someone to perform their job.* Note the distinction.
4. You must be at-ease and proficient *with the speed you transition* from science to art and from art back to science during the interview. *Interviews are not linear, predictable, scripted events.*
5. The analysis of the applicant's answers in relation to the question asked *is an art, not a science.* There are few rules to follow in the art of interviewing, but significant application of accumulated gut wisdom.
6. This process ends with you making a *judgment call*: do the answers you receive make cohesive and holistic sense in relation to the questions asked? Does each answer pass your own, personal, smell test? Example: do you detect the claimed ten years of job experience reflected in the answers given by the applicant, *or one year's experience ten times in a row?*
7. One can clearly see: the more interviews you conduct, *the more positional hiring wisdom you will accumulate.*

Do not look for a more concrete, substantive, or "scientific" answer than provided above—*because there is none in the art of hiring human beings.* Those of you seeking to remain in the comfort zone of a hard and fast rule to detect A-players, such as to be found in the more concrete nature of hiring science (i.e. fill out this form, you receive two weeks vacation, we provide the following health insurance options, etc.), must stop looking for such hiring guidance, *as no such guidance can or will be provided.* To look for such guidance—much less demand it—is to potentially paralyze your hiring process.

Success in hiring is both an art and a science, and if you do not master the art, while nobody is perfect in hiring an A-player every time, you will mostly fail at hiring. As the saying goes, while even a blind sow finds an occasional acorn, solely relying on luck is not the way to practice superior PMO hiring. But there is much more to add on the topic of A-players.

CHAPTER 68

ON APPLICANT CLAIMS OF PRIOR EXPERIENCE

The art of hiring or firing is also a part of the aptly named, "reading between the lines" process; the use of the wisdom gained in your life to date, and the subjective determination that the answers you receive ring true in your gut— yes, gut—determining if the answers you receive align with common sense, or if the claims of the applicant seem overblown in relation to their job title, current duties, claimed years of experience, pay history, etc. For instance:

When the person you are interviewing claims to have 20 years of experience in _____ (insert field of expertise here), do all of his or her answers to your questions probing this topical experience area make sense to you? Do the answers seem reasonable to you? Do all answers hang together? Do the answers complement and build upon each other? Do the answers correlate to common sense? Do the answers in your mind equate to someone gleaning, for example, 20 years of experience doing _____ (insert tasks here) over 20 calendar years, or do you detect this applicant actually possesses *the same one year of experience, repeated 20 times in a row?*

One year of experience repeated 20 times in a row is not the same as the claimed 20 years experience—*but the interviewer has to detect this fact, and I can assure you such detection will not come from simply reading the applicant's resume.* It is a rare applicant—*but it is an A-player applicant charac-*

teristic—who will truly report without embellishment his or her experience level, *which is to say perceive to diminish the chance of being hired*, during an interview. And while applicants may not deliberately falsify the number of calendar years of work experience they posses, <u>who cares solely about calendar years of experience</u>?

Do not overvalue how many calendar years of experience someone claims on their resume—*you only care about the applicant's true knowledge and true skill level*, his or her true level at whatever job skills you need. Do not be taken in by applicant claims of "years of experience," as you will clearly note in an upcoming chapter that this parameter of "prior experience" *is not one of our precursor ingredients to A-player hiring*. Further note it is not my intent here to globally diminish years of experience as a hiring factor. *Do not use this information on the value of prior work experience outside our context*. We are only narrowly discussing herein the art of hiring *for PMO employment purposes*—we are not hiring biologists, police detectives, surgeons, etc., where prior experience carries a different weight in an applicant interview. *This point is paramount.*

Note no amount of traditional book reading, study, hiring software analytical tools, etc., in other words the science of PMO interviewing, is going to definitively give you the ability to discern fact from fiction, truth from half-truth, in the answers given by an applicant during the hiring process. All you have now, and all you ever will have, *is your applied wisdom*, a wisdom that does not grow necessarily simply by the passage of time. *The mere passage of chronological time does not in and of itself convey experience and wisdom.* We all know people who are no wiser today than they were a decade or more ago—*but they will make nonsensical claims to having "more experience"* solely based on the passage of time. Therefore, a key ingredient to the art of hiring is to also note:

The passage of calendar time leading to the applicant's claims of "experience" guarantees nothing in relation to actually owning the claimed experience in a particular craft or profession. Further note this point is as true for the applicant *as it is for the interviewer*. During any interview you must not be taken in by applicant claims of calendar years of experience. Not only this, *you should never pay a wage premium for such resume claims unless and until the claimed level of experience can be demonstrated and verified to your satisfaction during the interview.* Even then, *in most cases in PMO there is no need to pay a premium for "prior experience."* More on this critical point follows.

If you request letters of recommendation that speak to an applicant's *character*, fine. But letters of recommendation that speak to an applicant's "experience" *are to be considered as secondary sources of endorsement, not primary sources.* What is the primary source of endorsement as it relates to experience? Only what you and/or the person(s) you delegate to, *actually discern and detect during the interview when you probe the applicant's claims related to his or her prior level of topical knowledge.* Why?

One of the most common hiring mistakes made is to rely at face value on an applicant's stated claims about level of experience, and then subsequently pay in salary or hourly wages for "experience" that in fact, *does not exist anywhere except as phantom claims in a resume and in the mental dream world of the applicant.* As such, note it is incumbent upon the person conducting the interview to discern if the number of calendar years of claimed experience is actually reflected during the interview. Which brings us here:

CHAPTER 69

ASK FOR INTERVIEWING HELP WHEN YOU NEED HELP

To the extent you have little to no knowledge of how a particular PMO job is performed, *how could you possibly determine much, if anything, about an applicant's level of true experience?* Let us be very clear here: you have little to no chance of applying the art of this portion of the interview process if you do not have a firm grasp on how the job you are interviewing to fill should be conducted. <u>This point is paramount</u>. However:

Insofar as it is not possible and/or reasonable to expect you to know the detailed ins and outs of every PMO position that reports to you, clearly you can see that to successfully conduct such A-player search interviews you must enlist the help of someone who does indeed know the operational details—the practice science of the position you are trying to fill—and just as importantly, <u>*also what defines an A-player in the first place for this position*</u>. As such, the technical portion of an A-player search interview can and should, whenever necessary, be delegated to someone more technical in that field than the PMO administrator, *but who is also read in and attuned to both A-player defining characteristics and your PMO culture.*

Clearly you can see if this interview assistance comes from someone you hired who has already been with you for some years, you have by definition built yourself an A-player on your PMO team who lives the correct culture on the job and can now help you interview—*or they would no longer be employed*. And you can just as clearly see: *there is no sense seeking interviewing help from any of your remaining B-, C-, D-, or F-players.*

Whether you conduct a portion of the interview or the entire interview, you must listen very closely to the answers you receive because at any point applicants may step on the figurative land mine and expose themselves as either unqualified, and/or they overstated their true level of knowledge and experience. And remember this well:

> *Most PMO applicants are unqualified for the position they are seeking when the filter we select for hiring is our "A-player" filter.*

Does this sound depressing to you? Well, this is just how it is; *this is the reality of any job applicant pool when seeking A-players only*. People have a natural tendency and desire to advance their careers. When an employee reaches the employment ceiling where they currently work, some will naturally look for upward advancement somewhere else—*potentially at your expense*. Just because someone is seeking upward advancement does not at all mean this person is upwardly qualified for such advancement. It could simply mean he or she leased a new car, and without a raise in pay, is drowning financially. Maybe the rent was increased; who knows. There are as many reasons someone is looking to change jobs as there are people looking to change jobs—*and none of these ulterior motives endorses them as A-players, nor are their personal problems your problems to solve.*

Type, duration, depth, and relevancy of prior work experience are the most commonly exaggerated points on an applicant resume, and you should by now clearly see that not only is it incumbent upon the interviewer(s) to test all such claims of knowledge and experience, but also realize *you have no chance to test*

ASK FOR INTERVIEWING HELP WHEN YOU NEED HELP

such claims if you are not an A-player yourself, or know little to nothing about the job you are interviewing. This is why it becomes paramount to split the interview, and ensure someone read into what constitutes an A-player profile for this position from a practitioner and technical perspective, is helping you detect if such claimed prior knowledge and experience is actually present within each applicant. When in doubt always reach out for interviewing help.

CHAPTER 70

THE PRIOR WORK EXPERIENCE TRAP

While it is important that the PMO administrator know the actual—not claimed—level of knowledge and prior experience in each applicant, *level of knowledge and prior experience are not the most important parameters you are seeking.* Now there's a provocative but extremely insightful statement. Why is this?

Is it important to know the level of actual knowledge and experience in an applicant? Absolutely. Why? *For the purposes of establishing precise starting pay within the available pay range.* We also want to know the actual knowledge and experience in an applicant so that we have some framework for setting our expectations for a learning curve and daily job performance. Clearly, logically, intuitively we know one thing for sure: the more "prior experience" a person has doing the job I am hiring him to do, the quicker he will be up to speed and the better he will do the job in question, right?

No. Not right. Wrong. *Wrong, wrong, and more wrong.*

To accept as an interviewing and hiring truism that actual, proven, verified prior job experience performing _____ (insert PMO job-related task of choice here) necessarily translates into quicker learning or better job performance under your direction in PMO *is a trap and the worst assumption an employer can make about an applicant.* Why?

> **Indeed you will say, "Branches were broken off so that I might be grafted in."**
>
> —*Romans 11:19*

We know every enterprise has an organizational culture. The culture may be good, bad, right, wrong, superior, mediocre, or somewhere in between—but every enterprise has a culture, and as you have already read: *it is the culture of an enterprise that animates and shapes all actions by the personnel in that enterprise.* PMO is no exception to this truth. We don't know the applicant's prior work environment culture, *but we do know our culture.* Thus, when you hire someone into PMO—and it does not matter what position on the Org Chart—*whomever you hire is told they are grafting into your existing culture. We are not grafting our PMO culture into the applicant's culture, as shaped by overvalued "prior experience."* This point is not only paramount, if you remember to establish this point <u>during the interviewing process</u> you will not have to work to establish this point *after* hiring someone. *This critical notion that in PMO your prevailing culture will guide this person will have been explained, understood, and acknowledged by the applicant* <u>before he or she ever receives a job offer</u>. Indeed, any job offer is by definition contingent upon the applicant verbally acknowledging he or she understands this point during the interview, before a job offer is ever made. But I cannot overstress how much easier your life will be as the PMO administrator if this point is made clear <u>during the interview process and before any job offer is made</u>, rather than after the fact.

As such, what relevant piece of PMO organizational culture is further developed and maintained *during the hiring process?* Precisely this: we exalt two characteristics when interviewing any applicant for any PMO position, <u>and neither of those two characteristics has anything to do with prior work experience</u>.

Oh.

THE PRIOR WORK EXPERIENCE TRAP

The fact is—*and only the wisest applicants will realize the following counterintuitive truth in advance of their interview*:

> *For applicant interviewers seeking A-players, prior work experience is at best neutral in weight, but in all likelihood a detriment to the applicant's chances of being hired.*

Say what? Prior work experience is a detriment? How so? Why? Because standing alone without the two ingredients that will be explained below, prior work experience is something that often falls into the negative category and actually *lowers* the desirability ranking of an applicant. Why? How is this possible? How does the notion of "prior experience" work against the applicant? Let us start here:

Imagine you want to hire someone for the _____ (insert PMO position you are hiring for here). The rookie interviewer mistakenly leans on finding the most "prior work experience" they can to define the "best" applicant. Why is this? First, not having really put much thought into all the consequences of over-ranking the value of prior experience, the interviewer simply assumes that is what you do, that this is the logical and correct approach to hiring—the "Everybody does it this way" school of non-thought. Secondly, the interviewer intuits—*incorrectly*—that hiring someone with prior experience in the field will shorten, if not eliminate, the need for training this new employee (or volunteer). After all, this person does have "prior experience," and I did offer to pay the going rate—if not a premium for the "prior experience." Obviously, I must want to hire someone with prior experience and pay accordingly for a reason. And what might that reason be? Not what you think, I can tell you that. What will happen in most such cases where "prior experience" is one of the most exulted hiring parameters during an interview?

> *You have just hired and catastrophically unleashed this applicant into the current PMO culture without this person's understanding and buy-in to the current culture.*

Oh. That doesn't sound good. In fact, it gets worse.

Such an applicant, by virtue of the fact you no doubt informed her you were not only impressed by her "prior experience," but indeed, *you were swayed enough by it to offer her the job because of it*, quite naturally assumes upon her first day at work and every day thereafter that…*she was hired to imbue your PMO with her knowledge, her ways, and her means such that her ways and means are to be the standard bearer of your culture and operations.* The reality?

Nothing could be further from the truth. Such thinking is a disaster in the making.

The last thing I want is an outsider unleashing an almighty "prior experience" gorilla into my PMO culture, *a culture I worked so hard to create and work so diligently to maintain.* Why in the world would I want to hire and unleash people in PMO to operate *their* way, animated by *their* views on what "prior experience" means, *when by definition I already have a way I want the job to be done, which I hired them to do, and I intend to train them into our culture rather than allow current PMO personnel to be assimilated into their culture?*

In this light, "prior work experience" should be viewed for what it really is: code talk between applicant and interviewer for, "If you hire me I'll come in and use my prior experience to solve your problems. I'll rescue you. After all, if you are valuing my prior work experience you are telling me that you not only want to hire me because of that prior experience, but you want me to apply that prior experience on the job." Eh, no. Prior experience often actually becomes baggage that must be shed by the applicant; otherwise, if this baggage is not shed one of two things will happen:

1. In a short time your new hire will pollute your culture, or;
2. You will have to fire this person.

What do you want in a job applicant? Keep reading.

CHAPTER 71

WHO AM I REALLY SEEKING TO HIRE?

It is usually a given that as the PMO administrator you will not be the best and most knowledgeable person at every PMO job. But note this is also true of the symphony orchestra conductor; just because one is the leader of the band, doesn't mean he is the best at playing, or even knows how to play every instrument under his direction. The same is true for a CEO, military general, elected official, etc. You must be conversational about every PMO position, but that does not mean you must know every technical operating detail about every job. Indeed, this is not possible. As you know, this is why we sometimes split the applicant interview, so that in cases where we are not the most knowledgeable about a particular PMO position, somebody with deeper expertise in the field can assist us in selecting the right candidate—provided our interviewing assistants know our culture and the attributes of an A-player applicant.

In light of the above, what then is more important and weighted more highly than prior work experience when interviewing a PMO applicant? (Continue to note here we are speaking about positions germane to PMO, not surgeons, police detectives, etc.) We are looking for two criteria:

1. A very bright, very smart, applicant, and;
1. An applicant who is always willing to take direction.

Note that the use of "1." above for both points is not a typo. Each point is mandatory, and both points are equally important, so you could reorder the points if you wish and it would make no difference. One without the other is fatal to an applicant, but with these two points alone you can create—not hire, *but create*—an A-player. Therefore, we arrive at the secret to hiring A-players:

> *You don't set out to hire an A-player, you set out to hire someone you can <u>build</u> into an A-player. You are always seeking A-player <u>potential</u>, not necessarily ready-made A-player applicants. If you actually find a ready-made A-player applicant, <u>that is just a bonus</u>—but it is not mandatory and not our primary hiring objective. When we interview an applicant we are simply seeking the <u>potential</u> in the applicant to <u>develop</u> into an A-player.*

You could pay a lot of MBA tuition and never pick up the above piece of real-world wisdom. Further, note that "prior experience" *is nowhere to be found as a prerequisite criterion for PMO hiring*. Again, understand we are not proposing this hiring philosophy for the Chief of Neurosurgery, for example—but anyone who thinks there is a position and job description akin to the Chief of Neurosurgery on the PMO Org Chart should reconsider their thinking. The science of PMO is just not that complicated; job complexity is not to blame for mediocrity. Mediocrity in PMO does not exist because PMO jobs are complex, *mediocrity or worse in PMO exists because of all the reasons and ways to fail you have read about to this point.*

Prior work experience is not a highly weighted PMO hiring criterion, as mentioned above it is neutral at best and usually a detriment. Again, what we are looking for in an A-player applicant is:

1. A very bright, very smart, applicant, and;
1. An applicant who is always willing to take direction.

WHO AM I REALLY SEEKING TO HIRE?

In relation to prior experience and PMO hiring, how many academic degree letters one has after his or her name—including the fact some may not have any academic degree letters after their name at all—*is not a disqualifier for any PMO position*. Oh my, how many job opening advertisements I have read that ridiculously and without merit require a "four year degree" when the job does not require any degree whatsoever, much less a four year degree. On top of this, when you additionally demand prior experience in your job posting—shazzam! All parties to this decision quite naturally assume there must be a reason the employer demanded prior experience, and obviously that reason is they want me to apply my prior experience on the job! Eh, no. In PMO hiring prior experience is either neutrally weighted as neither bad nor good, *or it becomes the land mine applicants step on to disqualify themselves from hiring consideration*. How so?

The art of conducting the interview is to at various points give applicants some figurative rope, and see what they do with it. How so? Ask the applicant to explain the value of his or her prior experience to your needs in PMO, <u>*and then immediately stop talking*</u>. Make the simple statement, "Tell me how your prior experience relates to this job you are interviewing for." At this point, <u>*say nothing more*</u>. Do not overrun yourself and continue talking by putting words on the table for the applicant to repeat back to you, such as, "Tell me how your prior experience relates to this job you are interviewing for. I mean, how do you think your prior experience as an office manager will help you here?" You do not want to give *any indication* to the applicant as to what form or direction you want the answer to take, no hint whatsoever as to the answer you are seeking—because there is a correct answer and a wrong answer. When the applicant quite innocently, and indeed, quite naturally based on the wording of your job post, assumes you want to hear how ___ years of prior office manager experience will enhance your PMO, fine. But the *wise applicant* will either preface or end comments with, "But what's most important is that *I do this job the way you want it* done, not the way I do the job for my current (or last) employer." Guess what? You will rarely find applicants with the wisdom to subjugate the perceived value of their years of prior experience *to the more open-minded A-player defining characteristic that <u>you</u> will be teaching <u>them</u> how you want the job done, and not vice-versa.*

So, given the above insights, why would you even value, much less hire at a premium, someone strongly peddling "prior experience" to you? As busy as you will be, you need to understand *the last thing you want to do is unwind the ways the person you just hired goes about his or her job*, before you can even begin to teach this person to accept the ways *you want the job done in your culture.* This point gets to the heart of the matter: why would anyone pay a premium for something they do not want, cannot use, and that is ultimately detrimental to their organizational culture? Why do you want to pay a premium for "prior experience," when in fact the first thing you are going to do with all new hires is instruct them to subjugate all those years of prior experience to the PMO culture you have worked so hard to create, a culture that values two other propositions over prior experience:

1. Are you really smart?
1. Are you always willing to take direction? Can you be trained to do things in our culture precisely how I want them done, or do I have to deal with your pushback every step of the way?

While it is theoretically possible to teach people your culture while simultaneously asking them to divorce themselves from applying their prior experience—this request borders on a pipedream in the real world. *It is far easier for you to request this subjugation of prior experience than it is for the person to actually subjugate it.* Notwithstanding his or her comments to the contrary, do you really think an applicant steeped for years in a particular way of thinking, animated for years by a particular culture with little to nothing in common with your culture, is your best hiring option as opposed to working with a far more malleable, indeed blank, "prior experience" canvas?

The choice is yours. But in my experience, "prior experience" applicants are train wrecks waiting to happen, folks just looking for a place to draw their next paycheck, essentially in the same manner as they have done so in their life to date. I don't need to hire such people. *I don't want to hire such people.* Instead I very much prefer the more cooperative and malleable canvas, someone who interviews as the epitome of the above two points, *because that is someone I can build into an A-player.*

Note the science of asking an applicant the right questions is easy to do well. Make a list, work from memory, whatever—the science of forming questions to ask on an applicant's technical competency and proficiency is the check-a-box easy part of the interview process. The primary reason people chronically fail at hiring is that they over-focus on an applicant's technical competency, and not enough focus is placed on discovering the two aforementioned key factors that reveal A-player potential:

1. Are you really smart?
1. Are you always willing to take direction?

CHAPTER 72

LET ME TELL YOU WHAT YOU WANT TO HEAR

If—and this is the BIG if—if you can find an applicant who is really smart, and is always willing to take direction, and has prior experience? Of course this applicant is a superior candidate over the really smart person who is willing to take direction but has little to no prior experience. However, here's life in the real world:

> *I have very rarely found applicants with genuine years of prior experience who are always willing to subjugate their ego and fit into the culture I am either trying to create, or have already created. It is not impossible, but it is very rare.*

The above point is paramount and falls under the old but true expression, "You can't teach an old dog new tricks." Now, should you directly approach an applicant you would like to hire about your concerns that they might not be willing to take direction? Of course, but your problem is not expressing your concerns on this point to the applicant, *your problem is receiving an answer from the applicant that you can trust*. Why? Because:

Any bright applicant will now detect that you are concerned her prior experience might inhibit her from learning your ways of operating and accepting your culture (applicant's mental side note for next job interview: *determine if the interviewer values prior experience before overselling him on such experience).* Such an applicant would also naturally be confused as to why you would require experience in your job opening posting, and then proceed not to highly value it. Therefore, the applicant will logically follow your open invitation to lean on her prior experience to get the job…right up until the point she realizes, eh, maybe that wasn't such a good idea because that does not seem to be the two prized characteristics this interviewer is looking for. In this sense, if your job post specifically requested prior experience you have greased the skids as it were to fail the interview. You invited the applicant to fail by inferring she lean on prior experience *that you should have never requested, or at least exulted, in the first place.*

As such, what happens next is totally predictable: *the applicant is going to say what she thinks the interviewer wants to hear about her prior experience, instead of telling you what you need to hear.* At this point, the interviewer is left to make a subjective judgment as to whether or not the applicant is sincere, and to a large degree this depends upon what she said—in other words what she did with the rope—in answer to your prompt:

"Tell me how your prior experience relates to this job you are interviewing for."

How difficult did the answer to this question make it for the applicant to persuade you she is now oh so willing to always take direction within your culture, when a minute ago she just sold you that her prior job experience is paramount and precisely what you need? Did the applicant already step on a land mine when first answering this question, portraying herself as having all the answers? Did she tell you in full and glorious detail how, "I will really take charge of your office! I am a take-charge person! I have twenty-two years of Office Manager experience! You don't have to worry about the office anymore with me in charge!" And now the applicant realizes the error and backpedals from these previous remarks? Eh, next applicant, please.

LET ME TELL YOU WHAT YOU WANT TO HEAR

All of this brings us here: *when trying to build your new culture in PMO, why bother interviewing this heavily steeped prior experience applicant profile at all?* If you place a job opening notification that emphasizes, "Seeking highly intelligent person willing to take direction to fill _____ position," notice how you immediately minimize the applicant pool that is going to attempt to shape your culture and tell you how the job should be done, in return for a much larger applicant pool of people you can truly shape and mold into your culture, <u>and teach them under what culture you want all jobs done</u>.

All you need to do at this point is to verify the applicant is very bright and truly willing to take direction. I can assure you that these two tasks are much easier to detect, less time consuming to train, and ultimately more likely to succeed as A-players, <u>*than trying to unwind the tendencies of someone with a closed mind, brain soaked by years of "prior experience" mental obstacles, and then attempt to backfill your culture into such a hard-headed vessel*</u>.

So what's the catch to all this? There is only one drawback to this interviewing and hiring philosophy:

> *The initial burden of doing the job is first shifted to the person who will train your newly hired, really bright person who is willing to take direction.*

In other words: *you have to fulfill your end of the bargain and provide the necessary and requisite job training and culture direction to the newly hired employee.* You cannot shun prior experience in applicants, and then unleash them on the job without any training. However:

Does this sound like too much work to you? If so, look at it this way: there is no "free lunch" option. One way or another there is work to do and challenges to overcome in hiring and culture building. But I can assure you in relation to hiring someone with "prior experience" and spending countless hours subsequently unwinding what he "knows" in order just to bring him to culture ground zero level—and you really can't get to culture ground zero with such folks most of the time—then rebuilding him with the knowledge of how you want the job to be done in your culture, *that is far more time intensive and ultimately not worth it because it usually does not succeed.* Instead, hire a smart person who is always willing to take direction, accept the training burden, *and proceed to build a superior PMO A-player.*

Here we must stress there is no free lunch to building up any organization, but all PMO administrators have this option: commit to investing time at the front end of the building process to hire, train, and develop each new employee in the ways of your culture and the ways of how you want each job done, *knowing this will ultimately build a lasting and superior PMO organization on a foundation of A-players,* or; defer to finding and hiring the vastly self-overrated applicant who claims to have, "all the prior experience you will need," skip the new-hire training because after all, you are paying a premium for "prior experience," so why does this person need training, and subsequently live under a mishmash of mismatched individual PMO cultures animated by disparate employee attitudes and methods of doing their jobs by whatever culture "contribution" each person chooses to make for themselves.

How does that sound to you?

Choosing this latter option will inevitably and permanently result in mediocre or worse PMO, yet many do so. This is the PMO organizational equivalent of a symphony orchestra operating with as many different conductors as there are musical instruments, all at the same time. Such an orchestra can perpetually produce noise, but nothing resembling beautiful philharmonic music. This is the essence of broken PMO.

CHAPTER 73

THE HIDDEN BENEFIT: LOYALTY

In addition to the above-mentioned benefits of hiring a bright person who is always willing to take direction, and training this person to do the job within the culture that you are establishing/have established, and in the manner you want the job done, there is another benefit to this method of hiring: *employee loyalty*.

Let me explain this benefit as follows: given the choice between hiring a bright person who is willing to take direction but needs training, or hiring somebody with prior experience and relying on this prior experience to guide this person to do the job in a superior manner, ten times out of ten I will hire the bright person who is willing to take direction over the person who has prior experience, and provide the necessary training. Why? In addition to the reasons already spelled out above, it has been my experience that when you hire someone who has proven to you beyond a reasonable doubt during the interview that he or she is bright and willing to take direction, this person is basically saying to you:

> *"I can do this job. I know I can do this job. Please, just give me a chance and let me show you…because other people will not even give me a courtesy interview opportunity due to the lack of my 'prior experience.'"*

Now, the sad truth is most employers follow conventional thinking here and would not even bother interviewing this applicant because their misguided hiring parameters over-weigh and over-prioritize prior work experience, and/or academic degree requirements when no degree is necessarily required. This fact inevitably results in bright people who are willing to take direction—*the precise profile you want to hire and build into A-players*—being weeded out of your applicant pool before they are ever given an opportunity to interview for a job they would become supremely qualified to perform. Now:

Imagine how many rejection letters and emails this profile of job applicant has received prior to receiving your call to come in for an interview. Further imagine their internal amazement that your line of interview questioning seems to pursue trying to determine if they are bright, agile thinkers and if they are truly willing to take direction, instead of being quickly shown the door—never even being given a fair chance to show their intellect and willingness to take direction, simply because they lack the perceived, subjective, requisite number of, "prior years experience" somebody arbitrarily deemed necessary. Now imagine how such a person feels when he or she is not only given a complete interview, *but actually offered the job?*

I am here to tell you such people are generally *extremely loyal* to the person and organization that gave them this opportunity, and they do all within their power to live daily the two characteristics you stressed during your interview: to demonstrate their keen intellect, and to all the time and every time accept direction such that they can perform their job under the correct culture and in the manner they were trained to do. As such:

We come full circle back to the key hiring points: you do not want people with prior experience unless they are also bright and always willing to take direction—*a nearly impossible trio of factors to find singing in harmony in any applicant*. Therefore, if any one of these factors cannot be found in applicants, <u>let it be the "prior experience" ingredient</u>.

THE HIDDEN BENEFIT: LOYALTY

Do not fall into the trap of demanding excessive prior experience for PMO positions. Resolve here and now that you know your duty as a PMO administrator always includes new-hire indoctrination into the correct PMO culture, which includes a time investment in training the new hire on how to do the job the way you want the job done. You can delegate all or a part of these tasks, dependent upon the state of PMO where you are. Nevertheless, delegation or no delegation, the PMO administrator accepts the responsibility of *building* new-hire A-player employees for the reward of hiring loyal employees who are supremely willing and able to do their job, if only their boss would tell them what to do, when to do it, and how they want it done.

No PMO administrator need ask for more than this attitude from any employee or volunteer.

CHAPTER 74

ON FIRING

There are five primary areas of consideration to firing a PMO employee (listed in no particular order):
1. The administrative process.
2. Potential legal ramifications.
3. The internal impact on PMO.
4. The impact on the employee.
5. The impact on the parish.

The administrative process considerations simply have to do with mechanically following the policies and paperwork procedures for termination of an employee as set forth by the parish employee handbook. The parish employee handbook reflects all such policies and paperwork procedures of your diocese, as further reviewed and approved by the diocese law firm specializing in the legalities of personnel matters. If your parish does not have an employee handbook or if your employee handbook does not contain information on the procedures your diocese requires you to follow for terminating an employee, you would be wise to immediately contact the Chief Administrative Office and/or Vicar for Clergy in your diocese *before taking any action*.

Thus, concerning the *science* of firing—not the *art*—it can be summarized in three steps:

1. Locate the employee handbook for your diocese.
2. Read it.
3. Follow what it says to the letter.

From the above points you can conclude that after you have decided to terminate the employment of someone, the administrative process to terminate an employee is essentially mechanical, a series of approved and documented procedural steps that are to be followed by the PMO administrator as outlined and prescribed in the parish employee handbook. This process may be supplemented in your parish with an additional de facto policy, from, "Only the Pastor does the firing," to the highly lamentable, "Fire? We don't fire anybody here." (More on this point below.) Regardless, the precise process for terminating any employee varies according to the employment and labor laws of each state, but fundamentally, informing an employee he or she has been fired is usually the culmination of a lengthy administrative process of attempting, always in love and charity, to help the employee improve his or her performance via a written personal improvement plan, plus documenting and recording the employee's progress or failures over a period of time usually measured in months, not weeks or days unless there is an extremely grave reason to do so.

In terms of the legal ramifications of firing an employee, *there is no legal advice offered here*. It is beyond the scope of this book to offer any legal advice. All such legal advice must come from a competent attorney specializing in the employment and labor laws of your state. What can be said is that the PMO administrator must follow the labor laws as presented by all the written policies and procedures regarding employee termination, especially in the area of written documentation of below-standard employee performance. Furthermore, all such documentation regarding poor employee performance must not only exist in the employee's file, it must also *reconcile with other pertinent factors that also comment on employee performance*. For example, you cannot on the one hand claim poor employee performance, and on the other hand have the same employee's employment documentation *show a history of praise in job performance reviews, and/or a history of pay increases.* <u>Notwithstanding an egregious violation, in order to terminate an employee your subjective job performance commentary must correlate with the documented historical reality you are holding in your hand, and until it does you most likely should not do anything</u>.

If such accurate commentary and documentation does not exist in the file—and why that might be so will be addressed below—you have two options:

1. You must start to build an employee file that reflects current job performance reality before any termination action can be considered. Thus, for all intents and purposes, no matter the duration of employment, an old hire is essentially rendered into a new hire when the employee file historical documentation is inaccurate, incomplete, or empty. Or;

2. After consulting with the Pastor, labor attorney and all other necessary parties to the decision, you terminate the employee regardless of what the employee's file contains. You choose this course of action because in your judgment no matter how much further training is provided, this employee will not improve, and he or she is also extremely detrimental to PMO. Employee termination thus becomes akin to a moral imperative, as to delay dismissing this employee for the additional months necessary to document poor performance is to so grossly fail to serve the souls we have been called to serve, that no further delay can be justified.

Clearly, any previous written personnel file entries, even perfunctorily praising an employee's job performance and/or a history of pay raises, would not correlate well to your current observations of incompetent job performance. Now, one might legitimately wonder: but how is it possible to document satisfaction with an employee's job performance, give pay raises, bonuses, etc., *while at the same time actually being dissatisfied with his or her job performance?* Perhaps as hard as it is for you to accept—and it is certainly sad to accept—the answer is simple. The PMO administrator(s) prior to your arrival chose the more selfish path of least resistance: *no matter what your eyes tell you about employee performance, avoid confrontation at all costs, just go along to get along and don't make waves.* For example:

Upon your arrival you discover a woefully incompetent PMO employee, but when you open his personnel file—assuming there even is a personnel file to open—curiously you find a steady documented history of annual praise and salary increases for this employee. Or you find nothing per se written about job performance in the file at all—except a documented steady history of pay raises and Christmas bonuses, which is de-facto the same thing as documenting what? *Superior employee performance.*

Oh. That's not good.

Further note the status of "Church" does not mean the employment and labor laws of your state have been suspended or waived—you are an employer and barring any court ruling to the contrary you are subject to the same labor laws as any other employer. Just because you operate as a "Church" does not grant you the license to operate as you wish, nor does it grant you immunity from employee litigation. In the absence of a complete and properly annotated employee file, guess what you have? Historical employee performance has been...*pretty much whatever the employee claims it has been in all his or her months and/or years of employment.* (Memo to self: the parish is an employer and must follow all the best practices and rules of employment, *just like any other employer.*) Thus, when the personnel file is blank—much less filled with praise and pay increases—no matter what the actual truth may be, the benefit of the doubt in any legal contest will most likely flow to the employee, *not the employer.* In other words: *unless you have a written file, whatever the employee claims about his or her past job performance will be presumed as fact by those who hold your fate in their hands.*

Oh. That's not good. This may not be fair but this is the reality.

So, what if the employee file is empty and/or incomplete and you cannot show documentation to the contrary of whatever the employee is claiming? <u>Always speak with your labor law attorney about the circumstances before taking any action</u>. Again, your predecessor(s) chose to take the path of least resistance. Your predecessor(s) knew, as you must now know, *that confronting a poorly performing employee is the opposite of fun.* It is in my opinion the worst part of any managerial job. Nobody likes this aspect of the job. Such conversations can spiral down into brutally confrontational work—something that is easily anticipated and is precisely the reason people ignore doing their duty in this regard. Expect to discover this scenario of poor employee job performance hiding behind either the soaring language of false praise—perhaps perfunctory boilerplate language but nevertheless soaring, and wage increases to match—or no comments in the employee file at all. This is especially common when the PMO culture has been corrupted by the misplaced notion of, "We are all family here," a phrase used to avoid, cover, mask, ignore, or hide proactively addressing poor to abysmal employee performance.

Given this potential for grief, why bother with firing someone? Consider for a moment that others—including your boss—may not see what you see or understand what you understand about the negative ripple of consequences of poor employee or volunteer performance. Those you work with each day may make a misguided, but no less real, snap judgment about your actions, conjuring villain imagery while using words to describe you such as: atrocious, harsh, mean, not Christ-like, stupid, uncharitable—and those are just the words we can print. Ouch. The reality? We need and we have but one role model here and His name is Jesus.

> **Jesus entered the temple area and drove out all those engaged in selling and buying there. He overturned the tables of the moneychangers and the seats of those who were selling doves.**
>
> —*Matthew 21:12*

Rather than confront a person with the news that he or she is performing poorly—which of course you now realize shifts the burden of training the employee *away from the employee and onto the PMO administrator*—your predecessor(s) just looked the other way and swept employee poor performance under the rug. That is, if they were even capable in the first place of correctly defining and distinguishing between good and poor PMO employee performance. Why? It is so much easier in most cases to ignore poor employee performance to the detriment of those we are called to serve in PMO, and just allow poor performance to slide on by day after day. Pretty soon, poor performance becomes normalized within the culture. Indeed, "poor" performance simply becomes the new workplace normal, *the enshrined, accepted and transparent PMO performance standard.* Upon your arrival it will not take long for you to notice if this is your current inherited culture.

Further note, allowing poor employee job performance to continue unchecked—which is to say you fail to terminate an employee who should be terminated—is an internal cancer that will not only spread, *it will absolutely defeat all your efforts to create and install a proper PMO culture.* Wow. *That point is worthy of some serious reflection.* Do not even bother trying to install the correct PMO culture if you are going to even one time look the other way at current poor employee performance. *So long as you knowingly allow a <u>single</u> poorly performing employee to remain employed, you have no chance of installing the correct PMO culture.* Once you go down the road of turning a blind eye to poor employee performance under such broken rubrics as, "We are all family here," "We are all friends here," or, "I'm too busy to deal with this," *your culture is doomed and so is any chance at delivering superior performance to those we are called to serve.*

It must also be noted that when a chronically poorly performing PMO employee is allowed to remain employed, such employees not only fail to properly serve parishioners and the community at-large, *but they unwittingly are poorly serving themselves and their own careers and personal development.* Simply stated, such employees are not working where they belong. Look, when the job and the employee in the job are not a match, disingenuous allusions to, "We are all family here" and similar misplaced excuse-enabling imagery conveniently allows the boss—*who is clearly wearing the wrong hat at this moment*—to overlook chronically poor performance in the name of hollow-ringing "family" and "friendship" bromides. This is akin to putting lipstick on a donkey. The donkey is still a donkey and will always remain a donkey—*not the racehorse role you are trying to miscast the donkey into.*

In reality, casting an employee as a "friend" is simply hiding behind a label that has no place in this specific discussion. It is actually deploying a well-accepted canard the PMO administrator can use to avoid doing his or her duty: "They're my friends…They have been here for many years…I can't fire my friends." Such claims are actually detrimental to the career development of employees. When the PMO administrator allows poorly performing employees to remain where they are, *that is in fact the least loving and charitable response to the situation.* How so?

A poorly performing employee cannot be employed where God may desire him or her to be if poor performance on the current job is *chronically falsely rewarded* with unearned praise, unwarranted pay increases, and unearned continued employment. Who are you to say you are not acting as God's agent when you speak the bona fide truth to an employee about his or her job performance? Who are you to say that you are not doing the work of the Holy Spirit when you recognize a square peg, round hole, employee–employer job mismatch? How do you know you are not *defeating* God's plan for someone when you eschew doing your duty to terminate an employee? Why do you believe that terminating an employee is always and necessarily a bad outcome for the employee? Do you know this employee's future? No, you do not. I know many a prison inmate who will tell you that being sent to prison is—as bad as maximum security prison is—*the only reason they are still alive today.* Translation:

Sometimes things are not as bad as they appear, or even what they appear to be, *so who is to say who is the villain and who is the hero here?* When the PMO administrator allows poorly performing employees to remain where they are, *that just might be the least loving and least charitable response to the situation for everyone.*

CHAPTER 75

METHODOLOGY

Although it is sometimes necessary to terminate an employee, clearly note there is no connection between the fact an employee must be terminated, and that the manner and method of the termination by definition must be harsh, blunt, or accomplished without compassion. *There is no such connection*, yet this is somehow often assumed simply because the topic is "termination" of employment, a loaded word describing an action that admittedly carries some rather harsh imagery and overtones.

Notwithstanding how the employee may react when given news of his or her dismissal, from the PMO administrator's perspective the process of terminating an employee is always to be done with Christian love and emotional concern for the well being of the employee (or volunteer). No rational person takes joy in terminating an employee. But at the end of the day, the PMO administrator cannot allow a poorly performing employee to remain in a job that is clearly not a fit and not working for either the employee or the employer. However:

What is often overlooked is this notion that dismissing an employee is always a one-sided proposition that implicitly benefits the employer and explicitly hurts the employee. *This is not true*. We can actually be working with God—and certainly should be—when we are dismissing an employee. Because unless and until you dismiss individuals who are clearly not a fit where they are, they may never grow into what they could be, where they should be, doing whatever it is they should be doing. However:

More often than not, understandably the person who is the center of attention does not see this perspective when he or she is being dismissed. *But this is especially true after being misled either by silence, being ignored, or receiving unwarranted praise from the previous PMO administrator(s).* The employee's surprise when confronted with job performance reality is often understandable and is to be expected. Even after you give the proper job performance warnings and corrective training as called for by your employee handbook, ultimately how would you feel? How would you react to being fired after being told in many prior years by your prior boss that you have been doing a fine job—or even better than a fine job—and you have the historical pay raises to support your belief?

This is the grief we sow when we make excuses instead of doing our PMO administrator job in personnel management as proactively as we should. When we serve our time in a parish but deliberately ignore the obvious poor employee and volunteer performances, when we kick this problem down the road and pass the buck to the next PMO administrator, *we are planting the seeds of a broken culture and we are not serving the parish, the employee, or the Church.*

To assist you here are ten general insights on firing:

1. In conversation always be yourself.
2. Stay calm no matter what happens.
3. Do all your homework first.
4. Get to the point.
5. You are not compelled to answer all questions. In this context the less you say, the better. Why? Litigation must be assumed.
6. Seek approval from all necessary authorities before taking any action.
7. Do not be surprised at the amount or type of fallout from an employee

METHODOLOGY

termination, both within PMO and the parish at-large. Some employees may have connections you are not even aware of.

8. Do not be shy about using a termination as a culture-building lesson.
9. Always debrief yourself. You must understand why any termination was not preventable.
10. Be alert and aware for terminated employees who are so disgruntled they might hurt themselves and/or others.

Here's the bottom line: it is immoral to ignore doing our duty when we know our duty, simply because we are facing an uncomfortable task we would rather not perform. No rational person enjoys terminating an employee, and we are not asking the PMO administrator to enjoy the task—*just do your duty or vacate the PMO administrator position for someone who will.*

www.ingramcontent.com/pod-product-compliance
Lightning Source LLC
Chambersburg PA
CBHW030815190426
43197CB00036B/486